SHOPOMANIA

SHOPOMANIA

PAUL BERTON
OUR OBSESSION WITH POSSESSION

Douglas & McIntyre

DOUGLAS AND MCINTYRE (2013) LTD.
P.O. Box 219, Madeira Park, BC, V0N 2H0
www.douglas-mcintyre.com

EDITED by Peter Norman
INDEXED by Martin Gavin
DUST JACKET DESIGN by Naomi MacDougall
DUST JACKET ILLUSTRATION and interior illustrations by Raymond Biesinger
TEXT DESIGN by Libris Simas Ferraz / Onça Publishing
PRINTED AND BOUND in Canada
Printed on 100% recycled paper

DOUGLAS AND MCINTYRE (2013) LTD. acknowledges the support of the Canada Council
for the Arts, the Government of Canada, and the Province of British Columbia
through the BC Arts Council.

Library and Archives Canada Cataloguing in Publication

Title: Shopomania : our obsession with possession / Paul Berton.
Names: Berton, Paul, author.
Description: Includes index.
Identifiers: Canadiana (print) 2022024345X | Canadiana (ebook) 20220243514 |
     ISBN 9781771623346 (hardcover) | ISBN 9781771623353 (EPUB)
Subjects: LCSH: Consumption (Economics) | LCSH: Consumption (Economics)—
     Environmental aspects. | LCSH: Consumption (Economics)—Social aspects. |
     LCSH: Shopping—Social aspects. | LCSH: Sustainable development.
Classification: LCC HC79.C6 B47 2022 | DDC 306.3—dc23

CONTENTS

PROLOGUE

Perched on a mountainside high in the Himalaya, the stone house had neither heat nor insulation. It was cold, like every other place in Leh, the capital of Ladakh, a remote region along a border that India shares with China. The area is a high desert, so there was no firewood to speak of, at least when I was there in the early 1980s, but that didn't stop me from looking. When I wasn't searching for somewhere warm, I contemplated the community's raison d'être. People have lived there for twelve thousand years, and Ladakh once thrived as part of an ancient Tibetan trade route, but today it is a disputed area between the world's two most populous countries, and the border, such as it is, has been closed for decades. There is not much trade there anymore.

While Ladakh itself is too high and dry to get much snow, avalanches at lower altitudes made it inaccessible by road from October to May. In the 1980s, the only way to get in during winter was by plane, which arrived once a day from Srinagar in the Kashmir Valley to the south. Weather often prevented the trip to begin with, but once the aircraft arrived, it stopped only long enough to unload passengers and cargo, quickly reloading and promptly taking off before the afternoon winds made flying through the mountain passes even more treacherous.

Ladakh is a rocky place. Even in summer not much grows there, but the locals try their best with barley and wheat and root vegetables. A considerable military presence is evident, because the army likes to reinforce India's tenuous sovereignty in the region by marching purposefully through the desolate valleys and scattered villages. Leh was once dominated by a royal palace, but it was abandoned long ago, and is now open to visitors. Tibetan monasteries, remote shrines and other religious structures pepper the mountainsides. For decades, India has been promoting Ladakh as a hiker's paradise, so there is some limited tourism, but when I was there the tourists could be counted on two hands. Newcomers could easily be spotted because they would stand still in the middle of the street, gasping for oxygen as they tried to catch their breath in the thin mountain air. Hiking is impossible for the first forty-eight hours. And there was virtually nothing to buy, although you might have been able to pick up a turnip at the market or a prayer wheel at the monastery—if you really needed to acquire something. There was very little shopping in Ladakh, and, relatively speaking, there still isn't much.

The house where I lived, home to a family of five, clung to the side of a mountain on the outskirts of town. The woman of the house was Tibetan, aged perhaps thirty, but she looked older, likely the result of a hard life and severe climate. She sat on a low stool day and night in what passed for a kitchen, making dahl and chapatis over a single flame from a propane tank, the chilly room's only appliance, a lot in life that did not seem to affect her cheerful disposition. Her husband, a Kashmiri Muslim, was a soldier. His one desire in life was to someday travel with his son to Mecca for the Hajj. Their children were sisters Zarina Bano and Zahida Rashid, seven and six, and their brother Iftikhar, five. Bright-eyed, friendly and constantly smiling, they appeared to have no manufactured toys. There was of course no television, no packaged goods, no games, no puzzles, very little furniture. No Western items whatsoever. But they did not seem unhappy. In fact, quite the opposite. I thought about this, and about the region's clear lack of an economic engine: High on the cold and windy Himalayan plateau, the weather bleak and unforgiving most of the year, the visitors few and far between, modern entertainment in short supply and provisions scarce even if you could afford them. Yet life went on cheerfully. They did not appear to want for anything.

Five years earlier, in the late 1970s, I had had the great privilege of living in a barn on the top of a hill in the shadow of the Swiss Alps in a place called Le Mont-sur-Lausanne. I was attending school in the city below. The farm had a spectacular view. On a clear day, you could see the city of Lausanne far below and clear across Lake Geneva all the way to France. The weather was cold for most of the eight months I resided there, but the heat from the cows in the adjacent room kept most things from completely freezing. If it was raining in the city, I could count on it snowing by the time I made the long ascent to the farm. But on especially wintry nights, you could light a fire in the wood stove. The building next door—a short walk across the barnyard—housed a young family of four, plus an aging hired hand. They all got up each day at 4 a.m. to milk the cows, and went to bed every day around 7 p.m., after a long day of farm work and perhaps a little television. The family ate what the property produced and little else. Most dinners consisted of potatoes with a homemade sausage that left little to the imagination. A chicken killed on a Sunday was a rare treat. A slaughtered pig was a once-a-year feast. Early in my residency there, I was inclined, being a teenager, to raid the refrigerator, and so I ventured into the house late one night. When I opened the fridge, what presented itself was a giant pan of fresh cow's milk with a thick layer of cream on top. It took up the entirety of one shelf, and a huge wheel of Gruyère cheese resided on another. There was little else, save a tube of mustard on the door. I figured there was some bread somewhere nearby, but I could not find it. There were no leftovers. No snacks. No peanut butter. No packaged food. No pickles or relishes or chips or cereal or crackers or any of the predictable plenty you would find in many North American fridges at the time, let alone today. Neither the fridge nor the pantry could be raided—they were unraidable—and I never again even tried.

It would be hard to call a family with so much farmland and such a spectacular view poor, but I did not see much in the way of consumer goods around the place; the television seemed their biggest indulgence. And they clearly needed the rent from me to make ends meet. There were shopping centres in the city, but the stores in their rural area sold only—before the term became trendy—artisanal items: cheese, meat, pastries, yoghurt. There wasn't much in the way of shopping. They didn't consume packaged food, clothing or appliances in any great quantity. The rosy-cheeked children—Alain, six, and his little sister Christiane, five—were smiling at all times unless they were hungry. These kids made the farm their playground, skipping through the barnyard with the pigs and the chickens, running through the fields with glee, tormenting the teenaged tenant who lived in the barn. If they had plastic toys, I did not see any. Everyone was happy, or certainly seemed that way. They worked the farm, they visited with neighbours, they went to church. They did not do much shopping, and did not appear to want for anything.

I grew up with my parents and siblings in a house overlooking a scenic river valley in Kleinburg, which at the time was a farming village about an hour north of Toronto. In later years, it was swallowed by suburbia. Though my parents were well off, you might not have known it for looking inside the house, which was in a constant state of chaos and disrepair. Cats, dogs, birds, gerbils, goldfish and, for a time, even a pet raccoon were constant inhabitants. Dirty dishes and diapers were inevitably piling up. Doors, windows and furniture always needed fixing. It was, as they say, a well-lived-in house. Guests were constant, parties frequent. Visitors regularly slept on couches. We didn't take in boarders, but it certainly seemed that way. My dad worked a lot and my mother ran that crazy household.

My parents, like many who grew up during the Great Depression, were not big consumers by today's standards, but we had a lot of stuff nonetheless. Because there were eight kids, we all wore hand-me-downs and inherited toys and bicycles from our elders. Nevertheless, we exchanged so many gifts at Christmas that my dad would put some away in December and bring them out in April when we had forgotten them, an unexpected thrill. The house was warm, the fridge full. Sunday dinners were an event we were not allowed to miss. Roast beef and roast chicken. Green vegetables from the garden and the supermarket. Canned goods. Frozen foods. Potato chips. Ice cream.

Packaged cookies and crackers. Cereal. We had a TV, a hi-fi, a lot of unnecessary countertop appliances, toboggans, skates, skis, baseball gloves, board games, lots of toys and a swimming pool. We played outside in all four seasons: tobogganing and skiing in nearby cow pastures, climbing trees in apple orchards, organizing ball games with neighbours, catching frogs in the pond, getting stuck in mud, falling in the river, going on long hikes to explore the mysteries of the forest.

And we had a sandbox. It was in a field a short walk from the house. My brother and I spent a lot of time there, playing with Dinky Toys, miniature die-cast metal cars that we adored. We had a white 1960 Volkswagen pickup truck, a coral-coloured 1959 Chevrolet Impala and a two-tone blue 1961 Oldsmobile Starfire. I remember thinking the Chev and the Olds were the greatest toys I could ever have, and we played with them endlessly, moving them around in the sand and making little car sounds with our lips. But I remember this too: if only I could have one or two more cars, a Ford Falcon perhaps, just to round out the collection. I had more than most kids, and I was happy, but still I wanted more.

One day, when we had grown older, my brother walked away from the sandbox, and soon thereafter I did too, neither of us knowing we would never return. The 1961 Oldsmobile, that cherished possession, once the most important thing in the world to me, was left where it was parked. Over the following months, as the summer rains and the four winds swept over the sandbox, as winter snows arrived and receded, as grass crept into the edges and then engulfed it, the entire operation was swallowed by the lawn. The sandbox, and the treasured 1961 Oldsmobile, were never to be seen again.

INTRODUCTION

Shoppers have been at it since the invention of the arrowhead. But how long have we actually had a name for shopping? Only about two hundred years, it seems, a mere heartbeat in the history of consumerism.

The foundation was built in the late thirteenth century: the term "shop" was first recorded on paper in 1297, but only as a noun to describe a place where goods are bought and sold. In those days, of course, most things were made in a workshop and sold on site.

As for a word to describe the practice that would consume our lives, it took a bit longer. The term's use as a verb—"to shop"—did not become commonplace until another six hundred years later, in the late eighteenth century. Coincidentally (or perhaps not), that's about when the Industrial Revolution changed the course of history through mass production; when manufacturers the world over realized they just might be able to quench the insatiable human desire for stuff—or at least come close. Demand had existed for thousands of years, of course, but now they had supply. And, perhaps more importantly, not only could they satisfy demand, they could also create it. Workshops would no longer suffice. Factories would make stuff; shops would sell it.

Sometime after that, "shop" and "shopping" became all-purpose words, not just for a place, not just for a diversion, but for a lifestyle and, of course, the activity upon which the entire world economy now depends. Shopping came to describe both the purchase of goods ("I'm going shopping") and the goods purchased ("Can you please bring the shopping into the house?"). As for its use as an all-purpose root word, there is a long tradition of this also. By the fourteenth century, the English language allowed for such words as shopbulks, shopcloth and shopfellow. Or shopbell, shopshutter, shoptill or shopcoat, some of whose exact meanings have been lost to history.

And so it was that the lexicon at one time or another over the last five hundred years or so found room for dozens of words such as shopsign, shopstall, shopledger, shopthread, shopclub, shopmate, shopwife, shoprag, shopbreaker, shopcraft, shopdivine, shop-dropper, shopfinish, shopgaze, shopslop, shopticket, and on and on.

None of which you will find here.

This book is a dictionary of modern shoponyms. It provides mostly new words to help describe how, when, where and why we shop today. But there are four fundamental terms you need to know first: shop, unshop, reshop, deshop.

Just four words, but they are basic to an understanding of this new lexicon.

1. SHOP: to buy stuff.
2. UNSHOP: to return stuff for a full refund or unload stuff at a profit.
3. DESHOP: to get rid of stuff, sell it at a loss, take it to a consignment store or drop it at the dump.
4. RESHOP: to replace the stuff you unshopped or deshopped.

At some point in human history, these nudged aside eating, sleeping, working and sex as the new circle of life, and the activities that powered civilization. They are what separate us from every other creature on Earth. Without shopping, there would have been no exploration, no commercialization, no industrialization, no transportation, no globalization, no pollution. Without shopping, there'd be no economy, no work, no fun. Shopping is the mother of invention. Were it not for shopping, humans might never have invented writing, as it was the only way to record commercial transactions. After all, keeping track of one's stuff is almost as important as finding food, clothing and shelter. Shopping motivates explorers. Shopping makes nations.

Shopping powers innovation. And shopping, unshopping, reshopping and deshopping is the cycle that ensures the practice never ends. It is a perpetual-motion machine, powered by rapacious consumption and the unquenchable human need to acquire stuff.

We are all comfortable with the rhythm and we all recognize the theme that draws us inexorably closer. We shop at home and at play. In elevators and at bus stops. In stores and on computers. At sporting events and music concerts, driving on the highway or walking on the sidewalk. And we are abetted in the venture not only by manufacturers and retailers, but by governments, economists, industrialists, journalists . . .

Everyone wants us to shop—all day, all night, anywhere, anyplace, anytime. And we can see what happens when we are prevented from shopping—witness the chaos, consternation and economic calamity that accompanied retail closures, business shutdowns and store line-ups during the COVID-19 pandemic. It's not just individuals who are addicted to shopping; modern civilization depends on it—for better and for worse. But does it need to be exactly like this? Are humans, the smartest creatures on Earth and the only animals obsessed with stuff, able to recognize the insanity of it all?

Shopomania has engulfed the planet, and we need a more precise glossary to understand it. It is not, after all, just shopping—it's upshopping and predeshopping. It's autoshopping, aeroshopping and ultrashopping. It's about shoppability and shopomania, shopornography and shopaganda. And at the root of it all are four simple tasks: shop, unshop, reshop and deshop. These are the fundamentals, the substructure upon which everything else rests.

That is why this guide is not alphabetical, numerical or chronological. Once you understand the basic four concepts, it can be read front to back, back to front, from the middle out, or just picked up and read in no particular order like promotional material (shopaganda) from a merchandiser. Here, then, is a new lexicon to describe our shopping-crazy world.

SHOP

To buy stuff.

This is what we all do, whoever we are, wherever we are, whenever we can, however we can, no matter how much (or how little) money we have. People want stuff. It is an imperative, our raison d'être, the meaning of life, what makes the world go around.

UNSHOP

To return stuff to the shops.

This means getting a refund, or any activity that results in you getting *all* your money back—a full recoup of your purchase price—or even more. It's what we do Monday morning after we've spent the entire weekend in the shops. We bought a lot of things we're not sure we need and are pretty certain we can't afford. We get them home, feel guilty, realize they don't look as good as they did in the store and promptly return them for a refund before they take up valuable space in the closet. It's what we do when the Amazon package arrives, but the fit is all wrong. Needless to say, manufacturers and retailers hate unshopping, because it costs them time and money, and frankly, shoppers hate unshopping. It means getting rid of stuff, and that's always painful, no matter how big a mistake the acquisition was.

Some items can be unshopped without being returned to the retailer. But items resold for the same price or more than what you paid are few and far between. Corporate stocks or bonds can be unshopped, but just as often they are unloaded at a loss (see deshop). Many houses can be unshopped, depending on the housing market. But if a housing boom busts, unshopping houses can be a nightmare and crash the entire economy. Or, even if real estate prices stay the same, but you spent too much on luxury bathroom fixtures that are already out of style, appliances that are the wrong colour, or instituted a garden design nobody wants, then your house is not unshoppable, no matter how hard you try to convince yourself, your neighbours and your friends otherwise. Sure, you can still sell it, but after real estate fees, taxes, renovation costs and the inevitable heartache, it would be better described as deshopping. Very few homeowners were unshopping houses after the housing boom went bust in 2007. And while lots of condominiums in big cities are bought as investments and can easily be unshopped, others are not worth what people paid for them.

Despite the healthy market for used cars, most vehicles are not really unshoppable, because they lose so much value as soon as you drive them off the lot. Never mind all those classic Corvettes and Jaguars from the 1960s; they have hundreds of hours and thousands of dollars invested in them. They are fun to look at, but not to drive, so only art lovers can afford them. There are some exceptions. In 2019, a 1961 Rolls-Royce Silver Cloud II Drophead Coupé, once owned by jewelry-loving and serial-marrying actor Elizabeth Taylor, sold for more than half a million dollars. But it hadn't always been so sought after. The seller, Karl Kardel, a California collector who bought the car from Taylor in the late 1970s, put it this way: "When I bought it, my friends thought I was an idiot. But then about four years later, the car shot up in value enormously, and I became a genius. And four years after that, the values dropped again, and I became an idiot again." The bottom line: famous car fanatics such as talk-show host Jay Leno may make a profit on one or two vehicles in their impressive collections, but mostly these things cost lots to maintain and rarely get driven. Generally speaking, cars cannot be unshopped (see deshop).

Ditto most expensive watches and most jewelry, unless you weren't paying retail, and even then, it's a crapshoot. If you are a rich watch collector who understands the labyrinthine vagaries of this hobby, you might also be able to make a buck or two. Ignore marketers who say jewelry and watches are an investment—such items rarely are. Unless you really know your watches and jewelry, you're in for some deshopping sooner or later. Gold can sometimes be unshopped, but often not. And diamonds? Almost never. Diamonds are shockingly difficult to unshop.

Computers, cellphones, televisions and other electronic items are, of course, impossible to unshop. Electronics are almost always deshopped. That usually goes also for boats and planes, which give new meaning to the term deshopping, not to mention misshopping. Those who possess such vessels often describe the only two good days of boat or plane ownership as: "The day you buy it and the day you sell it."

Items from Amazon and other e-tailers are supposed to be unshoppable. If the reason for the return is the company's fault, you can easily unshop it. Even items you decide you simply don't like can be returned, but not always without complications. They might be flat out rejected, or you may be charged a shipping fee, and the bill can quickly escalate. That's not unshopping; it's deshopping.

But some retailers are beholden to promises such as "satisfaction guaranteed or money refunded." And many of us are quick to take advantage. Industry experts say one in five Britons is a chronic unshopper, indulging regularly in what is derisively known as "wardrobing" or "free renting," or "return fraud"—buying an outfit, wearing it to an event and then shamelessly returning it the next day to the store (see also contrashop), or buying a power tool, using it for a weekend DIY construction project and returning it Monday for a full refund. Retailers have lamented this scam for years while looking for new ways to fight it. Bloomingdale's, for example, began attaching bulky plastic tags, or "b-tags," to more expensive outfits in 2013. They are not removed at the cash register and are too big to render invisible, but once they are detached, the garment cannot be returned. Various studies put industry losses as a result of unshopping of used clothing in the billions.

Online purchases, meanwhile, are 40 per cent more likely to be returned than those bought at actual stores. It is estimated that merchandise worth $400 billion* is returned to retailers each year, sending five billion pounds of waste to landfills in the United States. While you may think unshopped merchandise is simply put back on the shelves or sent to resellers, in fact much of it ends up in the dump—brand new,

---

* Prices are given in US dollars unless otherwise noted.

unused items are crushed, shredded or destroyed before ever finding a customer, because it's cheaper.

Some items, such as wine and art, are not usually unshoppable, unless you really know what you are doing, and most of us simply do not (see misshop). That said, regular, everyday, strictly deshoppable items can sometimes be rendered unshoppable by rarity, a backstory or inexplicable demand from famous or rich people. Indeed, the very fact that a rich and famous person has owned something can elevate it from deshoppable to unshoppable. Take the case of a once-ordinary comic book, Action Comics No. 1, featuring the first appearance of Superman, which originally sold in 1938 for a dime. In 1997, Oscar-winning actor and outlandish overshopper Nicolas Cage bought one for $150,000. A comic book for $150,000 might seem like a lot to the uninitiated, but that price had already almost doubled since 1992, when the same book was bought for a trifling $82,500. Unfortunately—and fortunately— the flimsy publication, mounted inside a security frame in Cage's Los Angeles home, was stolen in 2000, but mysteriously reappeared eleven years later, when it was recovered from an abandoned storage locker (see predeshop). Cage, who had received an insurance payment for the loss, repurchased the book (see reshop), and then unshopped it at yet another auction for $2 million, a price likely related to its rarity and celebrity backstory. It remains one of Cage's few high-profile shopping ventures that actually paid off.

Even someone nominally rich and marginally famous, such as the late drug-addled mayor of Toronto, Rob Ford, managed to unshop the otherwise ordinary tie he wore on the day in 2013 when he finally admitted he smoked crack. After a false start, Ford realized a tidy profit on the garish tie when it sold on eBay for $1,445 in 2015. By 2018, the item was being unshopped again on eBay for $9,999.

And then there is the remarkable story of the so-called "Paul Newman" wristwatch, a previously deshoppable item that became eminently unshoppable due to the unwitting marketing efforts of the iconic actor. A half century ago, Newman's wife, actor Joanne

Woodward, paid a few hundred dollars for a 1968 Rolex Daytona as a gift for the famously blue-eyed movie star and car-racing enthusiast. Often seen on Newman's wrist in photographs taken around the racetrack, that model came to be celebrated far and wide as the Paul Newman Rolex Daytona. Each one became an object of desire for watch collectors the world over, some fetching $1 million or more for reasons only watch collectors can fathom. But when Paul Newman's actual "Paul Newman," the very one he wore in those photographs, and inscribed by his wife, finally emerged from oblivion and hit the auction block in 2017, it fetched more than a meagre $1 million. (Newman had given the watch years earlier to his daughter's boyfriend, who had kept it all those years.) In an auction that shocked even the auctioneers and made headlines worldwide, someone paid $17.7 million for it (see ultrashop). A backstory often makes deshoppable items unshoppable. And stuff owned by famous people is more than just stuff.

RESHOP

To buy new stuff after getting rid of the old stuff.

This is what we do on Monday afternoon after we get all the refunds and realize we are flush with all the money we didn't actually spend on the weekend because we returned stuff. It's what people do with what they convince themselves is "profit" from unshopped items, when they've sold their second home or an extraneous collector car they didn't need. Self-aggrandizing braggart and former presidential pumpkin-head Donald Trump did this in 1991, when he was forced to deshop his personal Boeing 727 and then buy one back again a few years later when he emerged from near bankruptcy.

The newly rich often become reshoppers when they realize they can finally afford the same old thing except newer and bigger and better and shinier—when they buy a new watch even though the one on their wrist tells perfectly good time. A better-looking bathroom sink, perhaps, or a more expensive handbag. Reshopping is what neighbours indulge in at street-wide yard sales, when they sell for peanuts all the stuff they purchased for a fortune, and use the money generated by that to buy the next door neighbours' junk moments later.

In the developed world, most shopping is reshopping. We are replacing a car, a suit, a dress, a pair of shoes, a phone, a kitchen counter or a bathtub. The one we have might be perfectly good, but it's not exactly in style, not what our friends and neighbours have and no longer what we want, so we unshop it or deshop it—and reshop for a more modern version in the latest colour scheme.

Everyone, to a greater or lesser extent, is like the mournful singer-songwriter Alanis Morissette, who once described dabbling in the deshopping and reshopping that consumes most of the planet's population: "I literally got rid of everything in my house and started over, and it's really minimalist now and I find I can focus and concentrate more when there's less clutter." Yet multiple published photo spreads of Morissette's various homes in later years reveal rooms that are not exactly "minimalist." Less clutter is a relative thing, obviously— and sooner or later the urge to reshop becomes too strong to resist.

Indeed, saying you are a minimalist is not like saying you don't like shopping or aren't addicted to lots of stuff. Though it often involves deshopping, being a minimalist almost always involves reshopping. Reality-TV regular, ubiquitous socialite and internet provocateur Kim Kardashian and her now-ex-husband Kanye West showed off their eccentrically austere home to *Architectural Digest* in 2020. In an accompanying video, Kim waxed materialistic: "I don't think I started off so minimal, but after being with you (West), I became way more minimal . . . I know where every last thing is, there's a place for everything even if it's like hidden in the wall in a cabinet that you can't see. Like, we do have a lot of stuff." Among that "stuff," as it turns out, is a Jean Royère Polar Bear sofa, one of which, according to *Money* magazine in 2018, "sold for up to $754,000 in recent years." Another reportedly sold for a relative bargain at $350,000. "I sold my Maybach to get the Royère," West said, explaining how he sold a luxury car to reshop for a couch. "People told me I was crazy for what I paid for it, but I had to have it."

Houses, of course, are regularly reshopped. And when it comes to homes, there may be no better unshopper and reshopper than committed humanitarian, talented comedian and alleged bully-boss Ellen DeGeneres, who felt compelled to write a book about the many homes she has bought, renovated, redecorated and then sold before she and wife Portia de Rossi got too comfortable. (As it happens, DeGeneres also has/had a Royère couch.) In 2014, she told the *New York Times* that "I've never bought to sell. I always say: 'This is it. I'm never moving.' People laugh at me now." She insisted then, after buying the so-called Brody House, a Romanesque-style villa in Holmby Hills, California, for $40 million and renovating it to her tastes, that this was finally it: "I think there's nowhere to go from here. It's the best house I've ever lived in. Where would I go?" A scant seven months later, the couple was clearly unhappy there. They unshopped it for $55 million—a tidy profit, perhaps, even after renovations, redecorations, time, tears, trouble, taxes and tariffs.

Not all unshoppers and reshoppers are so astute. There are always a few losers, such as ill-fated British garbage collector Michael Carroll—dubbed a "lotto lout" by the tabloid media—who won almost £10 million in a lottery in 2002 and blew it all within the decade: "I would buy these huge necklaces. One cost me around £2,000. All of it was robbed in 2004. There was about £100,000 worth of gold stolen. But the next day I went out and bought it all again."

DESHOP

To get rid of stuff.

This is what occurs when we sell stuff for a few pennies on the dollar or unload it at fire-sale prices. We toss it out, give it away, leave it on the sidewalk, put it in the dumpster. Or maybe we just plain lose it to forces beyond our control. It's the end of the line: the utter humiliation of the annual garage sale, where your eight-year-old kid generates more income from a one-armed 2011 action figure than you can from that $300 vase that looked so lovely in the store little more than a year ago. Or the auction, where nobody bids on the item on which you spent the equivalent of $1,246 and lugged all the way home from Kenya. It's usually what happens when you put stuff on Kijiji or eBay or Facebook Marketplace. You think something is worth $10, but you realize nobody will pay more than five. Deshopping is what Oscar-winning actor and failed land developer Kim Basinger did in 1993, when she and her partners sold the town of Braselton, Georgia, for $4.3 million after buying it for $20 million five years earlier (see also misshop).

It's what parents the world over do when they realize, to their dismay and alarm, that their grown children do not want the Wedgwood tableware they spent a lifetime collecting, the heirloom furniture for which they paid handsomely and then stowed in the basement, nor even the 1995 Mazda Miata they kept in storage for when junior finally got a licence to drive. It's what we do when all else fails, when we finally realize what everyone else seems to already know: it's all worthless. (The kids want cheap IKEA furniture and dishes, and junior wants a pickup truck.) "Old mahogany stuff from my great aunt's house is basically worthless," said one liquidator in a 2017 *Forbes* article entitled "Sorry, Nobody Wants Your Parents' Stuff." If we're really lucky, we call a local charity and drop it off for them, or better yet, get them to pick it up on the front porch—preferably in the dead of night so the neighbours don't witness the mortifying spectacle—and hope those charities don't realize until it's too late that this stuff is obsolete, worthless and deshoppable. Failing that, we haul it to the dump, where we pay one final time just for the luxury of disposing of it in one of the world's rapidly expanding landfill sites (see deshopping centre).

Deshopping is the ultimate punishment for shopping and God's revenge for our steadfast refusal to unshop, and our dogged insistence on reshopping. Deshopping is often the result of bargain hunting, where we buy a pair of shoes or a toaster for a price so low it almost defies belief, and then realize not weeks later that our purchase was not a bargain at all. With the shoes too painful to wear and the toaster already broken and unrepairable, we realize we paid full price after all, and off to the dump it all goes. The insane irony of modern acquisitive life is that it is possible the opposite is also true: you bought an item of exquisite quality and craftsmanship, but it is no longer in style, too bulky, too brown or white or harvest gold, too, well, old, and your kids and neighbours would much rather have the cheaply built silver, black or white ones at IKEA. Deshopping may soon be one of the most expensive activities on Earth, when the planet starts bending under the unbearable weight of all the dumps, when open space is worth more than retail space, and when landfill sites take up more space than shopping-mall parking lots.

Deshopping likely describes what oddball tech billionaire Elon Musk announced on Twitter he was going to do in 2020 at the height of the coronavirus pandemic: "I am selling almost all physical possessions," he tweeted. "Will own no house." Just because he didn't want possessions, however, didn't mean the controversial industrialist didn't care about stuff. In an interview only days later, he explained that he would keep some sentimental material. Furthermore, he said, whoever bought a certain one of his many houses, a structure formerly owned by comic actor and writer Gene Wilder, would have to agree not to tear it down, because it is "quirky" and should be preserved. As a result, said Musk, "it'll probably sell for less, but still I don't care." Musk acknowledged he bought a collection of "these little houses" in his neighbourhood (see supershop) so he could build something newer and bigger with a better view (see ultrashop), but then suddenly lost interest (see misshop). He did, however, admit he could simply reshop for the stuff he planned to unshop or deshop if the vagabond life didn't meet with his expectations.

Socialite and reality-TV pioneer Paris Hilton indulged in some serious deshopping after she announced that "I have, like, a million clothes and more than 500 pairs of shoes, so I'm going to give a bunch of them to orphanages and children's hospitals. I never wear something twice." Groundbreaking 1970s TV icon Mary Tyler Moore did the same thing when she unloaded an "extremely expensive" Russian sable coat only months after she bought it at the height of her fame. Somehow suddenly aware of the "pain" caused to furry friends in the creation of the coat, she described it as a "disgrace" she wore "only a half dozen times" before she was "ashamed to have it on" (see misshop). Moore, a famous vegetarian, gave it to People for the Ethical Treatment of Animals, where it became a travelling symbol of human excess and cruelty.

Deshopping is what questionable deal-maker Donald Trump, the man *Spy* magazine famously labelled the "short-fingered vulgarian," did in 1995 when he sold the Plaza Hotel, a New York City landmark, for $83 million less than he paid for it in 1988.

The late lunatic overshopper and evil mastermind Osama Bin Laden regularly dabbled in deshopping before he became the world's most notorious terrorist, according to an account from Christina Akerblad, former owner of the Hotel Astoria in Falun, Sweden, when Bin Laden visited in 1970: "On Sunday, I had no cleaner at the hotel, so I took care of the room myself, and I was shocked because in the big bag they had lots of white, expensive shirts from Dior and Yves Saint Laurent. When they had [worn] the shirt once, they dropped it. So the cleaner had taken these shirts to wash them, but they said, 'No, we are just using them once, so you can [have] them if you want.'"

Much to his chagrin, London mayor Sadiq Khan was forced in 2017 to deshop a trio of water cannons bought in 2014 by his loopy predecessor Boris Johnson, who never checked first if they could be used on the streets of the English capital. Taxpayers spent a total £322,834.71 on the vehicles (which never saw use) before unloading them for £11,025 for scrap.

For the unfortunate few, deshopping is not necessarily something they do, but often something that is done to them. Bankers, lenders, loan sharks and repo-men are forever lurking in the shadows. Deshopping is their business. Let's take as just one example the much-beloved but morally bankrupt American architect Frank Lloyd Wright. Often called the greatest architect of the twentieth century, Wright was also a collector and dealer in Japanese art in the early decades of the twentieth century, and he sometimes made more money from the sideline than he did from the commissions on his famous buildings. A cheapskate, a freeloader and a deadbeat dad who could not manage his money, he was forever broke and didn't pay his debts to friends. In 1926, Wright lost his home, Taliesin, to the Bank of Wisconsin, which deshopped thousands of his expensive prints for a dollar apiece to a single collector.

In 2010, cash-strapped eccentric Nicolas Cage, the fifth-highest grossing Hollywood actor in 2009 with an income of $26 million, lost a Tudor estate in Bel-Air, California, when the bank deshopped it for only $10.5 million, less than a third of what Cage had been asking a few years earlier. Formerly owned by, among others, philandering heart-throb Tom Jones and crooning Rat-Packer Dean Martin, the place was done up in a style one realtor called "frat house bordello" and entangled by six loans totalling $18 million. It wasn't the only home Cage would be forced to deshop (see also downshop). Rich or poor, the banks are always circling.

SHOPPER

A person who shops.

Almost all of us, some more than others.

NON-SHOPPER

A person who does not shop.

This is, of course, a distinct minority. Infants, usually. The aged and infirm, maybe. Monks and cloistered nuns possibly. Isolated tribes in the remote, sweltering jungles of Asia or South America, conceivably. The people of North Sentinel, for example, probably. The tiny island in the Andaman Sea has a population that shuns visitors, and to remind us, natives in 2018 speared to death the most recent visitor, John Chau, an American missionary who paddled ashore against all advice and common sense. The Andaman and Nicobar islands are 1,100 kilometres from the subcontinent, and the Indian government, to protect the tribes from outside interference, has outlawed all travel there. As a result, the Sentinelese have had little contact with the outside world, and their way of life has likely remained relatively unchanged for generations. As there is no recognizable shopping on North Sentinel Island, and as there is no internet, and as the tribespeople there never leave, and visitors do not survive, the North Sentinelese may qualify as non-shoppers, but only from a global perspective. After all, humans being humans, quite likely there is a booming internal shopathon there involving various local innovations. The Democratic Republic of the Congo, one of the poorest countries in the world, may have many citizens who are non-shoppers, on account of the fact they have no money, but even amid the widespread deprivation, people have to shop.

Indeed, there are many who claim they are non-shoppers, and many who are portrayed as such, but such assessments should be regarded with extreme skepticism in an acquisitive world. Brooding poet, notorious ladies' man and internationally beloved singer-songwriter Leonard Cohen, for example, did not accumulate much stuff during his lifetime, preferring to live for many years in dingy hotels, rented rooms, a simple home he paid $1,500 for on the Greek island of Hydra, and eventually a monastery. He griped about Suzanne Elrod, the mother of his children but not the subject of his well-known song, and her "Miami consumer habits" but said of himself: "All I need is a table, chair and bed." And he once wrote an earlier lover, the celebrated Marianne Ihlen of song, to say he finally realized what he must be: "a man who owns nothing." Well, almost nothing. His homes in Hydra, Montreal and Los Angeles were notoriously spare and spartan, according to many writers who profiled him, but there were, after all, three of them. Just because a famous person has homes that are not featured in *Architectural Digest* or *People* magazine doesn't mean they don't shop. Nor did Cohen's aversion to consumerism prevent him from drinking as many as three bottles of Château Latour, by his own admission a "very expensive" French Bordeaux, before each performance during his Future World Tour through Europe and North America in the 1990s (see ultrashop).

Despite being one of the richest men in the world during his lifetime, the demented aviator, filmmaker and industrialist Howard Hughes might have qualified as a non-shopper, at least by conventional standards, in his advanced years, owing perhaps to the fact that he was permanently holed up in various hotel rooms due to obsessive-compulsive disorder and an aversion to germs. In his youth, he acquired a predictable collection of clothes, cars, yachts and houses, but by the mid-1960s, as he descended into madness, he had little use for stuff as the rest of us might define it, because he never went out or even got dressed. But he managed to purchase a few things here and there nonetheless. In 1966, for example, Hughes checked into Las Vegas's Desert Inn on Thanksgiving, announcing a ten-day stay, but when he was still ensconced at the end of December, the hotel asked him to leave to make way for high-rolling holiday guests on New Year's Eve. Instead of complying, Hughes simply bought the hotel and stayed put for another four years, finding the arrangement so agreeable that he bought another five or so hotels in subsequent years. When Hughes, a famous insomniac and movie buff, became annoyed at the lack of a twenty-four-hour television station in Las Vegas willing to play movies through the night, he bought the CBS affiliate KLAS so he could dictate its programming, an arrangement that led to the frequent screening of the movie *Ice Station Zebra*, a 1968 vehicle for 1960s heartthrob Rock Hudson that received mixed reviews. That's not shopping the way most of us perceive it, perhaps, but it's shopping nonetheless.

Home computer pioneer, visionary Apple Inc. perfectionist and former deadbeat dad Steve Jobs qualified as a non-shopper in relative terms. An eccentric workaholic who in his twenties was worth merely tens of millions rather than the multi-billions he would eventually earn, Jobs was famously photographed for *Time* magazine in 1982 sitting on the floor of his expansive California home, which was decorated with little more than a light stand and a computer. "He's a minimalist," recalled former Apple CEO John Sculley, who recalled visiting Jobs and finding him alone at home with little more than a Tiffany lamp, a chair and a bed. Even in his later years, he appeared to shop for very few clothes beyond his trademark blue jeans and black mock turtleneck shirts, of which he reportedly had dozens, perhaps hundreds. "That's what I wear," Jobs told his biographer, Walter Isaacson. "I have enough to last for the rest of my life." Jobs was reluctant to buy appliances, furniture and other household items, because he could not find any with a design that met his particular standards.

J. Paul Getty, the avaricious, mean-spirited oil baron once known worldwide as the planet's richest individual, could perhaps appear at times to be a non-shopper, but "cheapskate" was probably more accurate. At best, he was known, as so many other rich people are, for his frugality. He wore tattered clothing, laundered his own socks, infamously installed a payphone in his home for guests, and notoriously refused to pay the ransom when his grandson was kidnapped. But he lived like a king in, among other residences on various continents, Sutton Place, a seventy-two-room English mansion, and had a collection of eighteenth-century European paintings, furniture and Greco-Roman sculpture numbering in the thousands, much of which is displayed today at the J. Paul Getty Museum in Los Angeles.

The writer Judith Levine might have once qualified as a non-shopper, but again it's debatable. Her engaging book *Not Buying It: My Year Without Shopping* documents her and her husband's twelve-month odyssey away from the shops, avoiding all but necessary purchases. The idea came to her at the height of the Christmas season (see shopathon) when she finally decided she could take it no more, and apparently neither could her credit card. But as she herself admits, she lapsed on more than one occasion. Being a non-shopper in a world of shoppers is no small challenge. Among the more notable segments of the book might be Levine's description of the last item she and her husband bought online before time ran out on New Year's Eve. You might think a couple going without buying stuff for a year would make this choice carefully, and search for something useful, helpful or convenient, but the couple's last indulgence before an entire year of abstinence was in fact "a small concrete baby elephant" to serve as "an ornament to place on a jutting rock in our perennial garden."

There are, of course, individuals who insist they are non-shoppers 24/7, distinct from those who may be just dabbling in it. The term "postmaterialism" was coined in 1977 by political scientist Ronald Inglehart to describe those who might want something more from life than just stuff. "The values of Western publics have been shifting from an overwhelming emphasis on material well-being and physical security toward greater emphasis on the quality of life." There are places, usually rich nations, where some people are actually living that dream (or nightmare, depending on your point of view), but for the most part we all still like stuff, and lots of it. Some people say they don't follow fashion, for example. They say they don't shop at trendy stores. They say they wear just any old thing, or buy the cheapest, simplest version of whatever trend was hot a few years ago.

But anyone who likes to think of him or herself as immune to the temptations or manipulations of the retailing business, and especially the fashion industry, should view (or more likely review, it's available on YouTube) the typically bravura performance of acting legend Meryl Streep in *The Devil Wears Prada*, a movie based on Lauren Weisberger's 2003 novel of the same name. It is the now-famous scene where Anne Hathaway's character, wearing a frumpy blue sweater, giggles about some high fashion items, dismissing them as "stuff." The room goes suddenly quiet, Streep's Miranda regards Hathaway's Andy with steely disdain, and then calmly but sternly schools her on exactly how the fashion industry, not Andrea herself, came to choose "stuff" like the very blue sweater she was wearing. Whether we are wearing haute couture or a sale-bin discount, we are all victims of fashion; we are all shoppers.

SHOPOPHOBIA

A fear of shopping.

Very few of us actually suffer from this. Certainly not people who already have everything a person could ever want and more. Not people whose (many) homes are already chock full of stuff. Almost everyone everywhere is looking for more, whether they need it or not. It's safe to assume most of us would agree with famous shopper, former drug abuser and gifted musician Elton John, who admitted to dispersing more than £40 million over a twenty-month period in the late 1990s, including £293,000 on flowers alone: "I like spending money."

But there are exceptions. Some people have a legitimate fear of shopping. They don't feel they deserve it. They don't think they look good in clothes, so they are terrified of racks. They don't feel they need another household item. They don't like crowds or lineups at the counter. "Nothing triggers my anxiety and depression quite like clothes shopping for myself," says writer Kristi Pahr. "Retail therapy is NOT therapeutic." Indeed, despite the unbridled joy it brings to billions, clothes shopping is pure hell for some. But compared to those with a shopping addiction, this kind of thing is rare indeed.

More often, shopophobia develops among the spouses, siblings, parents, children, heirs, business managers and various relatives of shoppers. Most of these victims are married to or associated with someone who is responsible for an awful lot of shopping and deshopping, and so the shopophobic becomes ill every time they encounter a quaint shop or an outlet mall or eBay on the home computer and contemplates the next credit card bill. And yet shopophobes often have another thing in common: they are often themselves overshoppers, but they hypocritically criticize others for it. Seventies movie star and wise-cracking nightclub owner Burt Reynolds, who at one time owned the typical assemblage of houses, cars, aircraft and 150 horses before declaring bankruptcy, may not have recognized his own shopping addictions, but he had no trouble declaring an allergy to the habits of his ex-wife, the actor Loni Anderson, whom Reynolds alleged required only half an hour to max out the $45,000 limit on an American Express Platinum Card he gave her: "The Countess bought everything in triplicate," Reynolds once told an interviewer. "China. Diamonds. Designer gowns. She'd pay $10,000 a pop for the dress. And being 'the Countess,' she'd only wear them once because, you know, she couldn't possibly wear a dress after it had been photographed. She'd say, 'I have to dress like a star, Burt.'"

SHOPIFICATION

The process by which stores carrying things you need are gradually replaced with shops carrying stuff you want.

A worldwide phenomenon, shopification is based on the assumption that shopping should not be a chore or a necessity, but a fun exercise, an enlightening diversion, a cultural experience in a manipulated commercial area vaguely reminiscent of Disneyland. The universal signposts of shopification are quaint antique stores, knick-knack emporiums, art galleries, tea rooms, places that serve lattes but aren't Starbucks. There are rarely ever any empty storefronts in shopified areas. They are pretty, perfect, predictable and safe. If not, they haven't been properly shopified.

It happens slowly, gradually, insidiously. Shopification is all about cute, genuine or manufactured, often for the sole enjoyment of tourists. Woodstock, Vermont; Aspen, Colorado; Carmel, California; Quebec City, Quebec, Niagara-on-the-Lake, Ontario; and Key West, Florida, have all been shopified. But it isn't restricted to quaint communities. Retailing "neighbourhoods" in big tourist cities are shopified annually, as residents are driven out to make room for droves of crap-crazy tourists. You can see it most acutely, perhaps, in places such as Venice, Barcelona and Dubrovnik, where city officials now worry that too many rich visitors shopping for curios are chasing away residents looking for a can of beans or a bathroom plunger. Nice places to visit perhaps, but you wouldn't want to live there.

The Canadian village where I grew up, a place called Kleinburg, Ontario, is a good example. Just north of Toronto, it was a rural farming community in the 1960s where everyone knew everyone. My friend Will Perry's mom and dad ran the drug store. Jim Shaw's folks owned the hardware store. Ralph Hank's parents had the bakery. Diane Hall's dad operated the gas station and Rick DeCaire's dad was the butcher. Gary Hilliard's dad owned Hilliard's TV Repair and Sales just off the main drag. In the village, you could pretty well find anything you needed and catch up on the local news to boot. My mother could easily spend an hour at the post office (in the days when post offices sold only stamps), and often did.

By the 1990s, it was all gone. The Perry family's pharmacy morphed into a place called the Rock Shop, where they sold polished stones. The old bakery became a purveyor of fine art and antiques. The butcher shop turned into a curio boutique. The hardware store and the Hall family's gas station are long demolished, replaced by a succession of cappuccino joints, fudge emporiums and a strip of quaint stores with names such as Harvest Treasures, Manhattan Shades and So Chic, once described on signage as a place "where girlfriends shop."

Unlike their predecessors, many of these operations come and go in a matter of years, regularly supplanted by the latest in shopification. The old general store became an elegant vendor of jewelry, handcrafted on site. My friend Randy Sweet would discover his childhood home on the main street had been turned into a bed and breakfast. The house in which my classmate Timmy Wheeldon grew up became, among other things, a café that also engaged in "floral artistry." Kleinburg was thoroughly shopified. Now, on warm summer days, the sidewalks teem with ice-cream-eating tourists and bridal-party photo shoots amid the few remaining historic buildings. Meanwhile, actual residents of Kleinburg don't shop in the village. If you require hardware, meat, a loaf of bread or gasoline, you must now drive to one of many gleaming new shopping centres and supermarkets a few kilometres away, park in a pristine asphalt ocean of automobiles that was once a cow pasture, and make your way through the checkout lines (see shopitization). Somehow, shopping in Kleinburg went from an old-fashioned necessity to a vacation activity.

SHOPITIZATION

The process of paving lush green fields or demolishing historic commercial, industrial and residential areas to create shiny, new, comfortably predictable and securely controlled retailing centres, outlet malls or so-called power centres.

While shopification is generally restricted to historic downtowns and can take years, even decades, shopitization can take place anywhere and comes all at once. Shopitizers are equally comfortable demolishing old buildings as they are building on a farm field, but their work almost always occurs suddenly and on a vast scale. It is marked by multinational name-brand stores, plus a few familiar fast-food outlets and several recognizable coffee shops. Shopitized areas are for those people who once shopped in what are now shopified districts. Unlike shopification, modern shopitization has no time for history, heritage or fake quaintness, and definitely no time for lattes, unless, of course, they are made by Starbucks.

Shopitization has occurred around the world for centuries, but in modern suburban instances it offers the promise of predictability, the illusion of convenient parking and the delusion of good deals. Shopitized areas in North America and beyond are utterly predictable and comfortably familiar, so even tourists who have never visited the place know exactly where to go, how to park, where to find the bathroom and what to eat. Unlike shopified districts, which exclusively sell stuff you want but don't need, shopitized areas sell stuff you need but don't want: gasoline, toilet paper, a snow shovel, plus a lot of clothes and home furnishings you somehow missed on your last trip. There are rarely any empty storefronts in newly shopitized areas, but such a transition is inevitable. They start out as handsome and safe, but sooner or later they start to deteriorate like any old Main Street as cracks form in the asphalt, parking gets farther away as the parking lots fill up, garbage gathers along the chain-link fences, weeds grow up along the boulevards, architectural fashion fades, ever-newer shopitized areas sprout up nearby, or everyone decides it's easier to shop online.

One of the first suburban (or rural) shopping centres in the United States created specifically for the automobile age is said to be a fifty-five-acre site near Kansas City, Missouri, called Country Club Plaza. Built in 1922 on what was then considered remote farmland, it would be the first in a long line of shopping areas designed with architectural flourishes to provide shoppers with the illusion they were somewhere they were not: in this case Seville, Spain. The developer, J.C. Nichols, enticed shopping away from what was then downtown and into the boondocks, where homes were nearby, parking was plentiful and everything was pretty—and white: Nichols, like many others, used restrictive covenants to prevent Black people from owning or occupying any of the houses in the area.

An early example of downtown shopitization is a nationally designated historic site in suburban Chicago. They call it Market Square, in Lake Forest, and it was bought by the Broadacre Management organization in 1984. According to Broadacre, when Market Square was conceived in 1913, the district was home to "an unremarkable clutch of ramshackle buildings. Situated directly across from the train station, these unsightly structures were a daily eyesore for the commuters on their way to and from the city." Enter Arthur Aldis and Howard Van Doren, courageous and progressive developers who bought up the shops, razed them completely and started from scratch. The result: the country's first planned outdoor shopping centre, and likely the first modern North American example of downtown shopitization.

Just as its inventors had planned, the mall became the town centre for many North Americans, whether it was downtown or in suburbia, in small cities or big metropolises. For me, it was never ingrained in my psyche, never the place be, to meet, to hang out, to shop. It was not the centre of the world as it seemed to be for other teens. Perhaps I had other diversions, or perhaps I simply had unfond memories of being dragged along while my mother sought shoes for my little sister, who needed to try on twenty pairs before choosing ones that fit. The only reward amid the ordeal was a corned-beef sandwich at the mall's deli. For others, however, the mall remains a place of euphoric shopping triumphs and embarrassing social tragedies. Only in the last generation has the romance—perhaps—started to fade.

And early signs of that began first in downtown cores. Despite the purported success of Market Square, many attempts at downtown shopitization failed miserably. By the 1970s and '80s, such "downtown revitalization" attempts were *de rigueur* across North America, and most were misguided. In too many cases, the malls failed as soon as the hype dissipated, and owners across North America deshopped them in the 1990s for a fraction of what it cost to build them.

Perhaps the best example is Detroit's Renaissance Center, a towering memorial to the Motor City built for $350 million in the 1970s. The brainchild of Henry Ford II, it was a thundering monument to glass and steel—and perhaps a metaphor for the industry that built it—and its builders hoped it would put the faded metropolis back on the map. Like so many other downtown shopping malls, the gleaming towers of the Renaissance Center were nothing if not imposing, and the development, typical of so much other ill-considered architecture, turned its back on the downtown it aimed to celebrate and revive. It stands guilty of the cardinal—and typical—architectural sins of not relating to its surroundings and frightening visitors away. By 1996, the Ford company had had enough. It deshopped the Renaissance Center to General Motors for a paltry $72 million, $280 million less than it spent to build it (see misshop).

Singapore committed the sin of shopitization in the mid-1980s, when developers bulldozed the city's storied and seamy Bugis Street, a twenty-four-hour *pasar malam* or "night market" known for its mysterious past as a haven for trans women and drag queens and a magnet for curious tourists. In its place, they plunked down glittering shopping malls, an ultra-modern subway station and newly regulated street vendors. The exotic air of mystery, debauchery and fun dissipated, the tourists went elsewhere and the hawkers packed up. Various attempts by the Singapore Tourism Board to recreate the history (see shopification) and carnival atmosphere that once made Bugis Street a destination largely failed. In 1991, Ronnie Chia, a developer overseeing restoration to remake the old Bugis Street, told the *New York Times*: "It's going to be a fun place, a partying place. We want to create the original flavor of Bugis Street. Good fun, 24 hours of fun."

It never happened.

Today, some in Singapore lament the city's loss of historic marketplaces—its heart and its soul—and the general deterioration of culture and historical perspective, as tourists flock to newer, better and flashier retailing opportunities in newly shopitized cities such as Dubai, a conservative Muslim community which lifted itself, through the power of shopping alone, into the highest echelons of the world's tourist destinations (see shopopolis).

RESHOPITIZE

To fix the place up.

Basically redecorating, remodelling, redesigning or renovating a store, a mall or a shopping neighbourhood. Retailers do it every six months or shoppers won't buy stuff.

SHOPPABLE

The degree to which a place or a thing is worthy of being shopped.

In the decades following the Second World War, the shoppability of much of the world was in question. We wrecked the place, after all, and people were focused on survival, not shopping. Even in North America, long after a war that barely touched its shores, there wasn't a whole lot to buy—yet. Take the North American service station, for example: it sold gasoline, oil, maps and, if you were lucky, Coca-Cola from a machine. And if you had a nickel, you might be able to pick up a gumball or a handful of peanuts from a dispenser. In other words: not shoppable. At some point, the service station began to sell all manner of items—candy, salty food, ice cream, pizza, cigarette lighters, sunglasses, fuzzy dice and lottery tickets—often jammed into a tin garden shed an eighth the size of the sprawling concrete bunker that was the 1960s service station. Today, it's difficult to find a North American gas station without an adjacent full-service retailing operation.

Ditto the pharmacy. While North American drug stores were famous in the 1920s for introducing the so-called soda fountain, by the 1970s they had retrenched to mostly medicines and a few other sundries. Today's drug stores sell everything from bread to birthday party decorations to kitschy craft items. Makeup and perfume. Some sell frozen dinners. Even fresh produce. You can spend hours strolling the aisles of the pharmacy finding useful items that have nothing to do with ailments. And, of course, there is almost no store in the developed world where you cannot acquire a bag of potato chips or a keychain flashlight at the checkout counter. The old-fashioned pharmacy was not shoppable. The modern pharmacy is a shopper's paradise (see shoptopia).

Once, the hardware store sold hardware; the lumber store sold lumber and maybe some nails. Unless you were building a deck, they weren't particularly shoppable. Today, the hardware store sells hardware, lumber, barbecues, kitchen utensils, lawn furniture, recreational items, garden plants, camping equipment. They have how-to demonstrations, craft activities, hot dogs, games for kids and dog runs for the family pet. And, of course, a lot of tools you'll never use and the predictable assortment of knick-knacks. The modern hardware store is shoppable no matter who you are.

The museum, the art gallery and the aquarium were once non-shoppable, but by the 1980s the shops near the exit had become widespread and often the main event (see shopapalooza). Universities have become littered with stores. Even hospitals, increasingly cash-strapped and always desperate for funding, are getting themselves shoppable. No longer are dried flowers, get-well cards and a few stuffed animals enough for the hospital gift shop—visitors have time on their hands and charity in their hearts. Savvy big-city health-care centres have gone from non-shoppable wastelands to shoppable paradises. Small-town equivalents will be following soon.

Some tourists in Europe may grow tired on day three of yet another church, another beautifully carved pew, one more stained glass window, a different candle to light. Fortunately, even churches frequented by tourists have shops, containing affordably priced icons and kitschy memorabilia we can peruse after a prayer. You can shop for jewelry at the Notre-Dame de Paris shop, for example, or a rosary at St. Peter's Basilica gift shop. Decorative crosses are popular at the Holy Sepulchre Store in Jerusalem. Westminster Abbey in London has a gift shop. The Hagia Sophia in Istanbul was shoppable, at least until it was converted back into a mosque in 2020.

Most cities around the world can be rated according to their shoppability. New York City, for example, is shoppable. So are Nairobi and Bangkok. These cities have a high shoppability quotient. But Flint, Michigan? Low shoppability, at least in comparison to Manhattan.

Then again, shoppability is in the eye of the beholder. Milan, Italy, is highly shoppable; Pyongyang, North Korea, is not, unless you are a rural North Korean with a pocketful of won, in which case it is likely highly shoppable. Neither is Havana particularly shoppable, unless you are Cuban, an art collector or a cigar-seeking tourist. Gaza City is not shoppable, even if you are a Palestinian without many of the basics the Western world takes for granted.

Iqaluit, Canada, is not particularly shoppable, owing to the fact it is largely cut off from the rest of the world each winter. Located on remote Baffin Island in the high Arctic, almost everything is imported, expensive and scarce. But if you've just put into the harbour with a bag full of cash after being trapped in the ice for months, well, it just might be the definition of a shopper's mecca. And there is some impressive fine art made there. Murzuq, Libya; Waldo, Kansas; Oymyakon, Siberia; and Marble Bar, Australia, are not very shoppable, unless you are a local treasure hunter or have emerged recently from the desert, the great plains, the tundra or the outback and are shopping for a bottle of water or some gasoline, in which case they might well be highly shoppable compared to some of their neighbours.

Until the final decades of the twentieth century, the shoppability of the entire nations of India and China was low for all but the most courageous, sophisticated, treasure-seeking, eccentric world-travellers and curio-collectors, and perhaps the Indians and Chinese themselves, but today, well, they're a virtual international shopper's paradise no matter who you are—as long as you have lots of spending cash. And many of the citizens of those nations have become supershoppers and ultrashoppers.

The transition to a shoppable destination may not necessarily require a societal transformation. Sometimes a place can simply declare itself as such. For example, Pitcairn Island (population fifty and dropping), an isolated volcanic outcropping in the southern Pacific Ocean made famous by desperate mutineers of the HMS *Bounty* and as the setting for incessant books and movies, is not shoppable. Unless, of course, you work for the island's tourist bureau, which trumpets the place as a shopper's paradise: "There is really something for everyone, including 'traveller staples' like Pitcairn Island T-shirts and Caps." (See shopaganda.)

If you are rich, own twenty-nine pairs of shoes, twenty-four scarves, seventeen watches, fourteen suits, eight cars and every countertop appliance that was ever invented, the Hermès store in London's Heathrow Airport and Bergdorf Goodman in New York still likely remain shoppable. Despite the fact that the Gucci stores in Beverly Hills, Toronto, São Paulo, Cape Town, Dubai, Vienna, Beijing, Tokyo, Sydney and dozens of other cities around the world are nearly identical, all of them, no matter how many you've been in, are somehow just as shoppable as the one you visited on a different leg of your holiday or business trip four days ago. For you, Walmart is likely not particularly shoppable unless, like so many rich shoppers, you simply must pay bottom dollar for everything. And although you probably wouldn't admit it, you could probably find something you "need" in a Walmart if you happened to find yourself trapped in one during some kind of nightmarish misadventure. But if you are among the working poor, have five kids, a beat-up automobile, threadbare clothes and holes in all your socks, then Walmart is indeed shoppable.

Deutsche Bank does an annual cost-of-living survey to determine which cities are most expensive for various products. In 2019, for example, Switzerland and the Scandinavian countries had the most expensive jeans, while Nigeria and Bangladesh had the least expensive. For "a summer dress in a High Street store (Zara, H&M or similar)," the most expensive were in Saudi Arabia, the least expensive in Greece and Nigeria. Not surprisingly, media organizations translate such information into listicles of shoppable and non-shoppable cities with headlines such as "The best and worst places to shop in the world."

In fact, a tourist town is only a tourist town because it's shoppable. A place can have the most spectacular and astounding natural wonder of the world in its midst; an ancient and fascinating architectural ruin and a rich social history; the nation's most famous native son or daughter whose childhood homestead has become a renowned museum and fascinating historic site; or all the amusements and rides that the mighty Disney corporation can dream up, but if it's not shoppable, visitors will be disappointed.

Meanwhile, the stores are littered with examples of formerly non-shoppable items that have been rendered shoppable through human innovation, interminable marketing, clever packaging and rampant globalization. A faucet was once a faucet. A sink was once just a sink. You might have been able to choose a round one over a square one, a pink one over a green one, and perhaps you could choose between a few national brands. But these things were not particularly shoppable. Now, in a globalized world, choosing a bathroom suite can take weeks for unprepared home renovators. Pull-out faucets or pull-down faucets or fusion-style faucets or waterfall faucets, single-handle, two-handle, old-fashioned, modern, black, stainless steel, red faucets and gold faucets. Hundreds, probably thousands of brands, styles, colours. Faucets today are totally shoppable. Discerning homeowners express themselves in faucetry.

Our grandparents might once have considered dirt non-shoppable. If you wanted some, you could dig it up in the backyard or sweep it off the front porch into a dustpan. Today, dirt is not just dirt. Dirt is "landscaping soil." It is sandy loam. It is rich in compost or manure. Or it has higher PH levels or calcium enrichments or nutrients. Designer dirt comes cleverly packaged in coloured bags, stacked to the ceiling at urban garden centres, guaranteed to grow stuff better, and marketed for upwardly mobile professionals who want their gardens to look lusher than the neighbours'. Today's plants simply won't grow in yesterday's dirt. Yes, grandpa, dirt is shoppable.

Sixties hippies lurked in alleyways to buy "grass" in unmarked nickel and dime bags (see contrashop). Today, in nations that have legalized marijuana, it can be shopped in showrooms offering a limitless variety of the formerly illicit material with trendy names in various forms, packages and potency. Marijuana was once marketed as a "take-it-or-leave-it" item (and let's face it, if you were a dope smoker, it was usually "take it"). Today, it has become shoppable, and as always, the type you favour reflects upon your person, and is a topic of conversation at parties (see convershopping).

Until the worldwide pandemic in 2020, vaccines were not particularly shoppable. You got the flu shot or the measles shot and that was it. By 2021, many Zoom conversations centred on which COVID-19 vaccine one had received, which ones their parents got and which ones were best recommended. Somehow, vaccines had been branded like watches and running shoes.

It turns out that anything is shoppable—just add unnecessary packaging, clever marketing (see shopaganda) and an ecologically suspect distribution system. In 1975, an advertising writer named Gary Dahl turned something utterly non-shoppable into something remarkably shoppable through the power of packaging. Dahl sold an astonishing number of "pet rocks" at $4 apiece over the Christmas season. Packaged in custom cardboard boxes with straw and breathing holes, they somehow became a hot item and Dahl quickly became a millionaire before shoppers came to their senses and the fad evaporated. By then he had sold 1.5 million, in what *Newsweek* magazine later described as "one of the most ridiculously successful marketing schemes ever." It was another indication that people are desperate to buy something, anything, no matter how useless, especially at Christmas.

Once upon a time, people drank coffee from ceramic mugs in their kitchens. Or they ordered coffee at the local diner. Today, coffee is shoppable. The idea of drinking it from a plain, unbranded, reusable mug is almost quaint. That same generation was also satisfied with the plain old gin or whiskey they kept in discreet glass decanters, but today we prominently display the brand that best reflects our lifestyle, our character, our refined tastes, our shopping prowess, our ecological or social wokeness or our desired social status, and few really stop to wonder if it's really worth it.

The one distinguishing feature of vodka, after all, is its utter lack of any discernible flavour. Indeed, US and Canadian laws stipulate it must be "without distinctive character, aroma or taste." Not exactly the building blocks for shoppability. And for centuries, vodka wasn't that shoppable—until the 1980s. That's about the time Absolut, a Swedish vodka maker for more than a hundred years, began marketing its stuff worldwide and enlisted experimental pop artist Andy Warhol and others to help make the brand a little sexier, the vodka a little more shoppable. The result was among the most successful advertising campaigns of the twentieth century—and an explosion of "handmade," "ultra-smooth," "premium" and "super-premium" vodkas such as Belvedere, Ketel One, Chopin and Tito's started pouring into the market.

Grey Goose vodka was invented from virtually nothing in 1997. It was the brainchild of schmoozer extraordinaire and legendary American promoter Sidney Frank, who had earlier transformed an obscure European herbal digestif called Jägermeister into a North American barroom sensation. Recalled Frank: "The nice thing about vodka is you make it today, you sell it tomorrow; even Jägermeister is aged for a year. So you don't have to put your money into buildings and machines and warehouses . . . The big-selling high-priced vodka at the time was Absolut, which was $15 a bottle. I figured, let's make it very exclusive and sell it for $30 a bottle. I said, France has the best of everything, I asked a distiller there whether they could make a vodka. They said sure." And so Frank and his partners tried a few recipes, quickly declared one the "tastiest," cleverly packaged it up, relentlessly promoted it, and the rest is history. "We made big, beautiful ads that listed Grey Goose as the best-tasting vodka in the world, and we indoctrinated the distributors and 20,000 bartenders, and when somebody would come in and say, 'What's your best-tasting vodka?' they said 'Grey Goose.'" That's how something without taste and only mildly shoppable became something tasty and highly shoppable in a few short years through the power of shopaganda. Only eight years after Frank created Grey Goose from thin air in 1997, he unshopped it to Bacardi, which paid him $2 billion. Frank immediately went upshopping for cars: "First I bought two Maybachs. Two big Maybachs, not the little ones . . . I bought a Bentley. Little toys." (See ultrashop.)

Perhaps there is no better way to understand the word shoppable than to consider the outrageous popularity of bottled water. Water was once mostly non-shoppable. If you were lucky enough to live in a country with access to clean drinking water, you simply leaned into one of many public fountains, turned on the tap in your home or (in rare and rapidly disappearing cases) dipped your hand into the stream *et voila*: the liquid of life was yours for the taking.

Today, while many countries in the developing world would put running water at the top of their wish lists (even survival lists), and more than one billion humans (and growing) do not have access to safe drinking water, H_2O has become a shoppable item across the developed world, where the masses have been brainwashed by conspiracy theorists and clever marketers not to drink the tap water (see shopaganda). Water has been rendered shoppable. Dozens of companies offer a dizzying array of bottled water, some promoting its shoppability by saying it comes from "springs" or "glaciers" or "artesian wells," others simply packaging, reselling and marketing the stuff that comes from the tap and shipping it back and forth over continents in trucks, and across oceans in container ships to people who want foreign water with a fancy label. Canada, a nation blessed with so much fresh water it makes the majority of other countries on the planet desperately envious, is a major importer (and exporter) of bottled water from Europe. Yes, gas-guzzling ships pass each other in the middle of the Atlantic Ocean, each carrying different waters in either direction for bottled-water addicts in both hemispheres.

Most of it, of course, comes in a conveniently disposable plastic bottle. It's not just ships and trucks carting this stuff around for our drinking pleasure; many of us are giving ourselves hernias hauling this stuff back from the grocery store by the case in the back of the family pickup truck. Worldwide sales of bottled water have grown almost every year for the last four decades. By 2017, water had become so shoppable that humans were buying a million plastic bottles per minute, and less than 10 per cent of them are being recycled. Despite the floating islands of plastic in the ocean and the constant scolding by environmentalists, experts, authors and civic leaders, and indeed a growing grassroots revolution against plastic bottles across many developed countries, water's shoppability shows no signs of abating. Humanity bought an estimated half a trillion plastic bottles in 2020. The bottled water industry will be worth $350 billion annually by 2025. In the United States, bottled water, imported or domestic, began outselling soft drinks in 2016 and hasn't looked back. It is, writes Elizabeth Royte in her book *Bottlemania: How Water Went on Sale and Why We Bought It*, "one of the greatest marketing coups of the twentieth and twenty-first centuries." According to Royte, selling bottled water in the United States is more profitable than selling gasoline: "The outrageous success of bottled water, in a country where more than 89 percent of tap water meets or exceeds federal health and safety regulations, regularly wins in blind taste tests against name-brand waters, and costs 240 to 10,000 times less than bottled water, is an unparalleled social phenomenon."

Shoppers can now choose between hundreds of different brands, some selling for a buck a bottle, others for more than $100. It comes from remote mountain ranges, from pristine streams, from isolated and ancient underground aquifers. There is distilled water and mineral water. There is purified or sparkling water. You can even get ethical bottled water and bottled holy water, a wide variety of which is available on eBay, or Kabbalah water, made famous by revolutionary performance artist Madonna, who allegedly once wanted to fill her swimming pool with the stuff. Water sommeliers help thirsty customers impress their friends by choosing a brand from water menus that can stretch to dozens of pages. These sommeliers join bottlers, well-diggers, industry leaders and thirsty observers at an annual "water summit" each year in exotic destinations around the world, including Barcelona, Los Angeles, Shanghai and, in 2019, Stockholm, all in an effort to get shoppers to buy something their grandparents would have regarded with utter befuddlement.

SHOPRENEUR

Someone who owns a little shop.

These are people with the courage, the impudence, the temerity, the audacity to open an independent store, on a main street, with no franchise support, no national brand names, no fancy store designers, no shoperative research, no bulk-buying or logistics advantage, who somehow think that they can possibly compete against the multinationals. A classic mom-and-pop operation. They tend to be interesting places that shy away from recognizable labels. They support local artisans and producers. They have friendly and knowledgeable service from the actual owners.

SHOPERATOR

Someone who owns more than one shop.

This is a shopreneur who, against all odds, has made a go of it. A franchisee perhaps with multiple locations.

MEGASHOPERATOR

A person who owns an awful lot of shops.

In the past, impressive success and excessive wealth have often been associated with the likes of John Jacob Astor, an opium smuggler, fur trader and real estate investor whose name is synonymous with wealth, privilege and high society. Later, so-called robber barons such as ruthless steel magnates Andrew Carnegie and Henry Clay Frick, and relentless oil tycoons Andrew Mellon and John D. Rockefeller, became symbols of entrepreneurial success. Hard-working railway pioneer Cornelius Vanderbilt and anti-Semitic manufacturing titan Henry Ford are among America's industrial legends. By the twenty-first century, energetic Microsoft boss Bill Gates, laser-focused Apple head Steve Jobs and other digital entrepreneurs had taken centre stage with a variety of other investors, bankers and tech billionaires. These names have been burned into our psyches and immortalized by history simply because they are associated with so much wealth—and so much stuff.

But through it all, an impressive number of mega-retailers—megashoperators—have maintained a place on the "richest lists." Marshall Field, Richard Sears, Rowland Hussey Macy, Alvah Roebuck, Frank Woolworth, John Wanamaker, Timothy Eaton, Robert Simpson, Charles Henry Harrod and Harry Selfridge were all pioneering retailers—megashoperators who made themselves a lot of money and a place in history. In 1962, a poverty-stricken southern boy named Sam Walton started out as a trainee for J.C. Penney, and then founded what would become the biggest retailer in the world. Famous for grinding its suppliers and insisting on lower prices, Walmart is today the world's largest corporation by revenue, with Amazon closing fast.

Walton was once the richest man in America, and the combined wealth of his heirs approaches $200 billion. Various family members collect the usual stuff favoured by the rich—cars, horses and art—but Sam himself was not fond of shopping for high-end goods any more than his stores were known for selling them (see non-shopper). He lived in a relatively modest house in Arkansas and famously drove a beat-up 1979 Ford pickup truck to work. Ingvar Kamprad, known for his heavy drinking, his ties to Swedish fascists and what the *New York Times* called his "almost monastic frugality" (despite the ownership of several luxury homes), made billions as the founder of IKEA and changed the way many of us lived in the process. Kamprad's compatriot Stefan Persson runs the fashion behemoth H&M, which was founded by his father. Among the many properties in his possession is the entire village of Linkenholt in Hampshire, England.

American entrepreneur Leslie Wexner made so much money as the founder of L Brands, an empire that began as The Limited and grew to include Victoria's Secret, Abercrombie & Fitch and Bath & Body Works, among others, he couldn't seem to keep track of it all. He told the Wexner Foundation in 2019 that his former financial advisor, the lurking deviant Jeffrey Epstein, had "misappropriated vast sums of money" belonging to himself and his family. More than a decade earlier, in 1996, Wexner had mysteriously gifted to Epstein his French neoclassical townhouse in New York known as the Straus House, said to be worth $77 million.

Megashoperators such as Amazon's Jeff Bezos, the richest man in the world, and Alibaba's Jack Ma, once his trailblazing Chinese competitor, began enterprises that are taking over the planet. Their virtual shops may be the biggest on Earth, and getting bigger by the day. Also battling for first place on the "world's richest person" lists is art collector and overshopper Bernard Arnault, the boss of LVMH Moët Hennessy—Louis Vuitton SE, and the man the *New York Times* called "the godfather of modern luxury industry. He pretty much invented the whole idea (this is not overselling it)." Energy, mining, manufacturing

and transportation have always been big business, but selling consumer goods has often been the biggest. People like shopping, and
those who know how to make things shoppable for individuals remain
among the richest people in the world.

UPSHOP

Trading up.

This is the joyful act of replacing obviously lousy items with presumably better ones. Or simply buying more of them than anyone you know. It usually involves unshopping or deshopping an item you are unhappy with, usually because of its insufficient price or prestige, and reshopping for something more befitting the income you recently acquired, hope you will soon acquire or think you should have acquired. Or simply adding more items to those you already have in existence. This is what legendary economist and the granddaddy of consumer economics Thorstein Veblen called "pecuniary emulation"—an effort to pass another in status associated with wealth. In other words: keeping up with the Joneses, a phrase that existed in a cartoon strip as early as 1913 but was said to be popularized by James Duesenberry in his book *Income, Saving and the Theory of Consumer Behavior* in 1952. It is what Juliet B. Schor, author of *The Overspent American*, calls "competitive consumption."

In the early days of human evolution, it meant moving from a barren hillside or a sweltering jungle into a cave. Then, a cave into a straw hut. Then a straw hut into a log cabin and so on. Finally, rich humans could barely survive without multiple mansions, one for each season at least. More recently, it meant buying a Cadillac when everyone else had a Chevy or perhaps a Buick. Or buying a Rolex when a Timex would do. It is what makes us uniquely human: we are forever searching for something better—and more of it. We can't help ourselves. Items that serve no obvious practical purpose, like jewelry, are often the focus of upshopping (see also ultrashop). The nouveau riche, young movie actors and current sports icons are inveterate upshoppers, buying stuff to fill their heart's desire, impress their friends or lord over others.

Today, upshopping is not just about being able to afford stuff our neighbours and friends have but keeping abreast of the latest in consumer trends. Who is the hotter artist? David Hockney or Judy Chicago? Jeff Koons or Georgia O'Keeffe? What handbag is more chic: Gucci or Prada, Balenciaga or Birkin? What scholars call the "bandwagon effect" or "bandwagon consumption" can also be a challenge for retailers and manufacturers. Luxury brands can capitalize on their reputations to supply mass markets and make billions in the process, but if they are too good at it, they'll erode the brand. The quandary was noted in an article for the *Journal of Business Research*: "These lines must keep a tenuous balance between top-end luxuries and the larger market of ordinary premium products, so that they are not seen as a downgrade of luxury."

After all, everyone wants the same luxury brand until everyone has it. Then nobody wants a luxury brand that just anyone can have; they want something better. Again, it's innate: First, we upshop for what everyone else has. Once we attain that, we immediately upshop for what everyone else wants but can't have. It never ends. Monster-home owners, even those living in expensive cities, are somehow impressed by luxury watercraft a piddling seventy-five feet in length, but the true yacht owner knows that, to truly impress those he cares about, he must upshop for a garishly outfitted vessel that exceeds one hundred feet and has a helicopter pad. Take the case of over-achieving entrepreneur, software wunderkind and university dropout Larry Ellison, the co-founder of Oracle Corp., and his sometime rival, brilliant Microsoft co-founder and college dropout Paul Allen: In the mid-2000s, flush with tech money and unable to spend it all on houses, cars and various other luxuries, the two billionaires were building new, bigger yachts to replace their old, big yachts. Allen had several already, but this one, *Octopus*, was making headlines for its astounding length—416 feet, perhaps the longest on the seven seas.

Miraculously, Ellison had his, *Rising Sun*, extended to 452 feet from the skimpy 387 that was originally planned. There was rampant speculation in the media and beyond about the possible reasons, practical or psychological, for the extension, but *Rising Sun* now had room for a personal submarine (as did *Octopus*) among other amenities. That could be considered upshopping (and ultrashopping), but in the world of yachts, you can hardly finish gloating before someone somewhere is launching one that is longer and bigger and better than yours and upshopping you. Indeed, the two infamous vessels were barely in the water before Sheikh Mohammed bin Rashid Al Maktoum, the Crown Prince of Dubai, launched *Dubai* at 531 feet. Almost immediately thereafter, it was eclipsed by the *Eclipse*, owned by mysterious Russian billionaire Roman Abramovich, whose boat just happened to be twenty inches longer. Today, big yachts are approaching six hundred feet in length. Ultimately, Ellison decided *Rising Sun* was just too big and sold it (see downshop) to music and movie mogul David Geffen, who himself owned several yachts and was indulging in a little more upshopping. Besides, in terms of size, it is now way, way down the list. *Octopus*, bequeathed by the late Paul Allen to his sister, is even further below. One day you are showing off the biggest boat in the harbour; the next day your vessel is written off as a garbage scow. Sooner or later, the same fate awaits all stuff.

Even if you can't get the biggest, you can still pretend you're getting the best, as vainglorious liar Donald Trump alleged in 1987. Trump bought the vessel originally built by the notorious arms dealer Adnan Khashoggi, an infamous and profligate overshopper who had himself upshopped the vessel seven years earlier. The third-largest yacht in the world at the time and built for something close to $85 million in 1980, it was acquired by Trump for the supposed bargain price of $29 million. Trump felt the purchase was somehow worthy of a press release: "Donald Trump is pleased to announce that he is bringing the most spectacular yacht ever built, the Trump Princess, to the United States, where it will be anchored off the shores of Manhattan; Atlantic

City, N.J.; and Palm Beach, Fla." (See also convershop—and probably shopaganda). Trump then sank another $8.5 million into retrofitting the vessel to his own lurid tastes and then was obliged to deshop the thing for $20 million after only three years in 1990, when he faced money shortages of his own. Just a few years after that, in 1993, he commissioned a Spanish company to build an even bigger yacht and frittered away $170,000 for the plans (see reshop and upshop) without ever actually building it. The entire escapade was another obvious mis-shop, especially considering Trump had inexplicably declared he didn't like boats (see misshop).

Upshopping has clearly motivated humans for, well, our entire existence. We want more stuff. We want what others have, and perhaps just a little bit more.

By the time of Ancient Egypt, and even long before it, stuff had become a status symbol—the bigger, the rarer, the more exotic, the better. Egyptian pharaoh Khufu demonstrated this when he gave the world the Great Pyramid at Giza, which for 3,800 years stood as the tallest manufactured structure on the planet. Perhaps built as a tomb, perhaps a monument to the glory of the gods or perhaps just a big shiny thing that reminded all who encountered it how magnificent was Khufu: "I have stuff, therefore I am. I have a lot of big stuff, there-fore I am bigger." These structures were invariably filled with other smaller, shiny things, useful or otherwise, in order perhaps that those entombed nearby might possess them in the afterlife. Khufu's son Khafre built the Sphinx, for reasons nobody yet knows but at which most of us can guess. The Egyptians were still at it several millennia later, when Ramses II went on a building spree that would put his ancestors to shame. Like so many other humans before and after him, he demonstrated that it was not enough simply to be king; he must also remind people at every turn by flaunting his stuff—temples, grand pal-aces and towering monuments to himself across Egypt, such as the one described in 1818 by Percy Bysshe Shelley in his poem "Ozymandias," the Greek name by which Ramses II was known in antiquity:

And on the pedestal, these words appear:
My name is Ozymandias, King of Kings;
Look on my Works, ye Mighty, and despair!
Nothing beside remains. Round the decay
Of that colossal Wreck, boundless and bare
The lone and level sands stretch far away.

This is why so many modern despots are still given to building garish palaces and plastering their photographs and names on everything from coins to buildings. It is why young millionaires and the nouveau riche today build towering homes close to traffic-clogged thoroughfares, for all to see. People are impressed by stuff. In the twenty-first century, unless you are a thieving autocrat in the developing world, it's not really *de rigueur* to erect huge monuments to yourself. But that doesn't mean you can't disguise such statues or edifices as something supposedly useful like a huge home with stone gates, an architecturally significant "cottage" that soars high above the trees, a sprawling ski "chalet" on the precipice of a mountain or, in the case of Donald Trump, garish casinos and lurid hotels festooned with your name.

Others disguise this need by installing ostentatious art. Frank Stronach, the free-spending Austrian-born Canadian auto-parts entrepreneur and racehorse enthusiast, commissioned in 2012 a twelve-storey bronze statue of Pegasus fighting a dragon, which, according to an article in *Toronto Life* magazine, was a "statement piece and tourist attraction" for his company's racetrack in South Florida. It was originally budgeted at $6 million but eventually rang in at $55 million, probably qualifying it as misshopping, and perhaps part of the reason various Stronach family members, like so many other dynasties with tons of cash and plenty of stuff, spend so much time (and money) suing each other.

A millennium after Ramses II, some of the mega-building had subsided, but Egyptian leaders were not yet beyond one-upmanship as demonstrated by Cleopatra, the shrewd and resplendent Egyptian leader who is now an icon of popular culture. According to a famous story told by Pliny the Elder, Cleopatra crushed a single pearl, whose estimated value in today's dollars exceeded $10 million, into a glass of wine and drank it to impress her visitor from Rome, the hapless Mark Antony. Destroying expensive but useless stuff (see deshop) has always been as much a hallmark of the ultrashopper as buying it in the first place.

DOWNSHOP

To deshop and reshop because we upshopped
when we should've unshopped.

None of us really wants an item of lesser value and prestige. Alas, the excessive price of some items and the burden they place on our credit cards can sometimes force our hands. We simply can't make the payments on them or feel we need the money to pay the heating bill. This means removing the Rolex we upshopped for recklessly and proceeding to a pawn shop, deshopping it for half the price we paid, taking a fraction of that to pay some bills, reshopping for some other stuff we don't need and using the remaining $55 to buy a Timex. It means having a shiny Jaguar repossessed and going to the used car dealer for a rusty Ford. Obviously, downshopping is not as much fun as upshopping. Just as all the neighbours noticed your Jaguar, they will also notice the rusty Ford. It's humiliating. Not surprisingly, downshopping is a common pastime for former upshoppers, who, having bought something they wanted but didn't need, are now forced to trade it for something they need but don't really want. It is usually performed with less fanfare.

While Old Money rarely involves itself in blatant low-level upshopping, it is inevitable that such folks—or their offspring—will one day become mired in the humiliation of downshopping, for financial, practical, social or even environmental reasons. They may never have owned a Rolls or a Rolex, but you can be sure they own some art or an exotic carpet that will satisfy a creditor or two, and there's probably a bottle in the wine cellar that some crazy upshopper will want. Or maybe they just feel guilty about owning all that big stuff and want something a little more manageable. Lev Parnas, the mysterious Ukrainian-born

American who became famous in 2019 as a pal of wacky former New York mayor Rudy Giuliani, described his rollercoaster life of upshopping and downshopping in 2020: "Sometimes we were buying Rolexes, and sometimes we were selling the Rolexes to make the rent."

Fearless performer Nicolas Cage, a famous shopper, unshopper, deshopper and reshopper, is probably one of the better examples of an upshopper and downshopper on a grand scale. Cage, the owner of nine Rolls-Royces at the time, somehow felt it necessary in 2007 to buy three residences, in addition to a dozen or so others he already owned, including two run-down castles, several Caribbean islands and a "haunted house" in New Orleans. But by 2009, despite a reported income that year of $40 million, Cage was mired in downshopping. He lost several of the homes in foreclosure auctions and blamed his financial situation on his former business manager, Samuel Levin, whom he sued.

Glimpses into the ordeal—and into Cage's overshopping—are available in a counter lawsuit by Levin, who said in his filing he warned Cage, whose birth name is Coppola, that "financial disaster loomed" if he didn't control his purportedly uncontrollable overshopping habit. "Instead of listening to Levin, cross-defendant Coppola spent most of his free time shopping for high-ticket purchases, and wound up with fifteen personal residences, most of which were bought against Levin's advice," Levin stated in the complaint. "Likewise, Levin advised Coppola against buying a Gulfstream jet, against buying and owning a flotilla of yachts, against buying and owning a squadron of Rolls-Royces, against buying millions of dollars in jewelry and art." In 2007, Levin said, Cage's "shopping spree entailed the purchase of three additional residences at a total cost of more than $33 million; the purchase of 22 automobiles (including 9 Rolls-Royces); 12 purchases of expensive jewelry; and 47 purchases of artwork and exotic items."

Cage may be an egregious example of such behaviour, but he is not alone. Overindulgent '80s hip-hop artist MC Hammer faced inevitable downshopping tribulations following a spree of upshopping. Famous for the song "U Can't Touch This" and a fashion fad called "Hammer pants," the favoured trousers of hip-hop dancers, the artist declared bankruptcy in the 1990s. He sold for $6.5 million a California house on which he spent $12 million only a few years earlier (see misshop). "All the floors are marble," he told a reporter at the time. "My wife flew to Italy and picked it out of the mines. They cut it out of the mountain . . . but I've only used the marble steam room in my bathroom once and I've probably never even sat on the couch in the living room."

Overnight sensations in show business and sports often find themselves mired in the agony of downshopping, but some of those who win lotteries are even better examples. The British "lotto lout" and former garbage collector Michael Carroll bought a Spanish-style mansion in Norfolk, England, for £340,000 in the early 2000s after winning millions. He renovated the place for an additional £400,000, turned it into a party house, then downshopped it for a paltry £142,000 a few years later, finally moving into more modest lodgings, including a stint in prison.

Ten years after she won $10 million in a lottery, Canadian single mom Sharon Tirabassi downshopped a big house, fancy furniture, luxury automobiles and designer clothes after she blew most of her winnings in less than a decade. The personal-care worker in Hamilton, Ontario, was living in a cramped apartment with three kids in 2004 when she hit the jackpot. She married her boyfriend, and they immediately went on an upshopping spree for several homes, including a McMansion in an upscale neighbourhood and four vehicles: a Hummer, a Mustang, a Dodge Charger and a Cadillac Escalade with a custom sound system that cost more than $200,000. Her new neighbours were unimpressed, she said. Ten years later, Tirabassi had supershopped through the bulk of her windfall and was forced to downshop and deshop most of the stuff she had acquired. In the end, she was back living in a rented house on a quiet street near an industrial area, riding an electric bike and taking the bus. She told a reporter for the *Hamilton Spectator* that life has more purpose now that she's not shopping.

MISSHOP

A shopping mistake.

Often, we come across an item we believe is of more value than it actually is, something we think we want but it turns out we don't, or something we figure we'll be able to easily unshop but in fact will be forced to deshop. It's a bad shopping event. It might announce itself to us on the way out the door or not until we get it home and put it on the coffee table. It might not reveal itself until years later, when we try to unshop it and find it is an albatross we can't unload, like that one-of-a-kind house we have loved for a generation but now is considered an architectural curiosity that nobody else can bear to inhabit.

Misshopping is what your grandparents did when they bought an electric carving knife or a fondue pot but used it only once or twice. It's what your parents did when they purchased a bread maker or a raclette machine and used it occasionally at best. Or what you did when you acquired a sous vide machine or a juicer. A misshop might be a hot stock promoted as a winner but exposed as a complete loser. It could be a stamp collection you curated and always planned to sell and now realize is decaying and nearly worthless. It could be a flashy but finicky sports car you got fifteen years ago and drive only six times each summer, at best, and now want to get rid of because it's taking up too much space in your garage. Or it could be the boat your neighbour bought for summer vacations before he realized he couldn't afford the fuel to even power it out of the harbour. So he and his wife stay at the dock on weekends and barbecue hamburgers in the marina with the rest of the "boaters." Next summer, no doubt, it will remain under a tarp in the driveway next to your house.

Misshopping could include purchases that are just plain ugly, anachronistic, out-of-fashion or poorly made—stuff that you should have known better than to buy in the first place. Other typically misshopped items include motorcycles, uncomfortable furniture, linen suits, painful shoes and exercise equipment—stuff that seemed like a good idea at the time but now looks like a misshop. Misshopping (see also overshop) may be what half the world's interior decorators, professional or otherwise, indulge in during endless cycles of sprucing the place up.

There is really nothing more misshoppable, however, than the curio, the memento or the tchotchke—those things that pile up on shelves and in drawers and closets and finally end up in boxes in the basement. Once, while visiting Cornell University's botanical gardens in Ithaca, New York, I found myself in the gift shop there, perusing the predictable array of books, coffee mugs, coasters and knick-knacks. One such item was something called a storm glass, an old-fashioned weather predictor of dubious accuracy. I do not listen to the daily weather reports on television and radio, nor do I consult the forecasts and radar maps on various websites, but I was somehow drawn to this particular item, found it irresistible and was soon in possession of it. Alas, by the time it reached my home in Canada and was freed from its packaging, it revealed itself as little more than another piece of useless clutter. A thing of no practical value. A clear and embarrassing misshop. As punishment to myself, I mounted it on the wall, where it reminds me daily of the dangers of such ill-considered purchases and my own misguided self-indulgence.

Misshopping covers more than stuff that isn't useful. It can also describe a bad deal. It might explain how former drug-addled domestic abuser Charlie Sheen lost money on his Beverly Hills bachelor pad. Once described as a "Charlie Sheen Fun House" on *Mansion Global*, a luxury real estate listings site, the price dropped from $10 million in 2018 to $8 million in 2019 after the combative actor rescued it from foreclosure. He deshopped it for $6.6 million in 2020, a loss of

$600,000 from the price of $7.2 million he paid in 2006. Despite the fact that even the moderately wealthy and financially illiterate can get rich by investing in homes, some really rich people are more than adept at misshopping in the real estate market. A house, no matter how ostentatious, can be as deshoppable as a used car or the "art" you picked up while touring Indonesia.

Often, it's not simply the purchase of something you didn't need, or even overpaying for something you did need. Misshopping can also cover those acquisitions for which even the term "bad deal" does not suffice. It's what a lot of rich people did in the late 1990s and early 2000s when they bought art purportedly by Mark Rothko, Jackson Pollock and other abstract expressionists from New York's famous—now infamous—Knoedler Gallery. Turns out the stuff was made by a Chinese immigrant in Queens, sold for thousands to the gallery, which in turn sold them to rich people for millions. In 2004, Domenico De Sole, an Italian lawyer and fashion industry executive, and his wife, Eleanore, paid Knoedler $8.3 million for an apparent Rothko that turned out to be worthless. Pierre Lagrange, a flamboyant Belgian hedge fund manager, bought a so-called Jackson Pollock for $17 million in 2007. Also a forgery. Ultimately, it turned out that $80 million had been squandered by rich people misshopping for fake masterpieces.

In the late 1980s, billionaire collector and competitive sailor Bill Koch, brother of the prominent conservative political puppeteers Charles and David Koch, spent $5 million buying rare French wines, much of which revealed itself as relative swill. "I just had to have them," he said of bottles upon which he spent as much as $100,000 apiece. Turns out the bottles were the work of the now-notorious Rudy Kurniawan, a young Indonesian of Chinese descent, who put lesser wines in expensive bottles at his home in California. He did it so well that so-called experts and really rich people who wanted to impress others didn't seem to notice until it was too late. Tech billionaire David Doyle, the founder of Quest Software, estimated that

$8 million to $10 million of the $14 million worth of wine he bought from Kurniawan for his $40-million wine collection was counterfeit. Kurniawan went to jail.

A misshop of biblical proportions might describe what evangelical Christian and American business tycoon Steve Green did when he began, in 2009, spending millions to acquire supposed pieces of the storied Dead Sea Scrolls. Among the most historically significant and priceless relics in the world and buried for two thousand years, these manuscripts were discovered in caves during the 1940s in what was then part of Jordan. Green, the president of Hobby Lobby, a chain of successful US craft stores, displayed the fragments of Biblical text prominently in his enormous Museum of the Bible in Washington, DC, which opened in 2017. Alas, in early 2020, the museum announced that all sixteen pieces were worthless fakes.

Faddish fashion, untested technology, archaic items, decaying antiques or anything that is heavily promoted and deeply discounted tends to be of little practical use and to become a burden rather than a benefit. What is shoppable today is almost always deshoppable tomorrow, and, in retrospect, is often labelled misshopping. Such was the case four centuries ago when the simple tulip bulb gained popularity during what some call the world's first recorded commodity bubble, often known today as Tulip Mania. In the 1630s, all kinds of rich and not-so-rich Dutch citizens bought and sold the tulip bulbs, some of which, according to Mike Dash in his book *Tulipomania*, rose in price to ten thousand guilders (for a single bulb), "sufficient to purchase one of the grandest homes on the most fashionable canal in Amsterdam for cash, complete with a coach house and an eight-foot garden, and this at a time when homes in that city were as expensive as property anywhere in the world." Of course, not everyone could afford the most extravagant tulip bulb, but lesser ones were also hot commodities. "In the autumn of 1636," writes Dash, "many Dutchmen must have thought . . . that the profits being made on tulips were simply too good to be true. But thousands did not, and they took their savings and mortgaged their goods in order to take part in the hurly-burly of the bulb trade." Like the rest of us through time, they were hoping to get rich quick. Unfortunately, after several years of madness, one day someone realized something about these bulbs that had been obvious from the start: they had very little use other than as spring garden decorations. The entire venture promptly collapsed onto itself, sending investors to the poorhouse. It was misshopping on a vast scale. The scenario has repeated itself with different commodities ever since.

One recent and widespread misshopping adventure involved so-called Beanie Babies in the 1990s, when the cute-ish stuffed animals became briefly popular. Ty Inc., the company producing cats, dogs, moose and other creatures, deliberately controlled their supply to boost demand, and these "commodities" somehow came to be seen as a financial investment, selling for twice or even ten times the sticker price, gumming up the works on eBay and throwing owners into a tizzy. In a short movie, filmmaker Chris Robinson documented how the craze consumed his family, and how his father invested in Beanie Babies to finance his sons' university educations, ultimately spending $100,000 on fifteen thousand to twenty thousand of the cuddly creatures. It began innocently enough, recalled Robinson. First, the family simply happened upon a store that sold them. Then his father learned of their collectability and smelled an investment opportunity. After that, things spun out of control. "It became this all-consuming family activity, filling up any free time that wasn't already earmarked for school or our youth hockey teams."

Ultimately, we are all misshoppers, rich or poor, whether we're buying expensive wine or cheap blue jeans, whether we're in the stock market or at the farmer's market, Walmart or Fendi. In fact, some of these misshops are forced upon us by manufacturers or our own misguided frugality. We buy cheap shoes we wear fewer than a half a dozen times, because they don't fit or they fall apart and aren't worth repairing. We make regular visits to computer stores to upgrade or replace obsolete or broken gadgets (see deshop and reshop) because we haven't the time, energy or ability to fix them. We buy cheap floors, windows and furniture for our houses, despite the availability of those that will last longer, because, well, we're probably not going to stay long enough to realize the investment or we'll be tempted by the next design trend anyway. An aging handyman of my acquaintance, originally from Britain, once commented on the asphalt shingle roofs favoured by North American homeowners. "They don't last, you know?" he stated incredulously. "We put those on chicken coops back home."

It is, of course, nothing new. In 1834, the Scottish-Canadian economist John Rae discussed the human predilection for cheap flashy stuff over more expensive, sturdier products, even though we all know that better products will pay off in the long run: "We know not the period when death may come upon us, but we know that it may come in a few days, and must come in a few years. Why then be providing goods that cannot be enjoyed until times, which, though not very remote, may never come to us?"

Today, most of us accept the reality that a growing avalanche of stuff simply wears out sooner than it should. A brave few push back against such insanity, the results of which are Right to Repair movements everywhere, with advocates urging governments to introduce legislation that will force manufacturers to make it both possible and less expensive to repair their products. In 2021, the *New York Times* website *Wirecutter*, which recommends stuff to readers daily (and sometimes gets a piece of the action), ran the following headline: "Sorry, but It's Probably Time to Replace These 16 Household Essentials." Among the advice? Toss out your toilet scrubbers and mascara every few months, and your plastic cutting boards every few years.

Unfortunately, such behaviour has been well ensconced for centuries. In 1940, light bulb manufacturers realized their products were just too good—homeowners weren't doing enough reshopping. Their answer: create a consortium to make bulbs more cheaply. After that, not only did bulb makers spend less and charge more, their products obliged by burning out more frequently.

In 1932, a realtor named Bernard London coined the term "planned obsolescence" for this kind of thing. Worried the Depression was persisting because of a lack of reshopping, London said consumers were waiting "until the last possible bit of use had been extracted from every commodity" and proposed making planned obsolescence a legal obligation. "People everywhere are today disobeying the law of obsolescence. They are using their old cars, their old tires, their old radios and their old clothing much longer than statisticians had expected on the basis of early experience."

His proposal was deservedly ignored, but in 1954, a gifted and visionary industrial designer by the name of Brooks Stevens suggested a new tack: "Planned obsolescence: The desire on the part of a consumer to own something a little newer, a little better, a little sooner than is necessary." Manufacturers didn't need governments to mandate planned obsolescence and force people to shop; companies could do it themselves through the power of shopaganda: "Unlike the European approach of the past," said Stevens to anyone who would listen (and there were many), "where they tried to make the very best product and make it last forever, meaning you bought such a fine suit of clothes that you were married in it and then buried in it, and never a chance to renew it, the approach in America is one of making the American consumer unhappy with the product that he has enjoyed the use of for a period and have him pass it on to the secondary market and obtain the newest product with the newest possible look." Reshopping hasn't looked back since.

CRYPTOSHOP

To shop secretly or discreetly.

This is what some people call clandestine consumption. Or inconspicuous expenditure. Let's say your spouse thinks you're a shopaholic. Worse, and much to your dismay, a friend or two has "joked" about it. Even your mother has mentioned it. You know in your heart you are not, at least not compared to some people you know. But you don't want to make a federal case out of every purchase. So you sneak out to the mall and creep around the shops buying stuff but foregoing the utter joy of being able to tell anybody about it (see convershopping), using cash rather than credit. When your spouse asks you about a new shirt you bought last week but are wearing for the first time, you reply: "This thing? I've had it for ages." But maybe your spouse is one of those nutty weekend cyclists who somehow feels they needed a $10,000 ultra-light unit made of titanium to ride all the way to the countryside and back on a busy highway every Saturday morning. You think $10,000 is an outrageous amount of money to spend on a bicycle, but you have been told it is necessary for safety and fitness. In fact, they have already traded in the $10,000 Italian model for a $15,000 German model of exactly the same colour and size but made of carbon fibre and you haven't even noticed, because, after all, a bike is a bike (isn't it?). They are well aware of your ignorance, and they, too, are cryptoshoppers.

Hobbies and so-called collections are perfect covers for cryptoshoppers. Once you have eighty-five rare coins, your spouse would hardly notice another twenty. Even thirty or forty. Hundreds perhaps. Five $10,000 watches look the same as nine $20,000 watches when they are in a drawer or a safe. It's not until they reach twenty in number that it becomes necessary to cover one's tracks. Meanwhile, when stuff is small, it's hard to keep track. You might think thirty-five fishing lures or artificial flies would be plenty for even the most avid angler, but you probably won't notice if there are one hundred, and there probably are. Even something as large as a guitar can be hidden amongst the others.

Old-monied folks, never ones for upshopping, indulge regularly in what the rest of us would call cryptoshopping. They have never been much for showing off and they pretend to eschew it. These people drive a Buick and wear a Timex, they've always driven a Buick and worn a Timex, their fathers drove Buicks and wore Timexes and they see no reason to change. In fact, that's why they're Old Money; they still have most of it. Such parsimoniousness helps define them—not to mention sustain them. And showing it off is gauche. Of course, that is not to say the rich, whether they are new money or old, don't indulge in quiet cryptoshopping for things like fine wine, rare books, obscure art and secluded Bahamian islands. It's just that they don't recognize it as such, any more than they can identify with the kind of low-grade cryptoshopping practised by the rest of us. As Chrystia Freeland writes in her book *Plutocrats*, "even if the billionaire is in a T-shirt and drives his own car, his universe is very different from that of the call-centre worker." When an old-monied cryptoshopper buys a house, it's at the end of a long driveway, hidden by trees and forests, not front and centre and announced by a lion sculpture or two and a garish garden. They need not impress common millionaires; it is only the really rich they care about. A lowly Rolex wearer, for example, might not know the difference between a Château Margaux and a Colognole Chianti Rufina. One costs thousands of dollars for a bottle; the other runs about $20. Both are delicious. In his delightfully insightful book, *The Natural History of the Rich*, Richard Conniff explains how the wealthy consume differently than the rest of us: "The art of being rich, isn't, after all, about conspicuous consumption, but about inconspicuous consumption."

Abdullah II bin Al-Hussein, the king of Jordan, amassed fifteen luxury homes in places like Malibu, Washington and London in a $100-million house-shopping spree during the first two decades of the new millennium while his country suffered economic hardships and received billions in foreign aid. Like many other rich people, the king didn't want the masses to know he owned such bounty, so he used shell companies based in the Caribbean to keep his ownership secret. There is nothing illegal about an offshore account, and those who use them insist they seek nothing but privacy, but billions are hidden this way.

Others involved in opaque financial machinations hide their purchases in plain sight. Before he went to jail, infamous sex trafficker and monstrous predator Jeffrey Epstein managed to own a $57-million mansion in New York, a palatial oceanfront villa in Palm Beach, a luxurious apartment in Paris, a sprawling ranch in New Mexico and a private island in the Caribbean, plus several airplanes, the usual assortment of luxury automobiles and a collection of twisted, sexually suggestive art with few people knowing much about any of it, and fewer still questioning how he financed it all.

SUPERSHOP

To get a lot of stuff fast, usually at a shopitorium, often online,
sometimes in fancy stores, regularly in large boxes and big bags.

You may need a truck for this kind of thing, and chances are you
actually own one. Such vehicles dominate parking lots at Walmart,
Costco and IKEA stores, where hopeful suburban overshoppers work
geometric magic to fit their latest purchases into the back of a vehicle
originally designed for bales of hay, two-by-fours and garden tools.
The big-box experience has overtaken what we once called "The Big
Shop" before it became redundant, because every shop is a big shop
today. Supershoppers love a big-box store, because it allows them to
buy more of any one item than they actually need. Even though most
urban, suburban and even rural dwellers are surrounded in all direc-
tions by food stores, appliance stores, clothing stores and hardware
stores, supershoppers want to drive for hours rather than minutes and
are never content to let things linger on store shelves when they could
be taking up space at home. Supershoppers seem to plan for the worst:
an earthquake, a pandemic, an ice storm or the zombie apocalypse.
Filling our cupboards with cases rather than cans of soup. Buying soap
in a container large enough to fill an Olympic swimming pool with
suds. Stocking closets with sixteen kilometres of toilet paper. Getting
a restaurant-sized jar of mayonnaise that would last a family of six for
several years, even though there are only two people in our household.
Spending a goodly portion of our paycheck on the jumbo-sized package of forty flashlight batteries and then losing them in the oozing
mound of detritus in the basement until they're discovered during the
next garage sale and we realize they no longer fit any new electronic
item. We may need only a single screw or a simple bag of grass seed,

but we will bypass our local corner hardware store and drive all the way to the outer reaches of town to acquire this same item (in a larger package) at a big-box retailer, because it's supposedly less expensive and, well, it's fun to shop, and you never know what other ideas might be visited upon us while we're there, and we haven't quite reached the limit on our credit card, and we just can't bear to go back to our cluttered homes so soon and face the chaos.

Supershopping occurs beyond the big-box retailer. It can occur anywhere: at the Home Depot or the Gucci store, and especially at Amazon or Alibaba or eBay, where getting lots of stuff does not require you to even lift it into the shopping cart. Fabulously rich business tycoon Jeff Bezos got that way by making it easy for people to become supershoppers. Supershopping is not about what you shop for, but how you shop for it.

OVERSHOP

To acquire too many goods.

This, of course, is done daily by almost everybody nearly all the time virtually everywhere in the developed world. We wanted it rather than needed it and now we realize we can't use it but we're stuck with it. It looked so good in the store, we decided to buy eight packages. But now it's at home, we realize it is quite useless, and we put the other seven packages in the basement or garage, hoping to give them away but somewhere in our unconscious we know they'll end up in the spring garage sale two or three seasons from now. Or worse, our heirs will shake their heads in disbelief when they clean out the garage when we're dead and gone. We overshopped.

Overshopping is what renowned filmmaker and environmentalist Annie Leonard beseeches us to stop doing in the marvelous and alarming *The Story of Stuff* and other films, which are, encouragingly, widely viewed around the world. "We shop and shop and shop," says Leonard, reminding Americans they consume twice as much as they did fifty years ago. "Ninety-nine percent of the stuff we harvest, mine, process, transport, ninety-nine percent of the stuff we run through the system, is trashed within six months." (See deshop.) Despite her convincing argument that overshopping is unsustainable, it continues unabated—and the costs to the planet inflate with each passing year.

Overshopping was once easy to define. Your house was overflowing, your bank account was empty, the rusting hulks in the back forty were cluttering up the yard and spoiling the view. It's more difficult today: we hide our stuff in ever larger closets and garages and finally in storage units (see predeshop); we run up the balance on our credit cards; we ship the garbage to the developing world, or we celebrate our "collections," no matter how absurd and self-indulgent. We hide the problem from ourselves and we ignore the environmental consequences: dirty drinking water and polluted lakes; smoggy air and gasping urbanites; dead reefs, melting glaciers, forest fires and menacing storms.

Still, in its most basic form, overshopping is simple: we buy too much. Over the course of my lifetime, for example, I have purchased not one, not two, not three but four separate versions of a mandolin, a kind of vegetable slicer that clearly requires more skill than I seem to possess. Each one was used only once, deemed ineffective (and dangerous) and put in a drawer or the cupboard where it took up space until it was ejected years later into the trash, the recycler or the Goodwill store (see deshop, also misshop). Not long thereafter, I somehow felt compelled to buy another one not dissimilar to the first, and the insane cycle repeated itself over several decades. Even today, when I have learned that a good Japanese kitchen knife is far easier and more efficient, I am not convinced I won't succumb and buy another mandolin the next time it beckons, or perhaps even a Veg-O-Matic during a demonstration on TV or at a country fair.

My father, a bestselling author, journalist, historian and what he liked to ironically call a television personality, had perhaps 150 bow ties and fifty or more pairs of cufflinks, in addition to an inordinate number of what I would describe as loud suits, all of which he said he needed to fulfill his obligations on such a visual medium as TV. Appalled that I occasionally needed a refresher course from him before those rare events when I would need to tie a bow tie myself (the same occasions on which I needed to borrow a pair of cufflinks), he would wax enthusiastically about how such items could be useful. While skeptical, I would never argue. I did, however, come to understand how they may have been required by TV personalities. When CNN chief medical correspondent Sanjay Gupta was asked to be a *Jeopardy!* guest host in 2021, he learned the lesson quickly. "They wanted you to take 10 suits," the neurosurgeon said. "I don't have 10 suits." For many of us peering regularly into our crowded closets, the question of what is necessary and what is not remains top of mind.

The celebrated personal shopper Betty Halbreich, "director of solutions" for several decades at Bergdorf Goodman in New York, might as well have been talking about overshopping when she advised, in her first book in 1997, that shoppers must be on the lookout for things they "have a tendency to overdose on: Do you have six red sweaters? Five black jackets? Four navy skirts? You don't necessarily have to get rid of any of them (they're all *completely* different, right?), but just remember how many you've got the next time you're in a store and find yourself heading to the cashier with yet another red sweater, black jacket, navy skirt, or (fill in the blank with whatever you tend to collect)."

UNDERSHOP

To acquire an insufficient amount of goods.

It can be more painful than overshopping, but for better or worse, undershopping is relatively rare in the developed world. You were at the store, there were bargains galore. It wasn't just a deal; it was a steal. But you weren't sure, you hesitated, you held back, you were rushed, you thought about the balance on your credit card, what your spouse might say, the encumbered environment, those offshore sweatshops and your overstuffed closets. So you eased off. You bought only two pairs of shoes when in fact you had your eye on three. You got the shoes home, showed them to a friend, and she said they were fabulous. What's more, your spouse loved them. And worse, they acknowledged— and you later confirmed—that the shoes were indeed a bargain. And as an added bonus, they actually *fit*. You realized you should have bought more, but the opportunity is lost, others have won the bargains that were meant for you. There's nothing to do now but drown your sorrows in drink—or more shopping, and probably overshopping.

On the other hand, undershopping can be environmentally friendlier, fiscally responsible and mentally forgiving. Some people are easily capable of buying a flashy Lamborghini but opt for a Kia. Others may dream about a huge mansion but save themselves the trouble of getting lost in it, securing it, insuring it, maintaining it or simply cleaning the place, and, like Warren Buffett, choose to live in an understated bungalow instead. The bridge-playing Cherry Coke addict is not an ultrashopper or even overshopper of the kind you might expect from a man who is worth, depending on the day, $50- or $100 billion, which he made through value investing. Buffett lives in the same suburban house in Omaha, Nebraska, that he bought for $31,000 in 1958, and drives a mere Cadillac that he replaces every six or seven years.

The *New York Times* once reported the "comic frugality" of telegenic US politician Mitt Romney, once a Republican presidential hopeful. Worth hundreds of millions as head of a successful private equity firm in the 1990s before he became a senator, Romney chose to drive a Chevrolet station wagon with "red vinyl seats and a banged-up front end" and "play with golf clubs from Kmart."

Jeff Bezos, the nerdy founder of Amazon, often cited as the richest man in the world with a fortune approaching $200 billion, was once portrayed as an undershopper when he was worth a paltry $10 billion. "What's with the Honda?" Bezos was asked while appearing on the TV program *60 Minutes*, in reference to the late-model Accord he was driving. The now famous answer: "This is a perfectly good car." Alas, Bezos's tastes in luxury have grown considerably since then. By 2019, he owned multiple vehicles and multiple properties, including more than 300,000 acres in Texas; a sprawling home (or two) in Beverly Hills; a former museum in Washington, DC; three units in an art deco building in New York; and a couple of houses in Medina, Washington. In 2020, he bought the Warner Estate from art-collecting entertainment magnate David Geffen for $165 million, beating out right-wing News Corp. heir Lachlan Murdoch.

Less complicated items certainly have their advantages, as I learned once while shopping for a washer and a dryer at a local Sears department store. I arrived looking for the white ones with a single knob that I could easily operate. Like the one my mother had. Still, I couldn't help but notice the flashy modern models painted in luxurious red, blue or silver and buffed to a high gloss.

"What about those?" I asked the salesperson.

"They're more expensive," she replied. Indeed, they were almost twice the price.

"Why?" I asked.

"They have more buttons," she answered. "And they're shiny."

"They probably wash and dry clothes better," I said.

"No sir, they do not. And you can believe me; I'm on commission."
Just because stuff looks better does not always mean it is.

ULTRASHOP

To buy the best of the best, the biggest of the biggest.

To ultrashop is to upshop an upshopper. It means buying better stuff than even those who think they've bought the best stuff. To acquire more expensive, more elaborate, more profligate, more sumptuous, more lavish, more luxurious stuff than almost anyone else, which is a tall order indeed, given that everyone seems to be trying to outdo everyone else.

Even owners of Atlantic and Pacific islands appear to be a dime a dozen these days. In the twentieth century, only a few rich people and actors such as hard-drinking macho man John Wayne and troubled bad boy Marlon Brando owned islands. Now it seems every rich celebrity has one: idealistic environmentalist Leonardo DiCaprio, allegedly homophobic and racist drunk driver Mel Gibson, free-spending problem drinker Johnny Depp. Business tycoons too are in on the act, including shameless self-promoter and Virgin founder Richard Branson or the late guitar-smashing recluse Paul Allen, co-founder of Microsoft. On the other hand, yacht-racing philanthropist and over-achieving entrepreneur Larry Ellison owns more than 90 per cent of the Hawaiian island of Lana'i, so that might qualify as something more than ultrashopping, especially considering the size of some of his other properties scattered across the world.

People who own private planes are not necessarily ultrashoppers, despite all appearances, because there are simply too many of them. Then again, it could depend on the size of the plane, and where one parks it. Famous Scientologist and disco-dancing actor John Travolta, for example, once owned as many as six aircraft, which probably qualifies him. But the fact that one was a Boeing 707—a four-engine jet airliner that can carry between 140 and 189 passengers—and was kept on the runway at the back door of Travolta's house in Florida, pretty well ensures his entry into the club.

Some luxury-loving televangelists look like ultrashoppers, and they certainly make no apologies for it. In fact, ultrashopping is God's will, apparently. Smooth-talking Southern preacher Jesse Duplantis, who once told a congregation that "one of my chandeliers cost more than most people's house—I got 22 chandeliers in the house," made headlines when he appealed to his God-fearing congregation to help the church pay for a new jet to fly him about—a bigger, better and sleeker private jet than the one he already had, the new one costing $54 million. Said Duplantis to his many followers: "God told me to have that plane." His colleague, telegenic Texan Kenneth Copeland, meanwhile, not only has at least two private jets, he also owns his own airport, next to his mansion in Newark, Texas. Copeland has famously articulated his dislike of commercial airline travel, but says jets are necessary to do God's work. According to the US television newsmagazine *Inside Edition*, "God's work" included 143 trips from Fort Worth, Texas, to his ski getaway in Steamboat Springs, Colorado, between 2000 and 2019.

Many preachers have been leaders in the development of prosperity theology, which holds that God wants us to have stuff, and lots of it. Shopping, upshopping, reshopping, overshopping and ultrashopping is God's will. Televangelism pioneer Oral Roberts was an early leader of the movement, but its profile was raised considerably in the 1980s by the infamous fraudster Jim Bakker and his raccoon-eyed wife, Tammy Faye, who together developed a popular TV show called *The PTL Club* and a Christian theme park in South Carolina. That was before they ultrashopped the entire organization into bankruptcy— spending money raised through their ministry on homes in California, Florida, South Carolina and Tennessee, all the while living much of the time in a luxurious suite in the Heritage Grand Hotel at the theme park—before Jim was imprisoned for accounting fraud. "The motive," said Assistant US Attorney Jerry Miller, "was opulence."

Ostentatious jewel-bedecked or gilded items, no matter how tacky, are often evidence of ultrashopping. Ferocious boxer and convicted rapist Mike Tyson spent $2 million on a bathtub, either made of solid gold or encrusted with jewels, depending on various news reports. (The assorted extravagances of the ear-biting pugilist, who earned more than $300 million over a twenty-year career before declaring bankruptcy, included the purchase of three Bengal tigers at $70,000 each, a price that did not include the care and feeding of the hungry beasts.) Academy Award–winning filmmaker Ben Affleck was reported to have once spent $105,000 on a jewel-inlaid toilet seat for actor and singer Jennifer Lopez. Soccer heartthrob David Beckham unloaded £70,000 on a diamond-encrusted Hermès handbag for jewelry-loving wife Victoria, once better known as Posh Spice. Fashion-forward pop megastar Beyoncé Knowles was widely reported to have spent $300,000 on a pair of diamond-encrusted high-heeled shoes from the House of Borgezie for a music video. Eternally perky actor Jennifer Aniston is reported to have bought beau Justin Theroux a gold-plated motorcycle worth $1 million. And British socialite Tamara Ecclestone once spent £1 million on a bathtub made of a rock crystal her staff found in the Amazon jungle and lugged all the way back to her London home.

Glamourous journalist Barbara Amiel, sometimes known as Baroness Black of Crossharbour, the wife of convicted felon and former Canadian newspaper magnate Conrad Black, may have best summed up ultrashopping: "I have an extravagance that knows no bounds." She later added: "For some people, jewelry is a defining attribute, rather like your intelligence or the number of residences you have," a comment that may have been facetious. And she admitted to keeping "a fantastic natural-pearl and diamond brooch" in her safety deposit box because, well, it was just too big for her bosom.

Famous maximalist and ultrashopping rapper Drake once listed the material draping his body in an absurd 2019 YouTube video entitled "How Much is Your Outfit?" The bestselling musician displayed and discussed his attire for the evening and happily shared the approximate price of each item: Custom Brioni jacket, $11,000; Tom Ford turtleneck, $2,000; Tom Ford pants, $1,000; crocodile Tom Ford shoes, $15,000; diamond necklace, $200,000; Richard Mille RM 69 Tourbillon Erotic watch, $750,000. None of that may be surprising, at least for those who wear such things, but Drake is the guy who also somehow managed to spend $395,000 in 2020 on a mattress for his bed, according to reports. In an interview with *Architectural Digest*, Drake explained why he chose his over-the-top home design and decor: "It's overwhelmingly high luxury. That message is delivered through the size of the rooms and the materials and details of the floors and the ceilings. I wanted to make sure people can see the work I've put in over the years reflected from every vantage point." Or, in the words of another rap star, 50 Cent—who filed for bankruptcy protection in 2015—"Cadillacs, expensive jewelry" and other material possessions "symbolized financial freedom" and "if you don't want nice things in your life, I don't even want to know you."

In 2015, Wang Sicong, the son of a Chinese real estate mogul, posted a photo of his dog wearing two Apple watches valued at $28,000 with a caption in Chinese that was translated by the *Shanghaiist*: "I have new watches! I'm supposed to have four watches since I have four long legs. But that seems too *tuhao* so I kept it down to two, which totally fits my status. Do you have one?" (*Tuhao* is a Chinese word meaning "nouveau riche.") In an age when so many people covet such expensive anachronisms, perhaps buying two for your dog is no different than finding a chew toy for it at the local PetSmart.

The more money you have, the more difficult it is to avoid ultrashopping. It will certainly be a challenge for Manuel Franco, who won an almost unfathomable jackpot of $768 million in the Wisconsin Lottery in 2019. On the topic of ultrashopping, Franco said this: "I'm not a big guy that's gonna go buy fancy stuff." And then, seconds later, he corrected himself, allowing that, yes, maybe he might indulge in some limited ultrashopping: "Well, of course, I might go buy fancy stuff, but nothing too big." Likewise, John and Lisa Robinson announced they were unlikely to become ultrashoppers after they won one-third of a $1.8 billion lottery in 2016. They immediately announced plans to stay in their modest home in Munford, Tennessee. "We are common people, we're just like y'all. These big fancy houses are nice, but you gotta clean them." Less than a year later, they were ensconced in a ten-bedroom house with a private theatre on a 320-acre lot with a private lake.

The problem for ultrashoppers, alas, is they rarely retain the title in an ever-more immoderate world. There's always someone vying to take their place and bump them down to plain old supershopper—or worse, undershopper. And they themselves often play a key role in the descent. Take Stephen Hung, whom the *Washington Post* in 2014 called "the world's biggest spender," a distinction that has undoubtedly been eclipsed since. According to *Paris Match* around the same time, Hung "lives like a rock star. Eccentric wardrobe, sumptuous mansions, monstrous cars. He loves diamonds." He worships "supreme luxury" and "nothing is more hateful to him than mass consumption, including that of the superrich who pile up goods that are ultimately very common." At the time, Hung had come to the attention of much of the world's media beyond Asia as he was making plans to build an exclusive hotel in Macau, China, which he imagined as an over-the-top refuge for the world's wannabe ultrashoppers. To that end, Hung had made a historic purchase of thirty custom-built Rolls-Royces, painted bright red mixed with gold dust. The $20-million purchase generated an awful lot of media attention at the time, which all seemed part of the plan. Hung, who made his money in real estate, did not buy the cars for himself. He already owned a white-and-gold Rolls, not to mention a Bentley, a Ferrari, a Lamborghini and a Pagani Huayra, an Italian mid-engine sports car that sells for more than $1 million. The custom-built red Rolls-Royces were for his hotel guests, and he was happy to bask in their glow and share his own excessive tastes.

In 2013, with a reporter for the *Wall Street Journal* in tow, Hung entered a private room in a Graff Diamonds store, examined a $10 million diamond ring, and declared: "It's never too big. It can always be bigger." Indeed, Hung imagined just such a store at the hotel he was building, a hotel "that will be the most luxurious and exclusive casino resort ever imagined," where patrons would rent suites at $130,000 per night and be transported around in those red Rolls-Royce Phantoms. Hung envisioned that "patrons will need an invitation to shop in private boutiques at the resort. Jewelry items at the atelier will cost at least $1 million, with some priced over $100 million." Alas, by the time the hotel finally opened in late 2018 after years of delays and financial challenges, Hung was out as the operation's boss and the establishment focuses today on just staying afloat rather than improvidence.

House-building (and house-buying) can sometimes qualify as ultrashopping. Indian business tycoon Mukesh Ambani, called the richest man in Asia by *Forbes* magazine in 2019, spent a rumoured $1 billion on a home in Mumbai that is 400,000 square feet on twenty-seven floors. It has three helipads and a room where it snows during hot Indian summers, among other features. Often labelled the biggest and most expensive residence in the world, it has a panoramic view of the teeming masses in the slums below. Its square footage dwarfs the single-family dwelling known as Versailles, an over-the-top monument to excess which has been under construction in Florida for more than a decade. One of the biggest homes in North America—and named after the actual seventeenth-century Palace of Versailles in France—the ninety-thousand-square-foot, thirty-bedroom home was featured in the 2012 documentary *The Queen of Versailles*. Owners David Siegel, the embattled chief executive of the hugely successful timeshare company Westgate Resorts, and his beauty-queen wife, Jackie, unsuccessfully sued the filmmakers, with David stating: "The only thing that's true about (the documentary) is that my wife is a big-busted shopaholic." Alas, a decade after construction began, the house was still not completed, and the couple, who lost a daughter to a drug overdose in 2015, no longer seemed to care. "I don't care about houses, I don't care about business, I don't care about money," said David in 2019. Added Jackie: "We're sorry we ever started, but we're $50 million into it, so it really needs to get done."

Despots, dictators, lawless autocrats, African strongmen, Russian oligarchs, Central American drug lords, Middle Eastern royalty and fraudulent North American business executives eventually find themselves near the top of the list of ultrashoppers, seeing as how they are often spending other people's money (see contrashopper), and there may be no one more infamous than Ferdinand and Imelda Marcos, former lavish-living co-dictators of the impoverished nation of the Philippines. Imelda's shoe collection is notorious for comprising as many as three thousand pairs. In the 1970s and '80s, the kleptocratic couple looted hundreds of millions from the Philippines's national treasury, made off with planeloads of jewelry, collected stacks of gold bullion and a museum's worth of expensive art. Imelda once spent $3.3 million during a one-day shopping trip to the United States.

Speaking of despotic footwear, Grace Mugabe, the luxury-loving wife of the former Zimbabwean president Robert Mugabe, known as "the First Shopper" or "Gucci Grace" in media reports, was once asked by a journalist about her reportedly vast collection of Salvatore Ferragamo shoes. Mugabe responded: "I have very narrow feet, so I can only wear Ferragamos." She was reported to have spent $75,000 in a single store in Paris, a story she denies. One of her sons is famous for a 2017 Instagram video in which he douses a diamond-encrusted wristwatch with a $500 bottle of Armand de Brignac champagne with the caption: "$60,000 on the wrist when your daddy run the country ya know!!!" An estimated 70 per cent of the citizens of the country his "daddy run" live in poverty.

Almost as infamous as Imelda Marcos's shoe collection was the assemblage of furs gathered by contrashopping communist Elena Ceaușescu, the former first lady of Romania, which included everything from foxes and zebras to leopards, tigers and jaguars. Not to be outshopped, Ceaușescu's ill-fated husband, the wretchedly inept Nicolae, destroyed some seven thousand buildings in Bucharest during the 1980s to build a palace, which still today holds the number two spot on the list of the world's biggest office buildings after the Pentagon. That is certainly ultrashopping.

Iraq's late unlamented ruler Saddam Hussein was an ultrashopper: while he may not have constructed the world's biggest palace, he probably built the most—as few as twenty, but as many as one hundred, according to differing reports. Most were garishly decorated with gold-plated bathrooms, glittering chandeliers and ornate balconies. His son Uday had a collection of some one hundred cars—subsequently destroyed by Saddam in a pique of anger after Uday displeased him by shooting some innocents at a party.

Vicious and legitimately paranoid North Korean dictator Kim Jong-un may well be an ultrashopper, despite the fact his nation has one of the worst economies in the world, and his people face ongoing economic hardships, frequent food shortages, regular power outages and a lack of transportation infrastructure. But it's hard to know for sure exactly how much of an ultrashopper Kim is because he's so secretive. That said, there have been glimpses into his luxurious private life. The beloved supreme leader has at least ten and as many as seventeen palaces, a fleet of luxury cars, dozens of pianos and a two-hundred-foot yacht that his friend, professional wrestler and basketball curiosity Dennis Rodman described as "a cross between a ferry and a Disney boat." There is also a private island that Rodman famously depicted after a trip there: "Kim's island is amazing. It's like going to Hawaii or Ibiza, but he's the only one that lives there."

Meanwhile, the bloodthirsty Joaquín Guzmán Loera, better known as the Mexican drug lord El Chapo, was also once an ultrashopper before he took up residence in a US prison, where his shopping is mostly confined to the commissary and perhaps some low-level contraband. According to US prosecutors, El Chapo acquired an estimated $14 billion during his career trafficking illicit drugs. At his trial, a former colleague described him this way: "When I met Mr. Guzmán, he didn't have a jet. But in the '90s, he had four jets. He had houses at every single beach. He had a ranch in every single state." One estate in Acapulco had a railway running through it so guests could view Guzmán's zoo, which included a collection of big cats: lions, tigers and panthers.

Loathsome former Italian prime minister, convicted fraudster and sex-party host Silvio Berlusconi's villa on Sardinia, just one of his many homes, had not just one or two swimming pools, but six, plus a secret underground cave with private access to the sea. And a fake volcano that burps smoke. Still, such is the nature of modern capitalism that you need not be the leader of an entire nation to qualify as an ultrashopper. You only need a lot of money and the willingness to spend it on over-the-top stuff. God-fearing fraudster and former WorldCom chief executive Bernard Ebbers once spent roughly $50 million on a 200,000-hectare ranch, the largest in Canada and complete with twenty-thousand head of cattle, two fishing resorts, a timber enterprise and an entire town before he had to forfeit it on his way to jail for fraud and conspiracy. Definitely ultrashopping, and, again, contrashopping.

Ultrashoppers come from all wealthy walks of life. The only thing tying them together is an unquenchable desire for the most of the best, regardless of how they finance it. Nothing is too much. All kinds of kings and queens, including the Queen of England, have extensive and resplendent holdings: land, castles, jewelry, the usual (for them) array of cars and horses as well as various and sundry other items, just one of which would allow the rest of us to retire in relative comfort. Others spend their own legitimately hard-earned or inherited cash with enthusiasm. Politically incorrect CNN pioneer and philanthropist Ted Turner, for example, has property in Kansas, Montana, Nebraska, New Mexico, South Dakota and Argentina totalling more than two million acres. He is happy to tell us he is the second-largest individual landholder in North America.

Canadian business tycoon Paul Desmarais built his own personal golf course in the Charlevoix region of Quebec. Domaine Laforest, as it is known, is open only to family members and a few friends. "I'm very proud of that course," said golf course architect Thomas McBroom. "The only downside? Hardly anyone will play it." High-rolling ex-billionaire and songwriting timber baron Tim Blixseth carved his own golf course out of the desert in Rancho Mirage, California, spraying buckets of precious desert water to transform vast swaths of parched sand into lush green fairways. It was one of his many over-the-top indulgences before he faced bankruptcy. Larry Ellison bought it for half the asking price (see deshop). Few people except friends, politicians and the occasional high roller have ever played it. The Du Ponts, the Mellons and many others throughout the twentieth century have built their own golf courses, but such creations still likely qualify as ultrashopping if only because of the environmental destruction visited on so much land for the benefit of so few.

AUTOSHOP (SHOPOMATIC)

To acquire stuff without a particular plan.

This is increasingly common in a developed world where almost everyone almost everywhere has almost everything, even though they don't know it. You have no list, nor do you need anything. You go shopping to pass the time, wandering the aisles with your shopping cart, mindlessly tossing in stuff that reveals itself to be extraneous only after you arrive home. Rich or poor, we do this every week at the supermarket, acquiring another in a long line of the latest, the greatest, the all-new-limited-edition-commemorative-series products and items introduced daily. "I thought I'd try it" or "I'm a sucker for new products" are often the only explanation for such purchases.

A home cook without a recipe wanders the aisles to robotically fill his ever-expanding and newly renovated kitchen with various spices he has no idea how to use, packaged food his family will never eat, kitchen gadgets that won't make it out of the box, and pots and pans that may never touch a stove because, well, he really prefers Uber Eats. A DIY enthusiast without a plan fills her cart with various items, nails and screws of every size and type, shelving that will never be installed, tools that will never be employed. An artist with dreams of greatness fills the shopping buggy with canvasses, paint, brushes and frames for masterpieces that will never be created.

Meanwhile, the development of online shopping and instant delivery means some autoshopping unfortunates never get around to opening the boxes piling up around them before they order more stuff. Online retailing certainly made autoshopping easier for people such as Ryan Cassata, a twentysomething musician and actor who once explained the challenge in an interview. The Los Angeles resident got an Amazon alert that some socks and a fanny pack were being delivered, but he didn't remember ordering them. Turns out he did indeed—in the middle of one sleepless night. He admits to being on online shopomatic in the daytime too, having collected a variety of extraneous items: "I don't really need most of this stuff." (See overshop.)

Lauren Bowling, a personal finance and self-help blogger, once suffered from what she calls "buy-and-return behaviour shopping bulimia." Rampant unshopping mitigated some of her financial challenges, but it didn't solve her compulsive shopping. Snowed under by debt racked up by overshopping, Bowling recalls the insanity: "I remember one week I had $30 left to last until my next payday and instead of buying groceries (which I desperately needed) I bought the ugliest purse while out shopping with a friend because I felt like I absolutely had to buy something before I left the store. Said ugly purse came home with me because I convinced myself I loved it, and it never left the back of my closet after that day." Bowling articulates what most of us know in our hearts: "I just couldn't stop shopping. It felt too good."

Most of us also know that no matter how good it feels, it doesn't feel as good as it used to. And yet we continue, until it becomes shopomatic. The late pop idol and alleged child-molester Michael Jackson demonstrated it blatantly in a controversial documentary film by Martin Bashir. The performer was clearly on autoshop in a gift store at the Venetian hotel in Las Vegas while Bashir looked on aghast. In the 2003 film, *Living with Michael Jackson*, Jackson spends no more than one hour in the store, but purchases $1 million worth of household items (see also supershop). Walking by some paintings, he examines one for seven seconds and promptly orders two—"Excuse me, I want that one there, and this one"—at $50,000 apiece.

In her book *Overdressed*, the author Elizabeth L. Cline describes the phenomenon of possession obsession. "I was buying clothes all the time almost subconsciously, like a cow grazes on grass." Cline notes that shoppers buy far more than they need at a discount wholesaler for reasons even they can't explain: "this is called the Costco effect." Or, as the retailing behemoth HomeSense likes to remind us in advertising: "Find exactly what you weren't looking for."

PREDESHOP

To put something in storage.

You bought a lot of stuff and can't bear to part with it, or maybe you just can't face the fact you don't want it. There are often several stages of predeshopping: Into the basement it goes, and there it stays until finally the kids are off to college and announce they want nothing to do with it, whereupon you take it all to the garage, where it languishes for a few more years, until you discover you're snowed under by your own stuff—you can't even put the car in there—and you find a self-storage operation just around the corner. Yes, today's consumer looks beyond the family home for help with storage. Formerly known as warehouses, now called self-storage centres, these wretched and unfriendly structures began popping up in earnest several decades ago, and their growth has been exponential ever since, so much so that many municipalities are finally fed up, staunching the urban stain they present by banning them outright.

The predeshopping centre is the veritable last stop before the end of the line, where things go to die before they are actually dead and buried. There you take all the stuff and discover your home is actually much bigger than you ever imagined, and of course it can now fit the new stuff you've always wanted but felt guilty about buying because your house was overcluttered (see reshop). Americans have more self-storage space—nine square feet—per capita than in any other country in the world. Canada, although no slouch in the shopping and collecting department, has only two square feet per capita. This is at a time when the size of houses (and garages) across North America is growing, with the average new home adding almost four hundred square feet over the past two decades. It is estimated that 60 per cent of predeshoppers already own a garage, more than 40 per cent have an attic and more than 30 per cent have a basement. In 2011, construction costs on self-storage outlets across the United States was $241 million. By 2018, operators were spending $5 billion on them. In the United States, there is now more than 1.7 billion square feet of rentable self-storage space, and one in every nine households has a unit. The self-storage industry in the US alone is estimated to be worth almost $40 billion and growing. That these are needed in such growing numbers is proof that garages, closets, attics and basements across North America are already full of stuff. Such is the North American predilection for acquiring stuff and our subsequent reluctance to part with it that storage companies must auction off the contents of units whose owners have not paid rent and abandoned their stuff after all. And in true North American fashion, it's often all on TV.

Administering one's stuff can be complicated, especially when you have so much of it spread to the four winds. Provocative musician and *Sex* author Madonna found herself in the middle of a very public predeshopping court battle when she discovered in 2017 that her personal items were scheduled for an online sale without her knowledge. It seems the Material Girl had moved her stuff to a former employee's storage unit during a move years earlier, before the two fell out. The personal items included a pair of unwashed panties, a hairbrush and a letter from her ex-boyfriend, the late hip-hop pioneer and convicted rapist Tupac Shakur. Madonna claimed in a lawsuit that she did not know these things were not in her possession, proving once again that the more stuff you have, the more difficult it is to keep track of it all. Similarly, a "bureaucratic foul-up" was blamed for the fact that the contents of a storage locker belonging to celebrity party girl Paris Hilton were bought for $2,775 in 2006 by treasure-seeking shoppers. The lucky buyer estimated the contents, including photos of Hilton, personal diaries, computers, clothing, videos and furniture, were worth between $5 million and $20 million.

Paying the predeshopping bills for storing stuff can be complex when you have so much, as the late drug-addicted music superstar Whitney Houston discovered to her chagrin in 2007. The warehouse company holding her items conducted an auction to recoup at least $175,000 in storage fees. The predeshopped stuff included a clear acrylic grand piano and sixteen music awards given to her estranged husband, drug-abusing drunk driver and deadbeat dad Bobby Brown.

Despite conceding her own financial troubles, daddy's girl and '90s TV star Tori Spelling admitted to rampant predeshopping when she told the audience of her reality TV show in 2013 that she had 127 storage units, at about $50 each per month. "What I'm paying in storage is seriously a mortgage," said Spelling, launching into an emotional defence of her stuff, how she had earned it, why it's important to her, and how her dad would have approved.

SHOPATHON

A prolonged period of shopping. Christmas, for example.

It could be an hour, a day, a week, a month or even years, depending on your definitions of "prolonged" and "shopping." Increasingly, it is an entire lifetime. For some, it's a few hours at the local Costco. For others, it is an indulgent vacation in Milan or Dubai. Until recently, when shopping began to truly consume our lives throughout the year, shopathon has best described Christmas. You spent a few days in the shops, overindulged in mostly everything, and woke up on January 1 with a hangover, an extra five pounds of body weight and some unmanageable credit card debt, all the result of gift-giving, a tradition that helps power the global economy and damage the planet.

Year by year at Christmas, peace, goodwill and any celebration of the birth of Christ became secondary to the all-consuming battle for position at retail checkout counters or a prolonged period at the computer looking for stuff that can be conveniently shipped to your door or someone else's by a vast fleet of little trucks. Like everything associated with modern consumerism, Christmas today is bigger, the merchandise more expensive, the season longer, the excess greater. More people are shopping for more stuff. In North America and increasingly beyond, it somehow begins in earnest on so-called Black Friday, the day after Thanksgiving in the United States, when bargain-hunting crowds jostle for position to get the best deals in the malls and outlet stores, and now even sooner, with the skyrocketing popularity of online shopping.

It wasn't always thus. Gift-giving by humans has existed longer than civilization and has likely always been associated with big events, festivals, feasts, celebrations, solstices or the arrival of visitors. But in recorded history, the first evidence of gift-giving at Christmas may have been provided by the Three Wise Men, or Biblical Magi, who brought presents to the Baby Jesus little more than two millennia ago. Interestingly, and ironically, the bulk of the famous gifts offered to the Christ Child—gold, frankincense and myrrh—were likely of no practical use to his poor parents or their shivering newborn, despite their professed medicinal properties, unproven to this day. It was perhaps the beginning of a long and accelerating tradition of giving useless stuff like jewelry, perfumes and inedible oils that continues into the twenty-first century.

These very items are front and centre in department stores now, first placed there a century ago in an act of historic retailing bravado by American merchandizing genius Harry Selfridge. "No one man grasped the concept of consumption as sensual entertainment better," says Lindy Woodhead in her book *Shopping, Seduction & Mr. Selfridge.* He put stuff out where people could see it and touch it. One radical idea at the time was to create bathrooms for women. It worked brilliantly; shopping became fun—and business boomed. Selfridge, a free-spender himself whose name is now often synonymous with department stores, made millions in the endeavor but died penniless, a result of overshopping, high-living and frequent gambling.

Several hundred years after the birth of Christ, the practice of gift-giving got a nudge from Saint Nicholas, a kindly and generous Christian bishop from Greece who couldn't have known then that his fondness for material benevolence would one day be linked to the orgy of consumerism that now engulfs the entire month of December—and beyond—across much of the Western world. The tradition has had its ups and downs ever since, but it really took hold after 1800 and was given a particular boost in 1843 when writer and social critic Charles Dickens published *A Christmas Carol.* In it, he introduced us to the wretched Ebenezer Scrooge, a lonely miser who finds redemption in gift-giving, a practice taken up with half-hearted enthusiasm by aging and so-called "philanthropic" business titans for centuries thereafter.

Since then, Christmas hasn't been Christmas without gifts—and shopping. In 1905, the writer O. Henry pondered—and espoused—the value of impractical gifts in his now famous Christmas story, "The Gift of the Magi," in which poverty-stricken lovers make sacrifices to buy gifts that turn out to be even more useless than was first obvious: A wife cuts her hair and sells the long locks to buy her husband a gold fob chain for his watch, which she discovers he has sold to buy her ornamental combs for her hair. True love may well be the greatest gift of all, but using stuff to declare it these days can be economically challenging, environmentally destructive, socially fraught and personally stressful. For ample evidence of the latter, you need listen only to the convershopping between fully grown adults around many trees on Christmas morning:

"Oh look, it's a new top."
"Do you like it?"
"It's lovely."
"Because if you don't, I can take it back?"
"No it's lovely. I won't hear of it."
"Is it the right size?"
"It's perfect."
"Because if it's not I can return it?"
"No it looks terrific. I'll wear this a lot."
"Do you want to try it on and then if it doesn't fit I could
   exchange it?"
"No it's exactly my size. I love it."
"I know it's green and you like yellow but I didn't like the yel-
   low for some reason but they have blue, and I thought you
   might like that but I didn't know for sure but you could take
   it back and get the blue."
"No, the green is perfect, just perfect."
"Or the yellow?"
"This one is just right. I really love it."

"Are you sure, because I was looking for the ones at Banana Republic and I just couldn't find them there but they had these at Gap and they seemed to have your size but we can take it back to Gap and look for the ones at Banana Republic?"

"No I love this one. It's perfect. Really."

"Well, okay, but I have the bill just in case you need it, but it doesn't sound like you do."

"Well, perhaps leave me the receipt just in case."

For some, the shopathon at Christmas long ago descended into something darker. For me, it's not so much the jostling crowds, the jammed parking lots, the unruly lineups, the oppressive Visa bills or the subliminal sadness amid the pronounced joy. Instead, it's the very the stress of finding the right thing—or the anxiety of giving the wrong gift (see misshop). It can be debilitating in a world where so many have so much. Like others, I realized long ago that even high-school students in many middle-class families don't want or even need the items we can afford to buy them, and the rest of us already have what others can afford to give. So the enlightened few simply skip the gifts all around. Even as a boy, I remember the anxiety associated with gift-giving at Christmas. Having asked for a racing-car set and receiving a train set instead, the result of a catalogue mixup, I had to hide my devastation from my parents, who may have been more disappointed than I, despite the many other seasonal stresses that weighed on them. Meanwhile, was my measly gift to them useful, or appropriate? Would they actually like the ashtray I made out of clay or the knick-knack created from popsicle sticks? I was wracked with anxiety. Another year, I wondered if my siblings had more gifts than I under the tree; a few years later, I was concerned they didn't receive enough compared to me. I pity my poor parents, for I'm sure they too fretted about such nonsense. Later, when my life was saved (twice, once at age seven and again at age fourteen) by pioneering heart surgeons, I was showered upon recovery with so many gifts and cards that it embarrassed me; I thought it excessive even as a child.

All kinds of celebrations and the attendant gift-giving announce themselves as opportunities to shop a lot. Each one is a shopathon. In 2020, it was estimated that in the United States alone, Americans would spend more than $25 billion on Valentine's Day gifts (up $5 billion from 2019), powered in part by the likes of sultry actor and quirky humanitarian Angelina Jolie, who, in happier times, bought her former heartthrob husband, fellow actor and self-admitted boozer Brad Pitt, a two-hundred-year-old olive tree, estimated to cost more than $18,000, as a valentine in 2011. Or headline-grabbing rapper Kanye West, who sent his overexposed wife Kim Kardashian one thousand roses for Valentine's Day in 2014.

Easter, one of the holiest days on the Christian calendar, was forever besmirched by the backward-looking Russian autocrat Tsar Alexander III in 1885, when he gave to his wife, the Empress Maria Feodorovna, a now-famous but utterly useless Fabergé egg, crafted from gold and encrusted in jewels. Alexander was not normally given to the immoderation that defined his predecessors, but his wife was so taken by the egg that he had one crafted each year thereafter until his death, when his son, the ill-fated Nicholas II, took up the Easter tradition and presented one to his wife—and another to his mother. By the time the Bolsheviks took over during the Russian Revolution in 1917, there were dozens of these expensively exquisite eggs, most of which were removed from ransacked Imperial palaces.

Americans spent $9 billion on costumes, candy and decorations for Halloween in 2018. There's graduation spending and summer-camp spending and back-to-school spending. There's Mother's Day and Father's Day and Grandparents' Day. There's a day for administrative assistants, a nurses' day and a teacher appreciation day. They all signal gift-giving. And so the shopathon that begins at Christmas is still full-ahead flank at Valentine's Day and Easter. Lavish gift-giving and the attendant shopping are key to birthdays, bar mitzvahs, retirements, debutante balls, coming-out parties, births and even deaths, a tragic irony given the circumstances, but one which persists nonetheless (see necroshop). Each celebration is its own shopathon. Each is an excuse to hit the shops. Each begins as another ends. Even a simple visit to a friend's home is an excuse for gift-giving the world over.

Meanwhile, weddings are now so engulfed by wasteful overspending that they are described as an industry—and there too, gift-giving can be fraught. Kathy Mason, a resident of the Toronto area, learned this when she attended a wedding with her boyfriend in 2013. Mason gifted the happy couple a basket of gourmet foods with a note: "Life is delicious—enjoy!" In response, the bride texted back, asking for the receipt: "I want to thank you for coming to the wedding Friday. I'm not sure if it's the first wedding you have been to, but for your next wedding . . . people give envelopes. I lost out on $200 covering you and your date's plate . . . and got fluffy whip and sour patch kids in return. Just a heads-up for the future." The bride suggested Mason ask "normal functioning people" what they thought of her apparent lack of manners or protocol, so Mason brought it to the Burlington (Ontario) Mamas Facebook group, where it ignited the predictable debate, and to the *Hamilton Spectator*, the local newspaper, which detailed the testy digital exchange between Mason and the newlyweds:

> GIFT-GIVERS: ". . . to ask for a receipt is unfathomable. In fact it was incredibly disrespectful. It was the rudest gesture I have encountered, or even heard of."
> NEWLYWEDS: "Weddings are to make money for your future . . . not to pay for peoples meals. Do more research. People haven't gave gifts since like 50 years ago! You ate steak, chicken, booze, and a beautiful venue."
> GIFT-GIVERS: "It's obvious you have the etiquette of a twig, I couldn't care less of what you think about the gift you received, 'normal' people would welcome anything given, you wanna have a party, you pay for it, DON'T expect me to."

NEWLYWEDS: "You should have been cut from the list . . . I knew we were gunna get a bag of peanuts. I was right."

Never mind the chatter, said Louise Fox, an etiquette coach interviewed by the *Spectator* reporter, even asking for the receipt was out of line: "The wedding is never supposed to be about the gifts. It's a celebration of the union. You should be grateful that you got a gift and that's the end of it. You want to preserve the feelings of the giver."

Weddings have always been a big deal for brides, grooms and their financially burdened parents, but in the world of the shopathon, it is getting ever more difficult to keep up, especially when the rich and famous are showing the way. Fleeting lovebirds Mariah Carey and James Packer, for example, spent a reported $10 million on a diamond ring before they broke off their engagement (she deshopped the ring for $2 million). Acquisitive model, singer and performer Victoria Beckham somehow had a collection of fourteen engagement rings valued at more than $1 million, despite having only one husband. Academy Award–winning actor and reformed drug-abusing singer Liza Minnelli's fourth marriage to producer and gambling addict David Gest, which lasted less than a year, is reported to have cost $3.5 million. Vanisha Mittal, the daughter of Lakshmi Mittal, an Indian steel magnate and one of the richest men in the world, married British business executive Amit Bhatia in 2004 in a big, fat Indian wedding at a French château estimated to have cost more than $50 million. That's a shopathon.

UNSHOPATHON

A big unshop.

This is unshopping on a large scale, and it involves the return of not just a few items, but an entire carload (or in the likely event we own a truck—a truckload) or perhaps several. An unshopathon takes time and planning. This is the kind of thing you do with all the stuff you got from friends and family for Christmas. Or two weeks after the wedding, when you return not just one or two items, but the entire registry list and pocket the cash. Or Monday morning, when you wake up with a hangover and some newly found common sense and return all that stuff you shouldn't have bought while you can still get your money back.

Unloading it all at a garage sale or having it repossessed is not an unshopathon (see deshopathon). But auctions of famous art collections, car collections or miscellaneous stuff collected by rich and famous people often qualify as unshopathons. A 2018 auction held by volatile actor Russell Crowe after he split with his wife, which he marketed as "The Art of Divorce," was just such an event. Containing a lot of stuff he acquired from movies he'd acted in (his *Gladiator* breastplate, for example) and some personal stuff including watches, jewelry, a motorcycle and sports memorabilia, it generated more than $3.7 million in Australian dollars. "Not a bad hourly rate for a 5-hour shift," tweeted Crowe. Music diva and overshopper Barbra Streisand is evidently an expert at hosting similar events, regularly auctioning off clothing, furniture and memorabilia for charity.

Elton John may be the king of the celebrity unshopathon, often using it to unload stuff en masse. In 1988, he realized he could barely live in his London mansion for all the stuff in it. "It's become less of a home and more of a warehouse," he told an interviewer at the time. By then, his collections had become so profuse he said he and his husband couldn't find a place to sit. He did not rule out, however, reshopping for new stuff. Indeed, that auction was only one among many. In 2001, John auctioned off twenty of his cars, including nine Bentleys, three Ferraris, four Aston Martins and others because "they don't get driven." (See misshop.) John later launched an annual clothes sale with proceeds going to his AIDS foundation, saying, "there are clothes that haven't been worn," including an entire room of Gianni Versace shirts: "I have every single silk shirt that he made, probably twice over and sometimes three over." (See overshop.)

Finally, while unshopathons can be financially beneficial to those who organize them, they can be fiscal disasters for the hapless reshoppers in attendance, determined to outshop a competitor at an auction simply because an item was once owned by a celebrity. These are the folks who are somehow so misguided that they squeal "I won!" when in fact the truth is something a little different: "I paid the most!"

DESHOPATHON

Deshopping on a large scale.

A deshopathon is what Japanese organizing consultant and deshopping phenomenon Marie Kondo recommends when we realize we are surrounded by so much stuff we can no longer think. Famous worldwide for her 2011 book *The Life-Changing Magic of Tidying Up* and the subsequent Netflix series, Kondo suggests itemizing all your stuff and getting rid of anything that doesn't "spark joy." The trademarked KonMari Method urges overshoppers to "keep only those things that speak to the heart, and discard items that no longer spark joy. Thank them for their service—then let them go."

Conveniently, her popular website has an online shop featuring "a collection of items that spark joy for Marie and enhance your daily life," so when you have finally deshopped the stuff that does not spark joy you can reshop for stuff from Kondo that does. Kondo was such a phenomenon that the *Washington Post* wondered if she was responsible for a landslide of donations—a nation-wide deshopathon—to needy charities in 2019.

Meanwhile, the success of the show—and the popularity of decluttering—might have had something to do with the creation of another Netflix show in 2020, *Get Organized with The Home Edit*. Produced by Hollywood powerhouse Reese Witherspoon and hosted by professional organizers Clea Shearer and Joanna Teplin, the show displays the hosts' "enthusiasm for excess and their talent for putting finery on display," according to a review in *Variety*, the entertainment industry magazine, which describes the program as "the precise polar opposite" of Kondo's show on Netflix. "But if Kondo's ethos is all about shedding attachments, The Home Edit's show emphasizes a sort of fetishistic maximalism, purchasing and displaying new gewgaws at the Container Store in order to display, particularly on social media, all the proud abundance of one's life." (See reshop, overshop, ultrashop.)

Often, a deshopathon is an event associated not with joy but trauma, as evidenced by all those people who cry their way through decluttering exercises with professionals, often—inexplicably—for the benefit of an international television audience. Others must engage in deshopathons just to pay the rent, their Visa bills or the tax collector. Academy Award–winning soul singer and writer Isaac Hayes, famous in the 1970s for writing the "Theme from *Shaft*" and in the late 1990s as the voice of Chef in the animated TV-series *South Park*, lost most of his possessions in a deshopathon in 1977 after declaring bankruptcy. "Being a creative person, I didn't like to get bogged down in a lot of administrative things," he explained at the time, echoing the sentiments of many artists.

After trailblazing entertainer and big spender Sammy Davis Jr. died in 1990, he left his estimated $4 million estate to his wife Altovise. Unfortunately for her, his debts dwarfed his assets and the result was a painfully drawn-out deshopathon. He owed $5.2 million in federal taxes, and thousands more to various other creditors, including a clothier, a jeweler and a grocery store. Well-known for his vast collection of garish rings, Davis's stuff could easily have been turned into a triumphant unshopathon. But it was not to be. Some 185 items of jewelry and an Andy Warhol soup-can painting mysteriously disappeared during the preparations, and the deshopping event itself was labelled a sad spectacle by some who attended. The IRS cloud hung over the estate for years, and in the end, Davis's widow was left impoverished and descended into alcohol abuse.

RESHOPATHON

Repurchasing on a large scale.

Picture yourself on Boxing Day afternoon: You've returned all that stuff you got for Christmas (see unshopathon) and suddenly realize the refunds actually make your Visa bill manageable. It feels like cash burning a hole in your pocket. True, you didn't want any of that stuff under the tree, but look at all these bargains! You might as well mosey on over to the electronics store and check out the latest in big-screen TVs. Or maybe investigate a new sound system, plus another game console, and perhaps a complicated and finicky home security system. And, look, the hot tub dealer is having a blow-out sale! It's a reshopathon.

Empty nesters and retirees hoping to downsize their homes often rid themselves of truckloads of stuff in a deshopathon and then must replace the entire suite of items in an extended period of reshopping—a reshopathon.

DESHOPA-RESHOPATHON

A big, simultaneous deshop and reshop.

For most of us, there is no better example than the street-wide garage sale, those horrible events where rather than submit yourself to the singular humiliation of a yard sale to deshop your stuff, you join your friends and neighbours and do it together. It's kind of like a street party, a big flea market, where everyone deshops their stuff to you for 10 cents on the dollar and reshops for your stuff for themselves at a similar discount. At the end of the day, rather than decluttering their homes, people realize they've simply redistributed everything.

SHOPAGANDA

The sales pitch.

Marketing statements, usually exaggerated, often untrue, are a key motivator in our desire to shop. Words, pictures, photos and videos created by advertisers, marketers and sellers make stuff sound or look good and persuade us to acquire it. Some of it is pretty innocent, such as the preposterous campaign stating that drinking McDonald's Canada's McCafé coffee is "a simple way to help make a difference" because the company's coffee beans are ethically sourced and buying them "protects rainforests and the animals within them." Marketers learned early on that *people want to believe.*

Some of it is a little more creative, like the famous claim by 1970s television star Ricardo Montalbán that the seats of the 1975 Chrysler Cordoba automobile were covered in "fine Corinthian leather." Turned out the stuff was an invention of the Bozell advertising agency to sound foreign and elegant. Montalbán himself later quipped to talk-show host David Letterman that the fancy words meant nothing. This particular shopaganda has become something of a cult classic, and like so many others, nobody seems to care that it's all nonsense. Neither did anyone seems to mind the shopaganda spewed by belligerent developer and crude philistine Donald Trump, who insisted his buildings were taller than they actually are; Trump SoHo was advertised as forty-six floors when it is only forty-three; The Trump International Hotel and Tower is in reality a meagre forty-four storeys, but Trump says it is somehow fifty-two; the seventy-storey Trump World Tower was advertised miraculously as ninety storeys.

Some of it is more sinister, such as Volkswagen's criminal scheme to sell "clean diesel" vehicles with lines such as "now going green doesn't have to feel like you're going green." The whole thing was an elaborate fraud. While it may have felt like they were "going green," Volkswagen diesel drivers were in fact polluting as usual, and perhaps more so. In 2017, a US federal judge fined the company $2.8 billion for the scam, after tests showed it had secretly equipped eleven million cars with programming software to hide emissions. How many self-described environmentalists proudly own Volkswagens, or hulking pickup trucks, needlessly large SUVS, overpowered motorboats or even multiple aircraft?

Some shopaganda is dangerous to health, such as a slogan in the late 1930s by Craven "A" cigarettes that suggested you should smoke them "for your throat's sake" or another that suggested Camels are "for your digestion's sake." But as usual, it actually works, as illustrated early on by the meteoric rise in 1927 of an otherwise everyday brand of cigarettes called Lucky Strike. Advertising pioneer Albert Lasker started promoting the idea that smoking "Luckies" would improve your singing voice. In a classic piece of shopaganda, Lasker called it his "precious voice" campaign: "I thought of the idea of getting foreign women to testify that they smoked Luckies. There was no prejudice in Europe against women smoking. They smoked then as now—the same as men—in public, out of public, and whenever they wanted." So Lasker decided to get people who used their voice for a living to extoll the virtues of cigarettes: "It was very natural that my mind went to the opera stars, because at that time there were only one or two American stars, and the rest were foreign. Then we developed what we called our 'precious voice' campaign. As they were singers, they said, 'My living is dependent on my being able to sing, and I protect my precious voice by smoking Lucky Strike.'" Within months of the campaign, Lucky Strike was hot. "Overnight, the business of Luckies went up like the land in a boom field where oil has just been found. All other cigarettes went up, too."

Lucky Strike did not pay for the testimonials at the time, offering the singers exposure and perhaps greater fame, but the brand would later pay millions in the 1930s to movie stars such as Henry Fonda, Clark Gable, Carole Lombard, Barbara Stanwyck, Bob Hope, Spencer Tracy and Gloria Swanson to promote Luckies (see shopostle). After spending more than a century promoting cigarettes as fun and exciting, and decades baldly lying to us about the health hazards, the tobacco industry then spent millions on shopaganda vociferously denying the health hazards in the face of mounting scientific and obvious evidence. Finally, cigarette makers were forced to pay governments hundreds of billions in fines, some of which is now used to finance advertising to discourage smoking.

Some shopaganda is insidious, like the monotonous television programs on channels such as HGTV, which are devoted to promoting home improvement, renovation, redecoration and wanton shopping, unshopping, reshopping and deshopping. This is the place where good-looking "ordinary" homeowners and plasticized TV hosts take cinematic glee in destroying—one wall at a time—homes that 90 per cent of the world's population would be thrilled to live in for the rest of our lives. But for them, everything is hopelessly out of date, unlivable, not good enough, the wrong colour or needs an update. "That backsplash has got to go."

Ironically, advertisers don't like the word "advertising." They come up with words to describe advertising that are themselves shopaganda: "Advertorial," "sponsored content," "promoted," "supported," "partnered" and other terms disguise the fact that this is not what it may seem. Not that it really matters. Most people, especially shoppers, will do what we're told: If a sign says, "Buy now!" a surprising number of us will do just that, whether we need it or not. We just love to be talked into buying stuff, and frankly, we don't really require much talk. A few superlatives will do just fine. Somehow, *we believe.* This was learned by entrepreneurs and sales executives centuries ago when, in order to make an ordinary widget stand out among all the other ordinary widgets, they announced, with no proof whatsoever, that theirs was "the best." It continues apace centuries later. If a hamburger joint on a restaurant strip announces it has the "Best Burgers in Town!" on a large sign, many hungry travellers will endanger their lives crossing several lanes of traffic so they can eat a hamburger not noticeably different from the one served at the more conveniently located burger joint with shorter lines.

Nor do we hold such promises up to scrutiny. Since the beginning of, well, stuff, marketing gurus everywhere have combed the dictionary for useful shopaganda and ways of presenting it:

What They Say	What They Mean
Save	Spend
Built to last	Designed to fail
Futuristic	We painted it silver
New and improved	Same product, minus the toxic stuff our lawyers told us to remove
New, convenient size	Higher price, less product
While quantities last	Uh-oh, nobody seems to want this stuff
Certified	We hired our very own "certifier"
Farm-fresh eggs	Eggs
Fresh hen's eggs	Eggs
US Grade A eggs	Eggs
Handmade in small batches	Mass produced in huge vats
Tasty	Salty
Lightly salted	Call the doctor
No obligation	Please read these five pages of legal mumbo-jumbo in fine print and click the "agree" button
Easy to assemble	Put on a pot of coffee; it's going to be a long night
Simple instructions	Engineering degree required
Satisfaction guaranteed	Frustration assured

We know from experience that nothing is "absolutely free," but it has not inured us to the possibility that, well, something just might be. Retailers are regularly fined for announcing items "on sale" when in fact they are not. Check out the store windows next time you are in a mall: "sale" signs are conspicuous by their absence. Some shoppers don't need an excuse to buy things, but many of us want a justification, a bargain, or some kind of a nudge to help us take out our wallets. Conveniently, there is no shortage of people, and flowery language, to assist with this. The real estate industry, for example, has long employed shopaganda as a useful tool:

What They Say	What They Mean
Handyman special	It's a wreck
Lots of character	It's a wreck
Needs your personal touch	It's a wreck
As is	It's a wreck
Good bones	It's a wreck
Great curb appeal	Looks good outside, but it's a wreck inside
Great starter home	It's a wreck, and it's small
Charming	It's small
Cozy	It's small
Intimate	It's small
Custom kitchen	Jury rigged
Low-maintenance yard	Dirt and pavement

English menu writers long ago enlisted the French language in their pursuit of shopaganda. Everything, it seems, sounds tastier in French. Doesn't "soup du jour," for example, sound better than "today's soup" or even "yesterday's leftovers in hot water?" Thus, sometime toward the end of the twentieth century, cold cuts somehow became *la charcuterie*. Limp carrot and celery sticks don't sound as good as *crudités*. Your grandparents called it a French stick, but for you, a sophisticate, it's *baguette*. Plain old dinner rolls and tossable buns have been repackaged as *brioche*.

Vintners, sommeliers and wine snobs, meanwhile, will describe a wine as "complex and opulent with notes of tobacco, vanilla and mocha and chewy tannins." And how can beer drinkers have fallen face first for campaigns selling dry beer, cold-filtered beer, ice beer, micro-carbonated beer, and—arguably among the greatest feats of shopaganda in an industry foaming with them—"genuine draft beer" brazenly sold in a bottle?

OUTSHOP

To get a better deal on some stuff than someone else.

Let's say you buy a pair of gloves. They're the super-duper double-stitched real calves' leather Prada gloves with the inset pearl beads that you and your best friend have sought for six months. You finally find them, and you quickly phone her to announce: "Mission accomplished," only to be informed that, alas, she has found the gloves too, at a different shop, and she paid less than you did. You've been outshopped. There really is nothing quite as depressing, quite as humiliating, quite as awful as being outshopped. And there is nothing so delicious as outshopping someone else, or pretending to—and, of course, telling them about it (see convershopping).

If you and your spouse, for example, paid less for a bigger house with a grander foyer, better-outfitted bathrooms with fake silver and gold waterfall taps, and a more luxurious kitchen with the latest countertop material than your neighbours did, then you have outshopped them. If you held out for the latest (and less expensive) model of phone when your sister is stuck with the C-series, you've outshopped her. If you waited until the last minute to get this season's BMW with more features for $2,000 less than your buddy spent on last season's, you've outshopped him, and you should find a way to let him know it. On the other hand, your feat of outshopping might be so spectacular, so delicious, that you needn't tell him, because he likely knows already.

Perhaps outshopping explains why humans, from time immemorial, have been reluctant to discuss money matters. It's really all we want to know, but few of us really want to give it up. In spite of this, the price of houses, clothes and vehicles are increasingly discussed (see convershopping) and outshopping is laid bare at social gatherings, around watercoolers, or during business meetings.

This happens often in the stock market, when one stock picker buys lower and sells higher than another, or at least alleges to. To buy higher and sell lower is, after all, humiliating if common. It's not so easy in the world of professional sports, where winners and losers are always in the spotlight, on the playing field and off. For example, at trading time, which is one monumental shopathon for franchise owners and their minions, one team inevitably makes a better deal than another, and when they do, they continue to lord it over them season after season. Even fans get in on the action. Such was the case with one of the most famous baseball players of all time, hard-drinking womanizer Babe Ruth, who was sold by the Boston Red Sox to the New York Yankees after the 1919 season for little more than $100,000 and a $350,000 loan. It was a bad deal for Boston, and fans were reminded of it by gloating New Yorkers for the next eighty-six years. That's how long it took Boston to win another World Series; the Yankees, often with Ruth leading the charge, garnered twenty-seven. Along the way, a book was written about this particular shopping disaster, called *The Curse of the Bambino*, and the title is now part of the baseball-fan lexicon. NFL phenom Tom Brady is another example. In 2000, the University of Michigan graduate wasn't drafted until the sixth round. The now-famous quarterback followed 198 other players drafted ahead of him, including a quarterback who never played in an NFL game. Somebody got outshopped, and one day everybody would know it.

Getting a good deal on stuff is even better than getting a good deal on people—but getting free stuff is even better than getting a good deal on stuff. When you get something free . . . well, there's nothing better than getting something for "free," even if you are deluding yourself. This is why so many retailers and manufacturers often offer a little something extra to gullible customers. It might be as simple as "the prize" in a box of Cracker Jack—the company began including a worthless gewgaw in boxes in 1912, a practice that trained kids from an early age to look for free and largely useless stuff. The practice was picked up by the mighty McDonald's corporation when it started including a plastic promotional item masquerading as a toy in its Happy Meals. If your best friend used his dime to buy Cracker Jack, and you spent yours on a bag of chips, it looked for all the world like you were outshopped. Cracker Jack continued with the ruse for more than a century until the Frito-Lay company, which bought Cracker Jack in 1997, eliminated "the prize" in 2016.

It might be that "free tote bag" you get with a subscription to the *New Yorker* or the thirteenth doughnut in a baker's dozen. It might be a tiny bottle of Grand Marnier attached to the neck of a bottle of vodka or a cheap ceramic figurine in a package of teabags. It might be the "standard" electric windows or air-conditioning or automatic transmission on your car. It might be a $200 tie your clothier tosses in after you've spent $2,500 on a suit and $700 on two shirts. It is why a shocking number of highly paid celebrities and other rich people, despite already having everything they always wanted in triplicate, are still thrilled when they get a mysterious "loot bag" or "swag bag" full of meaningless stuff or a free iPad at an awards show. Everybody. Wants. A. Deal.

Outshoppers refuse to pay full price, list price, asking price or even the discounted price—any price that does not appear to be lower than the price everyone else paid. They simply must haggle, bargain, dicker or somehow negotiate a better deal. Most of us can't stand paying full price for anything. We love freebies and coupons, and are thrilled with the illusion of a good deal at a blowout sale. But most of us are not outshoppers; we are unwilling to put in the energy necessary to achieve a true bargain. Instead, we rely on luck to achieve one. We dread the thought of buying a new car (let alone a used one) because for some reason the industry is one of the few in North America that still insists vehicle prices must be negotiated, even when they are not really negotiable. No matter what price we pay, we feel we are somehow paying too much. But outshoppers have done their research. They know the MSRP, the markup, the ups and downs and ins and outs of every vehicle they covet (see shoperati).

There is a certain art to the whole affair, and some of us are simply not artists. It is evident in fresh produce markets around the world, where a cacophony of haggling floats through the air—a hip-hop symphony of retailing. Butchers, bakers, fishmongers, florists and farmers compete with each other for our attention and our money. For reasons which escape me (cowardice perhaps), I have never felt capable of holding my own among the hagglers, despite sampling hundreds of fresh produce markets from Lake Toba to Tangier. At a farmers' market in Canada, I once found myself in front of a table examining eggplants, when a woman beside me held up two of them and barked at the farmer "how much?" The answer was immediate: "$1.50." The woman responded: "I'll give you one dollar," tossed him a coin and walked away with the produce without even waiting for an answer. Astonished and clearly outshopped, I knew I was incapable of this kind of shopping chutzpah and instead paid the poor farmer what he was asking.

Everybody is a cheapskate, but some are more obvious than others. Outshoppers look for reasons to get a bargain. They case the shop for signs of desperation, a product that might spoil, an unfashionable item taking up space that a newly fashionable object might occupy, a hapless shopreneur with bills to pay and product to move. They tell her the item for sale is just not right. They complain about the colour, a fray, a scratch or a dent. Or they bulldoze the merchant and refuse to pay retail. In his bestselling book, *Stung*, Gary Ross recounts in gripping detail a particularly outrageous example. His book tells the true story of Brian Molony, a gambling addict who embezzled more than $10 million from his employer, the Canadian Imperial Bank of Commerce, in the early 1980s. Molony, as close to a non-shopper as they come, drove an old Buick and wore inexpensive clothes, but nonetheless would gamble away hundreds of thousands of dollars in a single evening at casinos in Atlantic City and Las Vegas. Harried and enroute from Toronto to Vegas on his final trip before finally being apprehended, he discovered he was without luggage. He didn't want to raise any suspicions among customs officials by travelling without a suitcase, so he ducked into a travel agency on the way to the airport for a prop—a travel bag. Normally, the receptionist said, the bags were gifts for clients, but Molony was told he could have one for $5. The man who later that evening would lose more than $1 million at the gambling tables balked at the $5 price for a cheap plastic travel bag. Ross described Molony's thinking: "Five dollars was exorbitant. Two was fair, he said, and two more than they usually got. Finally, the girl just shrugged her shoulders."

Indeed, the raison d'être of outshoppers is to wear down or wear out salespeople until they give you what you want. It's done regularly for big-ticket items such as homes and cars and maybe some antiques or art in North America, but the rest of the world is swarming with outshoppers bargaining for anything from a hotel bed to a pair of pants to a basket of hot peppers.

BALKSHOP

To refuse to pay for something you've already bought.

Balkshoppers declare that goods and services are not up to snuff, so they withhold funds—they balk at the price. They won't pay up. They bounce cheques. They buy now but won't pay later. They frustrate retailers, renovators and repair companies. They make work for collection companies. Balkshoppers basically fund repo men. Mean-spirited New York hotelier Leona Helmsley, dubbed the "queen of mean" by the media in the 1980s, was notorious for being reluctant to pay full price for anything, regularly grinding contractors or refusing to pay for work she alleged was not up to standards. She was, said her lawyer Gerald Feffer, "paranoid about being ripped off." Whether she sincerely believed she was being overcharged is difficult to know for sure, but there was little doubt she distributed her own money with extreme reluctance, and took the art of outshopping with other people's money to overshopping extremes. With a fortune of about $5 billion, she famously tried to cheat the government out of roughly $1 million in taxes, allegedly uttering the notorious phrase "only the little people pay taxes."

In a monumental spree of contrashopping during renovations to her Connecticut mansion, just one of her many homes, Helmsley charged a $13,000 barbecue pit, a $57,000 stereo system, and a $45,000 clock to her business. She bought a $500,000 jade figurine but categorized it as a business expense, and misrepresented $10,000 worth of dresses for personal use as hotel uniforms. In a statement that would become progressively ironic as the years went by, petulant landlord Donald Trump, himself notorious for allegedly stiffing contractors, piped up to call her a "disgrace to humanity." In her closing argument at Helmsley's trial for tax evasion, federal prosecutor Cathy Seibel summed up what poor people have known for millennia: "Just because you're rich doesn't mean you're not cheap."

Of course, all of us would like to buy but not pay (see shop-o-erotic). And many are not about to be discouraged by the mere lack of a bank balance or, worse, a growing debt to the credit card companies. Our shopping philosophy was delivered to us by the retailing industry: "buy now, pay later." We blithely acquire stuff on credit: big houses, expensive cars, ugly furniture, shiny appliances, impractical clothing, glittering jewelry, offensive art and worthless home decorations. We borrow from whatever and whoever is willing to lend money to us, which turns out to be almost everyone: governments, credit card companies, banks, mortgage lenders, car manufacturers, loan sharks, hedge funds, our parents, our children, our friends. Household debt grows each year: in the United States and Canada, it was almost nothing in 1950; today it is more than $14 trillion in the US and $2.3 trillion in Canada. We love overshopping even if we don't have the money, and we carry the debt and make the payments until inevitably we cannot, at which point we lose all the stuff we convinced ourselves we "owned," when most of it in fact belonged to the bank.

This is, of course, what happened during the world economic crisis in 2007–08. It was all a mirage, a pleasant dream in which we were wealthy and happy and we finally got some respect because we had nice stuff. Long before that economic calamity, economist and author Juliet B. Schor wrote about the inevitable disaster: "The total amount of debt held by the average household has increased relentlessly for decades, and it now equals just about what that household makes in any given year." Americans, she wrote, "spend more than they say they would like to, and more than they have. They spend more than they realize they are spending, and more than is fiscally prudent. And they spend in ways that are collectively, if not individually, self-defeating. Overspending is how ordinary Americans cope with everyday pressures of the new consumerism."

It is the way of the world, and has been since the beginnings of civilization. Indeed, without loans, without credit, without debt, there would be no civilization. Credit is a necessity for civilization, but civilization starts to erode when the bills come due. When people can't pay their loans, the cascading bankruptcies cause the house of cards to topple, and the entire world faces a crisis, as it did during the sub-prime mortgage debacle in 2007. Before that, bankers had told struggling workers across America they could suddenly afford to buy houses—and all the stuff we put in them—that had previously been beyond reach. When the payments came due and these hapless pseudoshoppers finally read the fine print, world economic chaos ensued.

But as usual, it isn't just the cash-strapped working poor and heavily leveraged industrialists who indulge in often irresponsible pseudoshopping. And it doesn't require a global credit crisis for many to face economic armageddon. Enthusiastic pseudoshoppers include the plain old rich-and-famous. Cash-strapped bankrupts such as the late alcohol-abusing former teen idol David Cassidy, pothead country singer and overshopper Willie Nelson and former NBA oddity and former deadbeat dad Dennis Rodman are seemingly everywhere.

Bizarrely plasticized man-child Michael Jackson was spending $30 million each year simply to service his personal debts before he died. "His largest expenditure," according to William R. Ackerman, a forensic accountant who, following Jackson's death, testified regarding the pop star's finances, "was interest expense. He spent a ton of money on interest." The amount Jackson owed grew from $30 million in 1993 to $140 million in 1998. When he died in 2009, Jackson owed $400 million. "He was tapped out," said Ackerman, in what may have been an understatement.

Jocelyn Wildenstein, an American socialite so infamous for her plastic surgery that she was nicknamed Catwoman, is another famous balkshopper. She filed for bankruptcy in 2018, despite having received $2.5 billion in a divorce settlement in 1999. How that would even be possible is hinted at in an admission Wildenstein made to *Vanity Fair* magazine in the late 1990s: she and her former husband, art dealer Alec Wildenstein, would spend at least $1 million a month. In filing for bankruptcy in 2018, Wildenstein indicated she owed hundreds of thousands to law firms, storage facilities (see predeshop), condominium renovators, as well as $70,000 to American Express. Plus $38,000 on a 2006 Bentley that was worth only $35,000.

BLOTTOSHOP

To shop while drunk.

eBay, Amazon and various other online operations have long benefitted from tipsy cybershoppers sipping a cocktail or two (or three). No public drunkenness. No impaired drivers. No embarrassing hiccups or drooling at the retail checkout. Just shopping. And bricks-and-mortar retailers have been luring pie-eyed patrons for decades, locating their shops within staggering distance of pubs and restaurants, fully aware that tipsy consumers tend to be loose with their money. Mall managers strive for the right mix of retailing and restaurants. Gallery owners serve cheap wine and bland cheese at openings so slightly drunk and financially strapped upshoppers can believe for a moment that they are rich art collectors. And bridal stores and exclusive retailers serve champagne in flutes if you look like a committed overshopper, supershopper or ultrashopper.

A few years ago, Lululemon started serving draft beer. Crate & Barrel introduced cocktails. Nordstrom opened a full bar—"and by 4 p.m. most days, it's packed," according to the *Washington Post*. Shoe Bar, as it's aptly called, specializes in $17 cocktails with names like Billionaire and Husband Daycare. Chief executive Erik Nordstrom states the obvious: "I don't know why it took us so long to put drinking and shoes together, but it's a great combination . . . it helps sell things." Some online merchants figure nighttime drinking is responsible for the fact that sales are busier then. *Fortune* magazine estimated that Americans spent more than "$39 billion while drunk shopping" in 2018, an increase over the $30 billion blottoshoppers spent the year before.

Go-Go's founder and substance abuser Belinda Carlisle admits to at least one incident of blottoshopping when she first became successful: "Once I went to the racetrack and woke up the next morning owning a horse. I'd been drinking, doing drugs and betting and it seemed like a good idea at the time." Turns out that, like Carlisle, all kinds of blottoshoppers are happy to share their misadventures. Social media is alive with examples of questionable purchases documented by formerly drunk people who inexplicably feel the need to share their misbegotten treasures with the world the next morning. These items include: a pet pig, a pet scorpion, a dog, dog socks, a triceratops mask for a dog, a cat house, one hundred top hats for a pet toad, giant googly eyes for an automobile, a life-sized cut-out of comic actor Danny DeVito, and various memorabilia related to quirky internet star Nicolas Cage, including T-shirts, cut-outs and pillows. Said one online commenter after reading a list of blottoshopped purchases: "I notice a lot of Nicolas Cage! Drunk people love him!!!"

SHOPOSPHERE

The planet.

There are still some places you can go where there is no shopping, but they are fast disappearing. Someone is always shopping somewhere. In Asia or Africa, in Norway or in Namibia. In Cleveland or in Cairo. Online or in malls. On radio or television. On a plane or in a car. At a museum or a football game. At 2 a.m. and 2 p.m. Dressed to the nines or stark naked. Rich or poor, healthy or sick, young or old.

CONTRASHOP

*Unethical, disreputable, dishonest, immoral,
amoral or illegal shopping.*

This means shopping when or where you shouldn't be, acquiring stuff
that is ethically questionable, buying stuff through improper means,
shopping with stolen money or plain old theft. It can include smuggling, cheating, lying about shopping, usually in the pursuit of the
elusive bargain. It can be as seemingly innocent as buying cheap
counterfeit goods—paying, say, $200 for a watch that normally sells for
$20,000—and pretending you somehow didn't know. Selling this stuff
is illegal, and buying it often is also. The counterfeit-stuff industry is
worth billions, and buyers are aiding and abetting the proliferation of
crap, mostly for the purpose of increasing their status among those
who have the real thing.

Also relatively innocent, if the endless lineups of startled travellers at airport customs counters are any indication, is overshopping in
other countries and bringing the stuff home without mentioning it to
officials. Many otherwise law-abiding Canadians buy too much wine or
cheese in Italy or France and fail to report it to authorities at the airport. Nobody likes to pay more taxes than they need to, but smuggling
is illegal, and in the case of some foods, plants and animals, it can be
dangerous.

Some pawn shops are hangouts for contrashoppers and those who
would illegally profit from them. Many are upstanding establishments,
excellent and legitimate places to shop, unshop, reshop and deshop,
contributing to environmental sustainability through the reuse of
material that might otherwise go directly to the dump—but some are
frequented by police on the hunt for stolen goods.

Government stimulus money generated the predictable array of contrashoppers during the COVID-19 pandemic in 2020. Mustafa Qadiri, a thirty-eight-year-old Southern California businessman, applied for emergency loans to prop up his mortgage and advertising business, but government investigators say he spent the money on various personal shopping sprees, including "lavish vacations" and a Lamborghini, a Ferrari and a Bentley, plus some other stuff he didn't need. Likewise, Florida entrepreneur David T. Hines got $4 million in loans during the pandemic and days later was driving a $318,000 Lamborghini Huracán EVO. Rather than paying salaries and other business expenses, trucking-company owner and reality-show star Maurice "Mo" Fayne bought himself a Rolls-Royce Wraith luxury coup and $85,000 worth of jewelry, among other things, after receiving $1.5 million in Small Business Administration stimulus funds.

Far more tragic is the catastrophic consumption of endangered animal parts. Contrashoppers who seek out stuff such as elephant ivory are as amoral as the brutal poachers who kill these beasts with AK-47s and rip the tusks from their skulls with chainsaws. It is worse than much contrashopping, but still somehow legal in certain countries. The gluttonous demand for this decorative dead material is responsible for the murder every day of dozens of these intelligent, social animals, slaughtered across Africa for only their tusks, the rest of their bodies left rotting in the sun, their surviving relatives shuffling about, clearly bereaved and confused. Tens of thousands are killed each year to supply upshoppers with little more than ghoulish, garish, grisly decorations. Penny-pinching narcissist Donald Trump once displayed a "carved ivory frieze" to a writer in his ostentatiously vulgar fifty-three-room apartment high above Manhattan, noting, "I admit that the ivory's kind of a no-no." It's not just endangered animal parts that find their way into lurid decor; rare wood is also a status symbol. Jackie Siegel, co-builder of one of the biggest houses in America, once boasted of doors made of Brazilian mahogany, which she acquired before that country stopped selling the stuff in 2001: "They had to stop exporting it because they were cutting down the rainforest, or whatever."

Ornaments, statues and jewelry carved from the head of the helmeted hornbill, a magnificent and critically endangered bird found in the jungles of Southeast Asia, are as gruesome and tragic as those made from elephant ivory. These horrific things are a hot commodity in China. Poachers roam the jungles hunting the creature to extinction and lopping off its head so that upwardly mobile Chinese overshoppers can have carved trinkets like their neighbours'.

Also despicable are products made from tigers and rhinoceroses: furs, medicines or lucky charms. Rhino horns are prized in many parts of Asia and the Middle East because of their unproven health benefits, but the main reason for the rampant poaching of this animal into extinction is in fact social status, a leading motivation for shopping the world over (see shopology). Rhino horn may not have health benefits, but there is no doubt that in Vietnam it is a symbol of wealth and power—not unlike jewelry, cars, yachts or big houses. A consumer research study in 2013 commissioned by TRAFFIC, an international conservation organization, found that in Vietnam "rhino horn users value this item because of its significance from a social point of view." Most purchasers are wealthy, educated and powerful, and "their main reason for purchasing rhino horn is to reaffirm their social status" when giving it as a gift. They don't care about, and may not even believe in, the rumoured medicinal aspects; like so much shopping, it's all about signalling their presumed greatness to friends and neighbours.

The totoaba, an otherwise ordinary fish once plentiful in Mexican waters but now on the critically endangered list, has a swim bladder with wholly unproven aphrodisiac and medicinal properties that makes it a delicacy on Chinese tables in New York and Asia. But it is more likely the outrageous price—a single bladder can fetch tens of thousands of dollars—and the fact that it is illegal to catch makes it an irresistible status symbol sought by contrashoppers. Never mind its suspect healing qualities, it's now often served simply because it is so costly and illegal and therefore indicates its possessor has power. Meanwhile, populations of the vaquita marina porpoise, also found in Mexico's Gulf of California, are disappearing at an alarming rate because they drown in nets aimed at totoaba.

Also popular in many parts of Asia and beyond is jewelry made from tiger teeth, claws and bones, and rugs made from its fur. The fact that such items are illegal hasn't done much to stem the slaughter of the biggest feline, of which there are now fewer than four thousand left in the wild. Indeed, the demand for this stuff remains so great that many shoppers are settling instead for teeth from the lion, which is merely vulnerable, compared to the tiger, which is endangered.

Any item—boots, curios, jewelry, musical instruments—made from most sea turtles is banned, as six of seven sea turtle species are endangered. Some people who buy bags, boots and other products made from crocodiles, caimans, lizards and snakes are contrashopping, as such items require a permit indicating they did not come from the wild. Ditto for some coral, the population of which has been decimated across the seven seas. Ignorance of such matters does not equal innocence.

Even a simple cotton shirt can qualify as contrashopping, depending on where the cotton came from and how it was harvested, not to mention who made it and where. And perhaps even how many you own. The clothing industry is not just an important economic sector, it is one of the worst polluters, as documented in an increasing number of books and research papers. Making a single pair of jeans uses up 3,625 litres of water and three kilograms of chemicals, not to mention energy and harvested land. According to a 2017 paper by researchers at the Copenhagen Business School, "the fast fashion industry is characterized by short-term use, symbolic obsolescence, and increasing waste generation."

As a particularly horrific example of the destruction the clothing industry has wrought, consider the Aral Sea. Once the world's fourth-largest lake, whose shoreline in the 1950s was dotted with fishing villages, wetlands and forests, it is now mostly desert. The cause is shopping and the culprit is cotton, which the Soviet Union began growing in vast quantities in the 1950s by diverting rivers feeding the Aral Sea to irrigate fields across modern Uzbekistan, a practice that continues today. The result is an environmental and social catastrophe: camels wander amid a graveyard of ships; winds whip up dust storms infused with toxic chemicals and agricultural pesticides from the former lakebed; cancer rates have soared—all so we can get cheap T-shirts and blue jeans, many of which clog our closets, some of which are never even worn.

The rising tide of opposition, over many decades, to the mysterious manufacture of much of this stuff, often carried out in Asian sweatshops by impoverished workers, may have improved some conditions in some factories, but the misery continues. In her acclaimed book *No Logo*, author Naomi Klein expressed hope for the future: "Ethical shareholders, culture jammers, street reclaimers, McUnion organizers, human-rights hacktivists, school-logo fighters and internet corporate watchdogs are at the early stages of demanding a citizen centred alternative to the international rule of the brands." And it's true, things generally improve. But two decades later, thanks to the insatiable desires of contrashoppers, better conditions are slow in coming. We continue to shop the planet into ruin, and the quest for more clothing and lower prices is contributing to environmental destruction on a grand scale.

Gold qualifies as a contrashoppable material, because the environmental cost of extracting it from the ever-deeper bowels of the Earth becomes steadily more prohibitive. Gold nuggets in riverbeds are a thing of the distant past; modern mining companies separate gold dust from plain old rock with the help of vast quantities of sodium cyanide, an inorganic substance with a terrifying reputation: more than nine hundred hapless cult followers of the lunatic preacher Jim Jones used it to die all at once on a sweltering morning in Jonestown, Guyana, in 1978.

And yet this is the stuff that mining companies around the world mix with ore to remove gold from the good Earth. For more than a century, gallons of by-products from cyanide gold mining have poured into various tailing ponds across the planet and, predictably, much of it ends up eventually and "accidentally" spilling into nearby rivers, killing everything in its wake, as it did in Baia Mare, Romania, in 2000, resulting in what has been called the worst environmental disaster in Europe since Chernobyl. A similar gold-mining disaster occurred in Argentina's San Juan province in 2014, and at Canada's Mount Polley mine the same year. Gold has some useful qualities in dentistry and medicine, as well as in the production of electronics, but mostly it is just pretty. It's a shiny rock. Humans have treasured it for millennia, stockpiling it, lugging it around, collecting it whenever they can in greater and greater quantities, oblivious or indifferent to the damage the quest is causing to the planet.

Ultimately, there is really no kind of shopping that is without environmental consequences (let alone social, political and economic consequences). Even buying too many plastic water bottles (see shoppable) or plastic shopping bags is contrashopping given the damage these things are doing to the planet. Sometimes contrashopping does not involve environmental trespassing, although sooner or later it all must be deshopped and it has to go somewhere.

Sometimes contrashopping is done by overshoppers and pseudoshoppers who are just too cheap to buy things honestly. That may have been what was at work in the case of US Congressman Duncan Hunter and his wife, Margaret. Hunter was an early supporter of Donald Trump's bid for president and his call to "drain the swamp" in Washington. Alas, the overindulgent couple hit the headlines in 2018 for illegally spending campaign funds, including $11,300 at Costco and more than $5,700 at Walmart, on a litany of personal items as well as travel to Italy, Las Vegas and Hawaii. During one shopping trip, Margaret Hunter spent $300 in campaign funds on "a tablecloth, three square pillows, a three-brush set, a metal tray, four temporary shades, four window panels, a white duck, two Punky Brewster items, a ring pop and two five-packs of animals," according to court documents. Exactly how they thought this kind of contrashopping could possibly be justified as campaign expenses remains a mystery. In the last days of his presidency, Trump pardoned Hunter. That is not surprising, perhaps, as Trump, always ethically challenged, also qualified as a contrashopper when he misspent funds from his charitable foundation, which turned out to be "little more than a checkbook to serve Mr. Trump's business and political interests," according to the New York attorney general. Trump was ordered in 2019 to pay $2 million to charities for the contrashopping, which included the purchase of two big portraits of himself at a combined cost of $30,000, but which Trump later valued at less than $1,000 (see misshop).

High-living big-spender L. Dennis Kozlowski, once chief executive of Tyco International, indulged in some now-notorious contrashopping (and ultrashopping) when he helped furnish his New York apartment by picking out a shower curtain for $6,000 and billing it to the company, along with a $17,100 antique toilet kit and a poodle-shaped umbrella stand for $15,000. He went to jail for various crimes connected to profligacy at Tyco. "I was piggy," he said many years later after emerging from prison.

Monumental swindler Bernie Madoff, the notorious New York investment advisor who by 2009 had defrauded rich people of $65 billion in what is, so far, the largest Ponzi scheme in history, contrashopped for the usual array of mansions, yachts and forty watches. But when law-enforcement officials finally hauled him off to jail in 2009, it was his 250 pairs of shoes, dozens of which had never been worn, that made headlines. His wife had an engagement ring that later sold at auction for $550,000 and a pair of earrings that brought in $135,000 (see also ultrashop).

Contrashopping is what the Oklahoma-based craft store chain Hobby Lobby did in 2010 following the Iraq War. The company, owned by the evangelical Christian Green family, paid $1.6 million for more than 5,500 Iraqi items from antiquity that they wanted to display at their Museum of the Bible, ignoring warnings that the artifacts might have been stolen from archaeological sites and smuggled into the United States. The company agreed to pay a $3 million fine and send the stuff back to Iraq (see also misshop). Contrashopping is what egregious overshopper Nicolas Cage unknowingly indulged in when he outshopped fellow bone-collector Leonardo DiCaprio for a sixty-seven-million-year-old skull of a Tyrannosaurus bataar, a terrifying T-Rex-like creature also referred to as Tarbosaurus, during an auction in 2007. He paid $276,000 for the thing, but agreed in 2015 to return it when it was found to be illegally taken out of Mongolia. It is not clear if the return qualified as an unshop or a deshop.

Contrashopping may be what best describes at least some of the expenditures of dubious political lobbyist and convicted felon Paul Manafort. Suspiciously paying for his stuff with wire transfers from foreign banks, Manafort spent almost a million dollars in a single New York clothing store between 2010 and 2014. The campaign chair for Donald Trump's first presidential campaign, Manafort was later forced to endure the humiliation of having his expansive and garish wardrobe displayed in the media after he was hauled off to jail for tax and bank fraud in 2018.

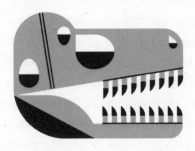

SHOP-A-GO-GO

A focused shopathon, often associated with a leisure activity.

This includes any shopping event that is not associated with a holiday or festival in which the majority of the population participates. The purchase of a new home, say. Or a cottage. Or the exploration of a new hobby. Let's say you have decided to take up fly-fishing. Like most pastimes, it requires gear. You have to go shopping. Rods, reels, flies, nets, different kinds of weighted line, tiny fake gnats made out of hair. A hat, a vest, hip-waders, expensive sunglasses and a variety of obscure but expensive fishing tools that complete the disguise and convince observers that you know what you're doing. And if you cannot find a picturesque river, in all likelihood you're going to need a boat, a motor and a raft full of safety equipment and angling knick-knacks and a special fishing cooler for beer and another for dead fish. Not cheap. If you do not have all this gear, and you do not catch fish, observers will tell you they are not surprised, because you don't have the right equipment, you cheaped out, you bought your stuff at Walmart rather than Bass Pro or Patagonia (see undershop). Or worse, you're just a loser. All those misty, nostalgic photos of you fly-fishing in a scenic mountain stream will not be worth distributing because you won't look like an angler; you'll look like a forlorn bum with some lousy equipment standing helplessly in a muddy river. You'll look like an amateur, and nobody likes those. But if you do indeed have all the right equipment, and you do not catch fish, it's just your bad luck, and your buddies will accept it: "The bite was not on today." Finally, you'll see the light, and as the tally for your "hobby" reaches into five figures, you'll realize you're in the midst of a shop-a-go-go.

Sooner or later, all "sports" become shop-a-go-goes. If you take up golf, you need clubs, bags, tees, ugly shoes, garish pants, loud shirts, ridiculous socks, a hat, a vest, a raincoat, special little ball markers, an extendable water ball retriever, a divot tool, an expensive and problematic distance-measuring device, a bottomless supply of pricey golf balls and a lot of other stuff you cannot yet imagine—and you need to buy it all festooned with the logo of an admired brand or people will look down their noses at you, label you an undershopper, or perhaps even turn you away at the entrance of any self-respecting country club. Even if you take up badminton, or perhaps even Frisbee, you probably need a lot of attendant stuff or you just can't play.

Meanwhile, don't even bother with cycling unless you are prepared for a major shop-a-go-go. In times past, you needed a bike and some weekend clothes. Today, to be a cyclist, you can't just pedal around, you need to look like disgraced rider and drug-abusing cheater Lance Armstrong. You need to have a $10,000 or even $20,000 bike made of carbon fibre. You need a brightly coloured European cycling jersey, preferably with some logos advertising your favourite brands on it, a special helmet, padded cycling shorts and other stretchy clothes, a cycling computer, clipless pedals, cycling shoes, cycling gloves, repair tools, a cycling water container and one of those little rear-view mirrors that clips to your head. And some other things you haven't thought of yet. If you do not have that stuff, fellow cycling enthusiasts will ride past without even acknowledging your miserable presence, and naïve passersby will think you are simply riding a bike rather than "cycling."

If you take up any hobby—scrapbooking or sewing or gardening—you need stuff. If you indulge in coin or stamp collecting, you need stuff. Any kind of collecting hobby is a never-ending shop-a-go-go, and often an unshop-a-go-go and a deshop-a-go-go.

Despite the fact they have spent their entire lives adorning their homes with the comforts offered by modern innovations and technology—plush furniture, large comfy beds, air conditioning, big-screen TVs and the latest in expensive kitchen appliances—many families insist on opting for a summer camping trip during which they "get back to nature." It's a low-cost alternative, they believe, to renting a cottage or going to a nice hotel on the beach. Or perhaps they figure it is just more honest or "real." But it inevitably turns into a shop-a-go-go because those embarking on such folly invariably find themselves first at the camping retail outlet, preparing for the great outdoors. Complicated tents, troublesome tarps, sleeping bags, uncomfortable inflatable mattresses, finicky and dangerous portable stoves, cumbersome water purification devices, compact cutlery and tableware, coolers, flashlights, foldable chairs, bug spray, bear horns, expensive and ill-tasting freeze-dried food and an endless array of other camping gadgets, many of which will not only prove themselves to be quite useless in the wilderness, but won't fit in the car or the canoe either and will end up forgotten and gathering dust in the garage or basement. Being involved in any pursuit means being prepared. Being prepared means shopping.

Families who shun camping and instead opt for the purchase of a cottage face a shop-a-go-go on a grand scale. No matter how simple and rugged the place, it's going to need housewares, deck furniture and, often, some kind of floating vessel. This is a joyful time—until we actually move in and discover the telltale signs of impending dock repair and watercraft maintenance. Dreams of relaxing on the deck and peaceful weekends nestled in nature, reading books and playing games, dissipate when we are greeted by one neighbour trying to keep the forest at bay with a variety of leaf-blowing, weed-whacking, chainsawing, hedge-trimming and lawn-mowing machinery. The other neighbour is an obsessive renovator fond of noisy power tools. And on the lake out front? Enthusiastic and tireless powerboaters, wakeboarders, water skiers or drunken teenagers intent on performing stunts on noisy aquatic machines. When this obnoxious symphony reaches its crescendo at cocktail time (or before dawn), the thoughts of the new cottager can be summed up in one word: misshop.

CONVERSHOPPING

Conversations about shopping.

Listen carefully: What do you hear? At dinner parties, at art shows, at the watercooler, at the ballpark? In the halls of justice and the houses of government? On factory floors and in office elevators?

Is it talk about politics or religion or philosophy? No.

The environment or internet privacy? No.

Workplace safety? Career advancement? No and no.

It's talk about shopping—convershopping. No gathering is complete without it. No get-together exists where it does not rear its friendly head. In fact, unless you mingle socially with egghead professors, nerdy scientists or boring politicians, it dominates all get-togethers that are not already consumed by sporting events.

Sooner or later, usually sooner, any discussion invariably turns into convershopping. Cars, cameras, phones, electronic gadgets, clothing, kitchen faucets, countertop appliances, designer vodka, bottled water and gear—it's all part of the never-ending conversation about consumables.

YOU: "Hey, got the new one, huh?"

THEM: "Yeah, it's the C series. Unbelievable."

YOU: "Oh, I thought it was the D series. They're smaller, but with a bigger microprocessor, and the colours are more vibrant."

THEM: "D Series? That's impossible. I just got this Tuesday."

YOU: "Sorry. I read about them yesterday in the *Times*. C series won't run the new software. Guess that one's obsolete."

Convershopping is heard during almost every TV morning show. It occurs frenetically in limitless and scandalously successful gameshows such as *The Price is Right* and *Let's Make a Deal*, and often on the evening news. Convershopping dominates the discussion on reality TV, and on programs such as *Antiques Roadshow*, where experts and owners discuss the stories behind items and art while viewers wait patiently for the estimated value of each to be revealed. Convershopping is an entire social media genre dominated by influencers. Convershopping is a certainty at family gatherings and community meetings, at cocktail parties and dinner soirees, at conventions and business conferences, weddings and anniversaries, joyful baby showers and sombre funerals.

Shopping without convershopping is like pizza without beer, a cottage without a view. If we can't tell people what we bought, what is the point? Sure, it is fun to buy stuff, but half the fun is telling people we bought it, often what we paid, and frequently what kind of a bargain we achieved. Isn't it why we wear expensive cufflinks or rings—so people will ask us about them, and we can both engage in convershopping? Isn't that why we drive an outrageously expensive car? The bigger and better and more impressive, the more convershopping it generates. We cannot really enjoy the thing by ourselves. We must boast about it, talk about it, expound upon it to others to really appreciate it. They must in turn say "ooh" and "aah" and then promptly share our shopping stories with others and their shopping stories with you.

Perhaps that is why former Canadian newspaper mogul and convicted felon Conrad Black felt the need to share information about his home with an interviewer in 2011, while he was still in jail for fraud: "It is a commodious property," he said of his family pile in Toronto. "It is very quiet. I have two libraries, both two stories in height. Twenty-five thousand books. I have an indoor pool, and a consecrated chapel—consecrated by cardinals when I was two years old. It is temperature-controlled, with all modern communications set up." And then, after all that, the great man adds this: "I have 12 cars there." The "12 cars" comment is rather gauche in the context of the twenty-five thousand books and the consecrated chapel, but one supposes there are indeed enough of them to warrant some kind of mention, even if it's just a vulgar afterthought.

The media has always been an obsequious partner in convershopping, especially when it involves the rich and famous. Architectural magazines, home and decor publications, *People* and others have always taken glee in celebrating supershoppers. In the 1980s, *Lifestyles of the Rich and Famous*, a show famously hosted by loud-mouthed sycophant Robin Leach, gave birth (or at least new life) to an entire television genre that memorialized ultrashopping. It was mimicked by MTV *Cribs* in the new millennium, wherein famous owners showed off over-the-top designs and garish decors in their homes, some of which, it turned out later, were not their homes at all (see shopaganda and contrashop). Today, celebrities don't need the help of adoring journalists or television producers. They are happy to share snapshots of their beautiful lives with fans on social media, sometimes with mixed results. When famous unshopper Ellen DeGeneres and dancing diva Jennifer Lopez, for example, shared videos from mansions during the 2020 pandemic, some of the responses were less than kind. DeGeneres likened being confined to her mansion to "being in jail," an assertion that sparked criticisms on social media that she was "tone deaf" and "insensitive." Lopez posted a video from the mansion of cheating ballplayer Alex Rodriguez saying "we can't go out to any restaurants or anything but the service and entertainment here is pretty good #staysafe," which generated comparisons to the film *Parasite*, about a rich family seemingly oblivious to the woes of their poor servants. And billionaire ultrashopper David Geffen sparked outrage when he tweeted a photograph of his superyacht in the Caribbean in March: "Sunset last night . . . Isolated in the Grenadines avoiding the virus. I hope everybody is staying safe."

Clearly, rampant convershopping can be frowned upon, depending on whom you are speaking to and where you reside. Showboating, celebrating and talking about what you own is easier in America than in

Europe, according to the millionaire German brothel owner and tax cheat Marcus Prinz von Anhalt. In an interview with a *Der Spiegel* reporter, Prinz von Anhalt, who owned homes around the world, announced he would soon be departing for America. "I'm flying to Los Angeles on October 3rd," he said. And then he added, unbidden: "There are two new Rolls-Royces waiting. A convertible and a limousine, both white. Before I had a silver, but now I think white is better. That's not possible in Germany, in the envious society. Someone like me who likes to show what he has doesn't fit in Germany." Years later, Prinz von Anhalt was still inexplicably convershopping about his cars (and—again—still somehow oddly obsessed with their colour) in a YouTube video featuring his mansion and crowded garage in Dubai, a place where such outlandish chatter may be appreciated even more than in America: "It's a pink Bentley, a Mansory," he said, dropping the name of a German aftermarket company that makes luxury automobiles look even more luxurious than they were when they rolled off the assembly line. "It's not wrapped. It's real colour, painted pink. It was Paris Hilton's car before and now it's my daughter's car. Even inside everything is pink. When she was five years old she said, 'Daddy, I need a pink car because when Momma drives me to school I need to go in a pink car.'" Moving on to his own personal vehicles, he waxes aesthetic for the camera: "Rolls-Royce Ghost. Also Mansory. Also not wrapped. It's painted in white with a little pearl effect. But this is a car I use with my driver. This is all white, white, white. I love white in a car. White and black, black and white." And moving on again to the next vehicle: "This is my Drophead [Rolls-Royce] also white, white, white, specially built for me."

Some old-monied folks would never dream of indulging in convershopping like that. They'd never mention their cars, but the helicopter might find its way into a conversation if it had not already made itself known by landing calamitously on the sprawling front lawn. And the wine collection? Sure, a few words perhaps, if you insist. We all have our limits, of course. Some won't acknowledge a car collection, but

Conrad Black will. Some won't talk about jewelry, but Elizabeth "Big girls need big diamonds" Taylor never hesitated: "The jewels were sumptuous, undulating the red colour over the blue water like a painting. I screamed for joy . . ." She thought so highly of her jewelry collection (as did many others), she wrote a book about it. You may not be capable of using such language to describe a new iPhone, say, but someone probably is. Today, young people have embraced convershopping with an enthusiasm that exceeds even earlier generations, write Kit Yarrow and Jayne O'Donnell in their book, *Gen BuY*. Shopping and the conversations around it help people understand each other in a universal language, they argue. Let's face it, a lack of any potential convershopping is another reason why buying underwear at Walmart is no fun. Nobody wants to talk about it.

TELESHOP

To buy stuff from afar.

There are many ways to shop, but marketers have been looking for ways to make it less strenuous since the invention of the catalogue. Now we order stuff over the internet, but before that, it meant purchasing things from TV. Or simply picking up the phone. No need to set foot in the store. No need to comb your hair or even put on a pair of pants. No maneuvering for a parking spot, jostling at the cash register or mingling with all those awful people on the sidewalk or in the mall. No grimy cash. No social interactions. Just pure, uninterrupted acquisition conveyed magically to your home. In a post-pandemic world, delivery may well be the way of the future, but it's always been the way of the past. Despite the modern popularity of Alibaba, Amazon and thousands of other companies that ship stuff directly to your door, teleshopping has been taking shape for centuries, and catalogues emerged soon after the invention of the printing press.

It's been big business almost since day one, but certainly by the mid-1800s, when mail-order operations emerged around the world: Pryce Pryce-Jones, in Wales; Eaton's, in Canada; Montgomery Ward and Sears, Roebuck & Co. in the United States, for example. By the mid–twentieth century, with more members of the household working, and with more money to spend and less time to shop, the mail-order business boomed. Retailers shipped stuff far and wide, especially to places without easy access to stores, making dull rural life worth living. People wanted stuff and they wanted it with as little fuss as possible. Trucks fanned out across the nations to deliver directly to homes, and they've been doing it ever since. With the invention of moving pictures and, later, television, teleshopping exploded like never before. It might be subliminal, like product placement in a movie, or it might be subtle, like a "news" report about the latest iPhone. It might be explicit, like the fifteen to twenty (or sometimes more) television commercials that bombard us every half-hour. Whether we know it or not, we're all teleshopping when we watch TV.

But focused teleshoppers are a breed unto themselves. They don't merely ponder the products they encounter, they don't store them in memory to be considered on their next trip to the mall or contemplate later while surfing the internet. The bona fide teleshopper is action-oriented. The true teleshopper behaves decisively. The committed teleshopper moves at light speed. When they see something—anything really—they take out their phone and they "call now!" And there are millions of teleshoppers around the world doing just that "while quantities last!" Most of them operate in off hours—drawn to the unrelenting infomercial early in the morning or in the middle of the night. Such behaviour may seem quaint in an internet world, but there remain millions of teleshoppers who need help from a dulcet-toned TV presenter. Rather than waiting for home shoppers to peruse the catalogues, take their time and make their own decisions, TV salespeople (see shopostle) take control of the situation, getting immediate and direct responses from defenseless teleshoppers who didn't know until that very moment that they needed a new slow cooker and a set of knives to be delivered to their door within days. Teleshoppers will buy anything, so entire networks such as the Home Shopping Network, now just HSN, among many others, began multiplying in the 1970s and 1980s. Selling everything from jewelry to makeup to clothing to appliances twenty-four hours a day, this relatively old-fashioned industry was a billion-dollar business. Today, online shopping is worth trillions. The mail-order catalogues may have disappeared before the end of the twentieth century, but the delivery trucks have continued to multiply in the twenty-first.

CYBERSHOP

To buy on the internet.

Even if the malls stay open, even if TV doesn't disappear and even if bricks-and-mortar stores don't close forever, it's the future. At the time of writing, global internet sales were expected to go from $3.5 trillion in 2019 to $6.5 trillion in 2022, estimates established even before the coronavirus pandemic made cybershoppers of the biggest luddites and security-conscious consumers. And this was before Amazon declared during the pandemic that it would require hundreds of thousands more employees, and Walmart, Dollar General, Instacart and Lowe's followed suit with mass hirings.

Facebook, Twitter, TikTok and other social media platforms didn't exactly start as e-commerce companies, but it was only a matter of time before shopping invaded our feeds. A TikTok video can turn a dud into a dynamo. Instagram is more than just pictures. Facebook is a social network where you can buy stuff. And the hashtag #TikTokMadeMeBuyIt had been used more than four billion times only three years after the platform launched.

And every celebrity who is anybody seems to have a website that sells stuff, from Kate Hudson's Fabletics to Reese Witherspoon's Hello Sunshine to Jessica Alba's Honest.com.

Getting stuff continues to get easier, and more attractive.

SHOPOSTLE

Anyone who promotes or endorses a product.

A shopostle can be a sales rep, peddler, celebrity, marketer, agent, huckster, influencer, TikTok star, you, me—even a computer-generated character such as Lil Miquela, a virtual model for the likes of Calvin Klein with millions of Instagram followers. Or a child, like Ryan Kaji, whose specialty is toys. According to *Forbes*, the nine-year-old made more than $29 million in 2020 by reviewing them on YouTube (he's known for his "unboxing" videos, in which he removes toys from their boxes and assesses them), a figure that excludes the millions more he makes in branded merchandise.

You may think of George Foreman as an Olympic gold medalist, an ordained minister, a father who named each of his five sons George, or a world heavyweight boxing champion who battled pioneering fighter and legendary social activist Muhammad Ali in the historic "Rumble in the Jungle" in Zaire in 1974. But 100 million purchasers of a modest kitchen appliance (and frankly, non-buyers too) know him best as a promoter for the George Foreman Grill, better known as "a George Foreman." Foreman is a shopostle extraordinaire. He is just one of many who have made a fortune selling us stuff on TV.

While it may look easy, mesmerizing crowds with outrageous promises, mellifluous reassurances and poetic utterances such as "it-slices-it-dices-it-julienne-fries" is an art. Even though we're all dying to buy anything, anywhere, anytime, these direct-response advertising salespeople, as they are officially and awkwardly known, offer a little something extra, a certain *je ne sais quoi* that helps close the deal. With now-famous lines like "and that's not all" or "if you buy now," these folks offer a ceaseless shopathon for people glued to their televisions and desperate to consume. Long before he became a TV pioneer in the early days of this multi-trillion-dollar industry, enthusiastic stuff-seller Ron Popeil worked as a shopostle drawing crowds at state fairs, hawking kitchen gadgets invented by his father. Television was still in its infancy, but Popeil quickly realized the potential of this emerging medium to help him sell a lot more stuff in a lot less time, so he created what he called "the first infomercial and commercials." Millions snapped up the Chop-O-Matic, Popeil's Pocket Fisherman, the Veg-O-Matic, the Smokeless Ashtray, the Inside-the-Egg Scrambler, the Ronco 6 Star Plus Knives, the Showtime Rotisserie and BBQ ("set it and forget it") and more. He was followed by various other famous pitchmen including smooth-talking writer, director and comedian Vince Shlomi, who sold the ShamWow, the Slap Chop and the Graty cheese grater—"and watch this!" for "tacos, fettuccine, linguini, martini, bikini . . ."—among other items. The late loud-mouthed Billy Mays pushed the Big City Slider Station, and favoured such phrases as "no more squishin' and squashin' or flippin' and floppin'." Mays later became famous on the Discovery Channel docudrama called *PitchMen*, which ended when Mays died suddenly in 2009.

Celebrity chef Emeril Lagasse, famous for coining culinary phrases such as "bam" and "kick it up a notch," is not just a star in the restaurant business and the cooking-show industry. He's not just a sitcom actor who worked with perennial TV star Robert Urich and rapper and kickboxer Queen Latifah. And he's not just a food journalist and a philanthropist for children's charities. He's a shopostle for a variety of stuff including frying pans, pressure cookers, deep fryers, air fryers, Dutch ovens, knives and more, pitching some of it himself interminably on TV. Lagasse is a shopostle.

Slightly more sophisticated is culinary hero and kitchen wizard Jamie Oliver, who realized quickly his viewers wanted more than just food. He manages to advertise his own stuff without missing a beat during a demonstration for Potato al Forno: ". . . and then I want eight cloves of garlic, and we're going to crush this garlic if you've got a nice little crusher"—and here he examines the one in his hand—"who makes this? Oh, Jamie Oliver. Subtle plug, that's what you like, so garlic goes in and . . ." Subtle indeed. He continues: "What I want to do now is put about fifty grams of parmesan into this cream off the heat. And these fine graters are just fantastic for getting the hard cheeses sort of really nicely grated, and another wonderful product available in Jamie Oliver's shop." He does it so seamlessly and sheepishly it's actually charming.

Then we have a revolving door of thousands of ordinary movie stars and celebrities and even the odd average person, who are willing to be a shopostle for a product if the price is right. And the price is usually right, because people will buy anything if celebrities say it's good. Former child actor, brainy Princeton graduate and one-time Michael Jackson sweetheart Brooke Shields became famous for, among other things, modelling Calvin Klein jeans. Convicted felon O.J. Simpson was a shopostle for Hertz rental cars long before he went to prison. HIV activist and peace ambassador Charlize Theron endorses Dior. If movie-set prankster and *Vogue* coverboy George Clooney says Nespresso is good (and, hey, fun!), it's a reasonable bet at least some of us will buy an expensive machine and the coffee to go with it in little tiny packages just so we can feel we're as good-looking, talented and cleverly mischievous as he seems to be. If suave Irishman Pierce Brosnan and rugged Englishman Daniel Craig like Brioni suits and Omega watches (respectively), perhaps we should too. It can't hurt, after all, to look like James Bond.

Like George Foreman, many stars have gone from being shopostles for other people's stuff to creating their own products, often adorned with their celebrity names, or investing in companies interested in being associated with celebrity. Many don't even pitch the stuff; they simply let it be known they are involved; others put their names front and centre. Troubled former teen idol Britney Spears, pop and fashion diva Rihanna, and fashion-forward singer and television judge Katy Perry, among many other stars, have their own makeup.

Oscar-winning actor and often-parodied entrepreneur Gwyneth Paltrow sells an infamous and expensive array of health and lifestyle-related products under her company's name, Goop.

While lots of famous men have their own clothing and cologne lines, what they really seem to like to invest in is booze: *Saturday Night Live* original funnyman Dan Aykroyd has a vodka. Grumpy actor and SNL alum Bill Murray invested in one too. Shock-rocker Marilyn Manson made absinthe. Leading man George Clooney sold a company that made tequila he helped create on a lark with friends in 2011 for as much as $1 billion in 2017. Songwriting legend Bob Dylan has a whiskey called Heaven's Door; rapper and convicted stabber Jay-Z has a cognac, comic actor Danny DeVito went with limoncello . . . and everyone who's anyone seems to own a vineyard or a wine bearing their name or associated in some way with their greatness. Shoppers flock to this stuff whether it's any good or not.

Many shopostles don't have to say anything at all. They don't tell people what they like, or appear in tacky TV commercials. They simply use this stuff, and are seen to be using it, at sporting events in which they compete, awards shows they attend or while they go about their daily lives. Others get paid to show up at events unrelated to their sport or the product. Growing numbers, meanwhile, are leveraging their social media power like celebrity wife Hilaria Baldwin, whose Instagram posts were once brought to us in a "paid partnership with @cutiesbabycare."

Somehow the mainstream media has long been an enthusiastic partner in many such endeavours, which is why awards programs such as the Oscars are so often overshadowed by the pre-show on the red carpet. There, actors and other famous people, rather than talk about the movies, tell interviewers exactly who designed their dresses, dinner jackets or ridiculous getups. Of all the questions any number of self-respecting (or perhaps not) entertainment journalists can ask, it's a good bet one of them will be "who are you wearing?" And the answer is they are wearing what the highest bidder hired them to wear, explains Vanessa Friedman in the *New York Times*. All that stuff the stars wear has been draped upon them strategically by experts promoting a global brand for an international audience. And the media, all the media, even respectable "news" organizations including the *New York Times*, play the game, gleefully spending precious moments and untold paper promoting and discussing various brands adorning movie stars or crediting dress designers and the jewelry companies in captions below photographs and articles ostensibly about movies.

Meanwhile, the universal desire to be a celebrity *and* to get free stuff is what gave rise to the twenty-first-century phenomenon of influencers—ordinary people who generate a social media audience through convershopping with their followers. Today, you don't even need to be famous to move product. You can start your own YouTube channel or become a TikTok star and advertisers will find you. E-tailing envoys and digital shopostles are clogging up the internet like clever memes. Some of them are doing it for money—lots of money—and some are doing it for, well, who really knows? Some are getting free stuff, and everyone, no matter how much they already have, loves free stuff. Sellers of said stuff, meanwhile, are happy to have people wear it, drive it, eat it, flaunt it, promote it—the richer and more famous the better.

Some work at it diligently and strategically, others simply can't help themselves. Who can explain, for example, the now-infamous tweet by self-promoting clothes horse Louise Linton, wife of US Treasury Secretary Steven Mnuchin at the time, who took the role of shopostle to new heights when she included a photograph of herself exiting Air Force One in 2017 with the following hashtags: "Great #daytrip to #Kentucky! #nicest #people #beautiful #countryside #rolandmouret pants #tomford sunnies #hermesscarf #valentinorockstudheels #valentino #usa." No one is quite sure what compelled her to highlight the expensive brands adorning her body in a tweet, especially while visiting a state with so many economic challenges, but the blowback on social media and in the mainstream press was less than flattering.

Then again, many parts of the soulless Trump presidency seemed crowded with shopostles. Counselor to the President and alternative-fact enabler Kellyanne Conway famously raised the ire of the US Office of Government Ethics when she once promoted a line of stuff marketed by the president's daughter, Ivanka, on television's *Fox & Friends*: "Go buy Ivanka's stuff is what I would tell you. I'm going to give a free commercial here. Go buy it today, everybody." As for the obese junk-food-loving presidential pitchman himself, who once shilled for organizations such as Pizza Hut and McDonald's, Trump may be the greatest shopostle (of his own stuff) to lead a government anywhere, and that is saying a lot, although most of them do it a little more discreetly. Nobody likes the Trump brand better than Trump. He emblazoned his name on so many things and so many products it became insidious (and helped propel him to the US presidency), and shoppers love stuff they recognize regardless of quality. Trump steaks, Trump vodka, menswear, coffee, deodorant, perfume, bottled water, eyeglasses, lighting, home furnishings. A lot of it didn't get much uptake from shoppers, but the fact a tawdry realtor was able to move so aggressively into the business of licencing one's name and then plastering it on everything, a tactic pioneered in the 1970s by the enduring French designer Pierre Cardin, is a testament to Trump's abilities as a shopagandist—and perhaps an indication of the gullibility of retailers and manufacturers.

There is perhaps no more contemptible shopostle than the loud-mouthed conspiracy theorist Alex Jones, who was once told by Trump that "your reputation is amazing." Jones became rich by spewing outrageous conspiracy theories and hateful conjecture on an unfathomably popular syndicated radio show, and as the fabulist host at the website Infowars. But a great deal of his considerable fortune derives from his own products, which he sells on Infowars amid the hokum: dietary supplements, bulletproof vests and toothpaste. He also touted stuff that he claimed killed the coronavirus, but that the US Food and Drug Administration says doesn't work.

And then there are the rest of us. We are the biggest shopostles of all. We are better at it than Trump. Collectively, we influence more people than Gwyneth Paltrow. And we do it more often. We promote items every day to our family, friends and coworkers in casual convershopping daily.

"Nice shirt."

"Do you like it? Ralph Lauren."

"Ooh! Beautiful. Mine is Gap."

It is not for nothing that word of mouth is considered a key to the success of any movie, restaurant, book, shoe, jacket, household appliance. If a film is good, we'll tell everyone "you've got to see it." If it is bad, people will take note when we say "don't bother." What do you say about the car you drive? "It's a Ford, my dad drove them, I drive them, and we've never had a problem. They're the best." Or: "I got talked into this one and I'll never buy one again." Our clothes, our jewelry, our recipes, our restaurants, the granite we used for the kitchen renovation—we're selling it all at every opportunity. And in a world increasingly dominated by brand, we barely need to mention it anymore, because we're flaunting labels left, right and centre.

In the end, we are all shopostles, a fact turned into satire in the 2009 movie *The Joneses*, starring former substance abuser Demi Moore and recovered sex addict David Duchovny. The film, which received a lukewarm reception from both critics and moviegoers, follows the lives of a marketing team disguised as an all-American consumerist family, planted in a well-to-do neighbourhood to surreptitiously encourage— *influence*—the folks next door to buy more brand-name stuff. "They're not just living the dream," says the film's tagline, "they're selling it." And everyone else is buying it.

Some ordinary shopostles who lack celebrity, television chutzpah or formal employment find themselves drawn to multi-level marketing companies, selling stuff such as health food and personal hygiene items to their friends and relatives, and recruiting them to also sell stuff to their friends and relatives. Others are thrust rudely into the business, however temporarily, as I once was.

It was December, and I was volunteering with a local charity, selling Christmas trees. There I was, standing in an evergreen forest on the pavement outside a grocery store, waiting for customers. I figured the purchase of a dead tree that would be in the house for two or three weeks—something destined to be tossed to the curb on January 1— would require little or no consideration. But I was thinking like a volunteer salesperson standing outside in the dead of winter, not like a shopper. I'd forgotten how fraught the purchase of a Christmas tree could be, and in the early days of selling them, I failed miserably as a shopostle.

A Christmas tree is more than a decoration; it is a reflection on the family that allowed it into the house. Not one of my customers (and there were a lot of them) chose the first tree they encountered. Most of them hemmed and hawed. "Can you show me that one? How about that one over there?" They wanted to see various sizes, shapes and species. As I wrestled with one tree after another, holding them all up for inspection, they would finally announce they'd need to consult their spouses. "We'll have to come back later." Sure enough, a spouse would appear later and the entire process would be repeated. What would fit in the living room? What would look best in the corner of the den? Which one would be easiest to hang ornaments on? Suddenly, around about hour six of this torture, I remembered my own Christmas-tree-buying experiences, reminiscent of Charlie Brown's ill-fated misshop for a tree in *A Charlie Brown Christmas*. And that's when I understood what every good salesperson—and even bad ones—knows from the beginning. Everyone (and everything) needs a shopostle. People don't want to simply buy; they want to be *sold*.

From then on, rather than standing there helplessly, holding up one tree after another, I would *sell* the first one they chose like it was a one-of-a-kind work of art: "Good choice. That's a beautiful tree. Look at that symmetry. You can't go wrong with a Scots pine." Or: "Excellent decision. Of course, your Fraser fir is a little more expensive than most, but they keep their needles longer. Christmas is always greener with a Fraser fir." And if there was ever any indecision: "This spruce is just crying out for you. But there aren't many left."

SHOPOCRACY

A nation ruled by shoppers.

There is perhaps a select number of nations, such as Myanmar and Cuba, that are not yet full-on shopocracies, but they are few and increasingly far between. Some still consider themselves monarchies. Many are labelled autocracies. A few cling to the idea they are democracies. Political leaders pretend to heed the advice of scientists, generals, planners, engineers and the voters themselves, but the people who really matter are the economists, business leaders, manufacturers, retailers and shoppers, who power the economy and keep politicians in office. Woe betide the elected official who does not promise to make it easier for people to get more stuff. And good luck to the candidate who won't take money from rich entrepreneurs or corporations intent on nurturing shoppers.

The eighteenth-century Irish philosopher and statesman Edmund Burke posited that social stability can only be achieved if a nation's poor majority is ruled by its rich minority, but the poor tend to be more difficult to govern if they cannot shop. People want stuff. Stuff keeps voters happy. Stuff keeps the masses docile. And the only thing people like more than having stuff is getting stuff: shopping.

Many powerful nations have weapons that could turn the planet into a cinder overnight. Some have sophisticated and malign surveillance abilities that, if we truly grasped their ubiquity, would make us all paranoid hermits. A few have untapped natural resources and really smart scientists who could save the world. But the nations with a lot of shopping are those with real power. For example, the United States was once, apparently, the envy of the world because of its shopping malls. In 1960, the future crooked president Richard Nixon put this in perspective: "They say the United States has stood still over the past seven-and-a-half years. Anybody who has said that hasn't been travelling around the United States. If you think the United States has stood still, who built the largest shopping centre in the world, the Lloyd Shopping Center right here?"

Two decades later, the importance of shopping was again highlighted by aging cowboy and B-movie actor Ronald Reagan, who, during his successful campaign for president famously asked: "Are you better off than you were four years ago? Is it easier for you to go buy things in the stores than it was four years ago?" There was only one thing former baseball-team owner and president George W. Bush asked of patriotic Americans after the terrorist attacks of 9/11, and again after the financial crisis of 2007: shop. It's what former casino operator and US president Donald Trump asked Americans to do every day of his presidency, and it's what politicians mean when they advise citizens to "go about your daily business." In 2021, US President Joe Biden realized socially distanced citizens were not spending money on services such as restaurants, sporting events, movies, concerts and theme parks and were instead buying stuff. The result: inflation, global supply chain troubles and not enough stuff. "Because of the strength of our economic recovery, American families have been able to buy more products," he said, basically apologizing for the lack of shopping.

Despite its proud embrace of communism, China, a nation of 1.4 billion souls, quickly made the transition to a shopocracy as the twentieth century came to a close. Turns out the Chinese, like the Americans and the rest of the world, love shopping. Their pent-up demand for stuff has powered the world economy in the new millennium. Meanwhile, Indian governments for decades leaned toward socialism and favoured protectionism. When multinational brands exploded across the globe after the Second World War, government intervention and red tape in India made doing business there almost impossible for outsiders. As a result, the entire nation was largely unshoppable, at least for Western goods. No Gucci, no McDonald's, no BMW, not even Coca-Cola. By 1991, a balance-of-payments crisis convinced the government to liberalize the economy and open it up. Today, amid the poverty, starvation and slums that spread for miles, you can shop at the Gucci store in Mumbai, New Delhi or Kolkata. There are four hundred McDonald's restaurants in India, a nation with the world's highest population of vegetarians, where cows are literally sacred and hurting them is illegal in many states. Today, you can buy a BMW or another Western car at one of India's many foreign car dealerships, if you can afford it. By any definition, India is now a shopper's paradise—and a shopocracy.

Smart leaders appoint, hire, recruit and cajole brainy people to help them run the country, but chief among them are the shopocrats—people who will help them ensure the masses continue to consume and the economy continues to grow. And many people, whether they are deep thinkers or not, seem to understand that even if shopping is not the best for their bank accounts, their cluttered living rooms, their health or the environment, it is still good for the economy. Fashion icon Victoria Beckham once justified yet another outrageous shopping spree as patriotic consumption: "Anyway, it helps the economy."

SHOPONOMICS

The rules of shopping. (Or how shopping rules the world.)

The English economist Nicholas Barbon, a man considered to be among the first proponents of the free market, wrote in 1690 about the role of fashion in society and the economy: "Fashion or the alteration of Dress," he said, promotes trade, "because it urges people to spend money on new clothes before the old ones are worn out: it is the life and soul of commerce, it . . . keeps the whole merchant body in movement; it is an invention which makes man live in perpetual springtime, without ever seeing the autumn of his clothes." More than three centuries later, the idea that clothing must be replaced more quickly than it wears out was given new perspective by Betty Halbreich, the famous personal shopper at Bergdorf Goodman in New York: "After they leave my clutches, clients go out into the world in the clothes I put on them and expect to be congratulated on how they look. If they don't, I get a lot of blowback." Halbreich is quick to add that even when clients tell her people "loooved" the outfit, her response is similar: "Well, then you can't wear it again."

In 1803, the French economist Jean-Baptiste Say came up with what is known today as Say's law, sometimes known as the law of markets, by insisting that production creates demand, instead of the reverse. In other words, if you build it, the people will come. Or, as American moral and social philosopher Eric Hoffer said: "You can never get enough of what you don't need."

Norwegian-born American philosopher, economist and social critic Thorstein Veblen was another pioneer in the study of the relationship between consumption and wealth. Disapprovingly and perhaps satirically, he is famous for coining the terms "conspicuous consumption" and "conspicuous waste." The main occupation of the ruling classes, said Veblen, was to make more money and display their considerable wealth. "Since the consumption of these more excellent goods is an evidence of wealth, it becomes honorific; and conversely, the failure to consume in due quantity and quality becomes a mark of inferiority and demerit." Veblen also shared early insights on the reasons the wealthy pay so much for stuff: they assume the price is high because the quality is good. Therefore, posited Veblen, demand for an item increases as the price increases. Economists call it the "Veblen effect," but it is really just upshopping.

Even non-shoppers and anti-shoppers cannot ignore shoponomics, but it's a complicated subject. Some economists think we spend too much (see overshop); others think we save too much (see undershop). It seems disaster looms around every corner: less shopping equals less employment, lower GDP, lack of competitiveness, etc. More shopping represents a burden on the environment and a strain on individual savings that threatens our ability to pay our debts. Shoponomics tell us that not only do we all want stuff, we also need others to want it too if the economy is to thrive. Meanwhile, we all need some stuff, and many of us need—indeed *want*—to work. But do we need so much stuff (see overshop, supershop, megashop), and do we need to work as long or hard as we do to get it (see shopititis)? Economic growth is a generally accepted imperative, but how long can it last? Growth is not necessarily progress. There is evidence that a society which indulges in more modest consumption and responsible shopping is more sustainable, perhaps more equitable and even reasonably productive. "The Netherlands, despite its high number of postmaterialists and relatively slow growth, has extremely high labor productivity," notes Juliet B. Schor in her book *The Overspent American*. "It also has a government that invests heavily in education, research, and development."

Are shoponomics changing in a modern world? Politicians once considered "infrastructure" to consist of roads and bridges, and now it includes education—can "shopping," too, expand to include buying more than just the tangible? Elizabeth Dunn, co-author of *Happy Money: The Science of Happier Spending*, argues that experiences may be better investments than material goods. The latter, she says, offer mere "puddles of pleasure"—there may be a lot, but it evaporates quickly. "Abundance is the enemy of appreciation."

SHOPOMANIA

*What happens when desperate, overenthusiastic
shoppers get together.*

They call such things a shopping frenzy or a shopping stampede.
Shopomania could, of course, describe all day every day everywhere.
For most of the world, shopomania is our lives. But it most accurately
describes a single event in which a crowd of people jostle for bargains
or hot items all at once. Sometimes, perhaps, it's the latest fashion
that takes hold over a season or more: bell-bottoms or ripped jeans,
top hats or wide lapels. As such trends spread across continents, it
doesn't take long for everyone to look the same. But in more acute
cases, it involves a sudden rush by the mob for a certain item like toilet
paper, hand sanitizer or flour during a pandemic. People are trampled
in such situations, especially when there is limited supply and bargains
that generate demand.

When the coronavirus pandemic took hold in North America in
early 2020, various shopomania reports kept police busy. In Peoria,
Illinois, police were called to the local Dollar General store when someone phoned about "many people fighting" over a "run on toilet paper."
"Everyone is on edge now," Sheriff Brian Asbell told a local TV news
reporter. In Chino Hills, California, deputies arrived after getting calls
about a disturbance over shortages of toilet paper and other items.
"It's been nuts," said Costco CFO Richard A. Galanti in an earnings call
with investors in March 2020.

In 2019, shoppers stampeded during an event that mall operators
in Sydney, Australia, called the Ultimate Mega Balloon Drop, in which
shoppers competed (to say the least) for balloons filled with gift cer-
tificates. Free stuff or an advertised bargain often causes a stampede,

and this was no exception. The resulting mayhem sent five people to hospital. Organizers were clearly unaware of a similar incident in 2006 in Torrance, California, where two thousand shoppers fought over five hundred falling prize-filled balloons, leaving nine with minor injuries and sending one person to hospital.

On Long Island, New York, in 2008, a Walmart employee was trampled to death by enthusiastic shoppers seeking treasures such as a Samsung fifty-inch plasma high-definition TV for $798, a Samsung 10.2 megapixel digital camera for $69 and DVDs such as the Incredible Hulk for $9. "The crowd was out of control," a police spokesperson told journalists at the time, describing "utter chaos" as the thirty-four-year-old employee opened the doors for a waiting crowd of some two thousand people. Some noted it was a "doorbuster event" in which the door was actually busted. Several people, including a pregnant woman, were taken to hospital after the incident.

In 2011, a woman pepper-sprayed other shoppers at a Walmart in California in what police described as "competitive shopping." As many as twenty customers were hurt. "This was customer-versus-customer shopping rage," a Los Angeles police spokesperson told the *Los Angeles Times*. Newspapers recorded shoppers being trampled for laptop computers, pinned against the doors in the rush for faddish toys and game consoles and shoved aside by overzealous shoppers on the hunt for discounted materials.

Such events often occur on the eve of the busy Christmas season. One explanation for the insanity is that shoppers, already grumpy from sleep deprivation because many sales begin at midnight, feel cheated if they can't get what they came for. "Black Friday has become a setting for consumer misbehavior as shoppers compete for deeply discounted products," according to Jaeha Lee, an associate professor of apparel, design and hospitality management at North Dakota State University. "Being unable to purchase the advertised product seems unfair, leading to misbehavior and in turn making others more likely to follow suit."

Bridget Nichols, an associate professor of marketing and sports business at Northern Kentucky University, has also studied the shopping frenzy phenomenon. In particular, she examined the so-called "running of the brides" at Filene's Basement stores in some American cities, a scheduled event at which hundreds of people, mostly women, poured through the doorways, pushing, shoving and snatching up as many wedding dresses as they could, in order to barter later with other scrambling shoppers to find the perfect one. It was all an attempt to get a bargain on a dress costing thousands of dollars that was meant to be worn only once in a lifetime. "People want to feel they got a good deal," says Nichols.

Shopomania could accurately describe some aspects of Christmas (see shopathon), especially when desperate parents engage in physical and verbal combat with other parents while seeking out Cabbage Patch dolls, Buzz Lightyear toys, Tickle Me Elmo puppets, Pokémon figurines, Elsa dolls, Hatchimals, Fingerlings or whatever hot toy in limited supply is the heart's desire of their children in any given year. The phenomenon was illustrated to comic effect by muscleman actor Arnold Schwarzenegger in the 1996 film *Jingle All the Way*, in which Arnold battles other shoppers for a difficult-to-find toy called Turbo-Man, a replica of which was conveniently available to real-life moviegoers and random shoppers as part of the predictable merchandizing that accompanied the film's release.

Shopomania occasionally describes the rush for beer on a long summer weekend. Or the clamour for liquor to get us through Christmas. When people want stuff in short supply, or when there's a bargain to be had, there are no lengths they wouldn't go to to get it. Sometimes, though, a shopomania can be quite organized. Once, when my son was in his early teens and Nintendo's Wii console was introduced, he learned the local Best Buy was getting a shipment. He had saved the money and wanted my assistance navigating the anticipated shopomania. This meant, essentially, camping outside overnight in November to be first into the store in the morning—a scenario I frankly couldn't imagine. So I made him a deal: We'd drive over to the store at 10 p.m., before bedtime, to see if there was a lineup. If there was, we'd join it and stay overnight. If there was no lineup, we'd go back home to our warm beds and show up at the store first thing in the morning.

He took the liberty of packing deck chairs and sleeping bags into the car, just in case, and I dutifully drove him over to the store, fully expecting the place to be deserted. Instead, I was astonished to find half a dozen people already waiting outside in the icy darkness. "Quick," he said, "let's get in line." And so we joined the group, perhaps eighth or ninth in the queue, and waited as the temperature dropped to near freezing. All. Night. Long. By 4 a.m., some fifty or sixty people had joined this polite and organically organized shopomania, shivering, drinking coffee, eating doughnuts and hoping against hope there were enough Nintendo Wiis to go around when they opened up at 8 a.m. People want stuff.

SHOPERATI

Collectors. People who know a lot about a
certain type of merchandise.

The shoperati are rather more focused than your average overshopper, and usually have more resources with which to pursue their passions.

Jay Leno owns more than one hundred cars. Tom Hanks has more than one hundred typewriters. Roger Federer possesses more than one hundred pairs of sneakers. Why? Why do humans collect things? Psychologists have myriad explanations: childhood trauma, power, control, status, fun, emotional security, a desire to relive, reinvent or reimagine one's childhood, to step into the safety of a simpler era, to belong to a group of like-minded people. Some would say collecting is simply glorified overshopping. Others might insist collecting is little more than organized hoarding (see shoparrhea).

Meanwhile, it is almost a defining characteristic that an overwhelming number of collectors' items, while they may have once had constructive value, are no longer useful in the way they were intended. They serve no practical purpose. Yet they somehow have value. They are an investment. What else explains the fixation so many have with classic cars, watches, antique guns, vinyl LPs, clunky typewriters and dozens of other formerly deshoppable items that once had more use in everyday life? What is the point, after all, of glassware so precious that you cannot drink wine or water from it? Why did watch-collecting, especially among the rich, become insanely popular just as watches were made redundant by the smartphone? And how, in an age when the time of day is flashing at us from just about every kitchen appliance, automobile, street corner, elevator, subway platform and billboard, do so many people, even those who would not consider themselves collectors, continue to buy such items?

The answer may be that collectibles are often considered beautiful. They look good. Humans have, as only humans can, elevated everyday manufactured items to something more than the sum of their parts. We have deemed them "art"—over the strenuous objections of those who define the term more narrowly. To reinforce that view, the shoperati research their collections. They adorn them with stories, with histories, with character. They organize their items. They understand them. They pamper them. They *love* them. And they wish for the rest of us to understand that love, and appreciate that art—yes, art—as they do.

In this they are aided by marketers, influencers, TikTok creators and advertisers (see shopacademy, shopostle, shopaganda). We are endlessly advised to "Own it now!" or "Collect the whole set!" and so we are drawn into collecting baseball cards or *Star Wars* figures by the illusion of value—and because others are doing it. In the 1960s, clever marketers told gullible children that cheap plastic coins included in boxes of Jell-O were worthy of collecting—so we begged our parents to buy more Jell-O than anyone could possibly consume. In the 1990s, such fads included Pogs and Pokémon cards. While it takes a few years for most of us to realize to our horror that marbles are only marbles, a few collectors stick it out like the owner of all those Beanie Babies (see misshop), hoping that one day the rest of the world will realize their value (see shopomania). The fact your spouse or friend thinks you've wasted your money on worthless things doesn't mean it is true. As legendary stand-up comic and social critic George Carlin so perceptively said: "Have you ever noticed that their stuff is shit and your shit is stuff?"

This, of course, is the central question. *What distinguishes stuff from shit?*

How and why do humans attach value to some items and not others? How did we contrive to make one item of no apparent value cost more than something so obviously necessary? Known awkwardly as the paradox of value, many experts over many centuries have tried to explain it, but perhaps none so well as eccentric philosopher and brilliant economist Adam Smith: "The word VALUE, it is to be observed, has two different meanings, and sometimes expresses the utility of some particular object, and sometimes the power of purchasing other goods which the possession of that object conveys. The one may be called 'value in use;' the other, 'value in exchange.' The things which have the greatest value in use have frequently little or no value in exchange; on the contrary, those which have the greatest value in exchange have frequently little or no value in use. Nothing is more useful than water: but it will purchase scarcely anything; scarcely anything can be had in exchange for it. A diamond, on the contrary, has scarcely any use-value; but a very great quantity of other goods may frequently be had in exchange for it."

The overshopped and often misshopped collections of old cars favoured by aging men illustrate the point. Sooner rather than later, old automobiles stop becoming practical as transportation, especially if you can afford something newer. Old cars require maintenance. They rust. They pollute. They break down. They're unsafe. And relatively speaking, they are difficult to drive. They may be nostalgic, and they may even be enjoyable to operate, but not for any distance. What they are is fun to look at, and even then, only a nostalgic few even bother to look twice.

Indeed, New York's Museum of Modern Art, a collector of industrial and commercial objects for almost a century, owns nine automobiles, including a 1959 Volkswagen Beetle and a 1963 Jaguar E-Type Roadster. They are no longer used for transportation, obviously.

Leno has a collection of 180 cars and perhaps 160 motorcycles, depending on the day. His fellow funny guy Jerry Seinfeld also has many dozens. While they may have started as basic shoppers and descended into overshopping, today they are known as collectors, per-haps because they have so much money to take care of it all. Leno and Seinfeld are members of the shoperati—and perhaps much more.

Leno turned his venture into a small industry, what with garages, restoration crews, mechanics, maintenance guys and a popular YouTube show called *Jay Leno's Garage*, in which he shares a wealth of trivial information on obscure automobiles with millions of viewers. Seinfeld, too, has a popular Netflix show about cars and comedy. So the affable duo are also preservationists, educators, curators, employers—such are the lengths humans go to rationalize acquisitions. You need only watch an episode or two of either show to know they're pretty good at it too. (And, to be fair, at least this stuff is being re-used, and spared from the scrap heap.)

In his book *Enough*, John Naish shares the observations of Colin McCoy, the British operator of a storage depot for luxury cars: "I don't know why some people have them. One bloke with a £100,000 Ferrari just turns up, takes the car around the block and comes back. Others just sit in them, smell the leather and listen to the stereo." Natty dresser and late Rolling Stones drummer Charlie Watts did even less with slightly more. He admitted to owning a small fleet of cars even though he couldn't "drive the bloody things." The reason? He never acquired a driver's licence. "I can't drive, so I just sit in them and listen to the engine. I suppose you could call it a rich man's indulgence."

It is worth asking whether such possessions are any different than books, especially today, when books, like old cars, vinyl records and watches are competing with modern equivalents: e-readers, digital books and other various implements that take up a lot less space. Like many readers, I still favour paper and ink, but I am trying to get used to electronic alternatives. Some book collectors stack their books in bedrooms, store them in closets, put them in boxes in the basement or hoard them in the attic, but most of us escape that sorry label by treating books as wallcoverings and displaying them proudly in bookcases. Many haven't been looked at for years, or indeed ever, but perhaps we can demonstrate we know about literature.

Bookcases, unless they are in a public library, are not often used as accessible storage units, though they are exactly that. Some people read books twice or three times and refer to them regularly, but most of us read them only once, if even that. Books are not like oregano or cumin on the kitchen spice rack, intended to be accessed daily, or at least weekly by even the most amateur of chefs or families fond of takeout. Some bookworms love to fondle their books, organize them mysteriously and can find anything at a moment's notice, and they can probably cite passages chapter and verse. Others organize them by colour or size to better display their decorating prowess. A US company that caters mostly to designers, Books by the Foot, owned by Wonder Book, gives them a second life. "We had many books that nobody would buy to read," president Chuck Roberts told the *Washington Post* in 2015. "This re-purposes books we can't sell for reading or collecting. This gives a lot of books one more chance." Many readers get rid of books after reading. Others use them to impress us with the entirety of the collection. For some, bookcases are like trophy cases, displaying for all the world that "I have books, therefore I am smart" or at least knowledgeable, all other indications to the contrary. The illusion is buttressed by the fact that book collections usually require money and space. The more money and the more space, the greater the collection.

And again, what makes one book collection great, while another can't even be unloaded for free to a used bookstore? *Star Wars* creator George Lucas has twenty-seven thousand books in an impressive library with two floors of shelves, beautifully carved woodwork and a nifty spiral staircase. Lucas may be a knowledgeable guy, and has no doubt read many of these tomes, but in order to have read them all, he would have had to read more than a book a day since he was about five years old—and that would not have left much time for writing, directing and producing blockbuster movies, merchandizing all the *Star Wars* stuff and hanging out with his movie-legend buddies. It is possible that because his library is such a majestic place and a resource for Lucasfilm employees, Lucas may escape the description of over-shopper, but as most of us cannot visit, it's debatable whether it's a gift to humanity.

Also off-limits to most of us is the dazzling library of Priceline founder Jay Walker. He calls the thirty-thousand-piece collection the Walker Library of the History of Human Imagination and, being a wing of Walker's house in Connecticut, it is open to invited guests only. You can, however, see glimpses of the place on the internet, where Walker sometimes waxes scientific about the assemblage, and where it has its own webpage: "Constructed in 2002," says the description on Walker's website, "the 3,600 sq. ft. facility features multilevel tiers, 'floating' platforms, connecting stairways, glass-paneled bridges, dynamic lighting and music, and specially commissioned artworks that celebrate major achievements in the history of human invention." If this place—once described as "the bibliographic equivalent of a Disney ride"—weren't so grand, and Walker weren't so rich, his collection, gathered over several decades, would definitely qualify as overshopping and even hoarding. Which brings us to idiosyncratic fashion pioneer Karl Lagerfeld, whose collection was ten times the size of Lucas's or Walker's, and who once took the time to describe his passion: "Today, I only collect books; there's no room left for something else. If you go to my house, I'll have you walk around the books. I ended up with a library of 300,000. It's a lot for an individual." The Japanese have a word for new unread books that clutter up households: *tsundoku*.

Like Walker and Lucas and Lagerfeld, I too have a collection of books. It is small by comparison, perhaps several hundred, and displayed in too many bookcases, not to mention disorganized stacks, around the house. Long ago, I realized that in an internet world, my reference books were mostly redundant. If I couldn't find that information by pressing a few buttons on the smartphone in my pocket, I could get a copy or the equivalent in one of many local public libraries within walking distance of my house, or a variety of university libraries not so far away. As for the novels and non-fiction tomes, it became apparent I was never going to reread them, as much as I hoped I might. Unshopping them was impossible, and deshopping books is painful for a book-lover. Most used bookstores look down their noses at works that are not bestsellers (or anything that looks as if it has actually been read), and it is downright humiliating to lug in a heavy box of books to such retailers and be forced to haul out all but one or two books fifteen minutes later. Most won't even take them for free. Libraries have their own deshopping restrictions. And so it is off to financially challenged community centres, charities or thrift stores, many of which also turn away anyone showing up with a box of books. Those who have moved more than once know the burden books can present, and yet they continue to accumulate. (A friend who read an early version of the *Shopomania* manuscript recommended a title: *Don't Buy This Book*. Hypocritically, perhaps, I rejected it.) Even though I have reluctantly let go of thousands of books, ridding myself of those that continue to stream onto my nightstand and coffee table and various other stacks around the house requires constant vigilance and courage, and is clearly a losing battle, as I still somehow own several hundred.

Academy Award–winning actor and famous nice guy Tom Hanks at one time had as many as 250 typewriters and is the author of a book of typewriter-themed short stories, *Uncommon Type*. Like old cars, watches and books, the typewriter has been rendered all but obsolete by modern technology. A typewriter collection is eclectic at best and kind of wacky at the very least, so it's unlikely Hanks is trying to impress anyone with it (although countless other typewriter collectors are indeed impressed), but some might wonder about his hoarding tendencies. In fact, in a profile of Hanks in the *New York Times* in 2019, writer Taffy Brodesser-Akner connects Hank's odd collection to growing up in a dysfunctional family that moved a lot, a familiar theme among hoarders. "Somewhere underneath," writes Brodesser-Akner, "he must have known that something was off because he had started accumulating a lot of typewriters. Hundreds of them." Hanks, on the other hand, like so many other collectors, explains his collection in terms of art: "They're brilliant combinations of art and engineering. But art, engineering, and purpose." That kind of articulate description elevates its speaker from hoarder to shoperati. At the time of the article, Hanks had reduced his collection to just over one hundred, a realization perhaps that he had overshopped. It is not clear, meanwhile, if those he ditched were deshopped or unshopped. (The Southern gothic writer Cormac McCarthy had only one typewriter for almost half a century. On it, he wrote various plays, screenplays and novels, including the acclaimed *All the Pretty Horses, No Country for Old Men* and *The Road*. When this Olivetti, which he acquired second-hand at a pawn shop for $50 in 1963, sold at a charity auction in 2009 for $254,500, McCarthy immediately went reshopping and found an identical one for about $20.)

A writer friend of mine has a collection of typewriters, all of which he insists are useful art. He tinkers with them, he marvels at them, he researches them, and, yes, he uses them. Perhaps more significantly, he discusses them with anyone who might be interested, mostly others who also collect typewriters. And he makes pilgrimages to see other collectors. This may be another reason we collect such things: they allow us entry into a clique, a tribe, a society, a group of like-minded individuals. In an increasingly digital and isolated world, humans crave such community. That's why comic-book collectors go to expos. And it's why antique car owners go to picnics and "meets" with other antique car collectors, many of whom have travelled long distances in temperamental machines with uncomfortable seats and dubious safety equipment—to reassure themselves their collections are useful art. But for shoperati who have more than two or three such items and can use them only so often, it's debatable just how useful such art actually is.

Former rodeo champion Kiefer Sutherland, who collects guitars in inordinate numbers when he is not acting or country singing, attempts another explanation for his collection. "At first, it was very practical," says Sutherland, explaining how he got started. "You wanted a Strat, you wanted a Tele and you wanted a Les Paul. The big mistake I made was, we had a studio and I got the kind of cases where you would have all the guitars out, and you'd go, 'Well, there's two slots missing there.

I know exactly what I'd like to fill that with.' And before you knew it, you had eighty to one hundred guitars. Some people collect baseball cards, some people collect cars or art . . . for me, guitars are that. They are beautiful works of art."

Likewise, it is doubtful that iconic blues rock guitarist and ZZ Top frontman Billy Gibbons can find the time to play all of his 450-odd guitars, perhaps because he also spends a lot of time on his hot-rod cars, which he collects, curates and creates. Multi-instrument-playing peacenik and actor Richard Gere auctioned off 106 guitars in his collection for almost $1 million in 2011, some of which he labelled "my true friends." The money raised by Gere was dwarfed by the amount people paid for guitars once owned by legendary rocker David Gilmour. At a 2019 charity auction that generated more than $21 million, the Pink Floyd musician sold 127 guitars including his famous Black Strat for almost $4 million, the proceeds of which went to charity. (A single guitar for $4 million qualifies as ultrashopping, but only a year later a guitar once owned by deceased heroin addict and grunge rock superstar Kurt Cobain sold for $6 million.) Gilmour expressed mixed feelings about saying goodbye to the instruments, but was philosophical: "If I need a particular guitar, I'll go out and buy another one." (See reshop.) It could be argued that Gilmour's guitars, like those owned by sometime occultist and Led Zeppelin founder Jimmy Page, or guitar aficionado Eric Clapton, were not collections, but tools of the trade, and considering the "trade" for each of them was beyond impressive, it might be easy to argue they needed all that stuff simply to do their jobs. And guitars are still useful items.

So are sneakers, especially for professional athletes. But what explains the sneaker collections favoured by athlete and non-athlete, rich and poor, alike? Basketball veteran Jarrett Jack once claimed to own 1,500 pairs of sneakers, and confessed to paying as much as $2,000 for a single pair. "There are only 365 days in the year, so I can only wear so many," he said. Roger Federer once owned more than 250 pairs of sneakers, and perhaps even twice that.

The sneaker craze traces its beginnings to 1985 with the invention of the so-called Air Jordans, which sold for about $125. Over a dozen years later, Nike introduced Dunks. A pair of Nike Dunk High Pro SB Supreme Blue Stars that originally sold for $75 in 2003 sold recently for $10,000, and a 2005 Nike Dunk SB Low Staple NYC Pigeon that originally cost $200 in 2005 sold for $33,400 in 2021. Somehow, sneakers became more than sneakers: they became status symbols, fashion statements and finally investments. And there are now an awful lot of people with an awful lot of sneakers they cannot possibly wear. Potty-mouthed actor, director and unlikely fashion icon Jonah Hill, a self-described sneakerhead says, "I roll with Adidas." Stylish trendsetters such as deadpan comedian Ellen DeGeneres and prolific entertainer Justin Timberlake are also sneakerheads, as are rappers Kanye West, Jay-Z and Lil Wayne, and influential moviemaker Spike Lee, to name just a few. "I gotta stop," said comedic actor Ryan Reynolds, who admitted he may spend more on sneakers than anything else. "I've got only two feet. It's like, what's the point?"

Cars, guitars, sneakers, and similar objects may start out as useful, even necessary, for some people, who only eventually evolve from drivers and musicians and athletes into collection-obsessed shoperati. Less useful—and less explicable—are some of the other items that people collect. It is possible a team of psychotherapists could spend months or even years considering the reasons for a reported but never confirmed collection of coat hangers owned by Spanish sex symbol Penélope Cruz. Or actor and social activist Demi Moore's rumoured collection of two thousand or three thousand vintage dolls, which, according to some reports, were once kept in their own separate residence. Who knows why renowned pop artist and party animal Andy Warhol collected (among many other things) 175 cookie jars, which his estate sold for an astounding $247,830 in 1988? TV star Corbin Bernsen, who became famous in the 1980s for his work on the series *L.A. Law*, has eight thousand kitschy snow globes. Is that overshopping or something that transcends it? "There's something that happens to a collector, this

internal voice that says, 'I want to have one of each that is in existence,'" Bernsen once said. "That's easier to do with '50s vintage cars
than with snow globes, but snow globes are a lot cheaper to collect
than cars."

SHOPARRHEA

An overflow of shopped items.

We all have a mild case of shoparrhea, but hoarders are chronic. Stuff silts up in closets and attics and basements and eventually flows out uncontrollably into their living areas, restricting their movements, ruining their lives. It's more likely to affect older people, and not just because we have had more time to accumulate it. The older we are, according to the American Psychiatric Association, the less willing we are to get rid of it.

Reprehensible newspaper mogul William Randolph Hearst had serious shoparrhea. The early-twentieth-century media magnate and rabid promoter of yellow journalism is said to have paid more than twice what his multi-million-dollar art collection was actually worth (see misshop). Hearst autoshopped for so many items—statuary, tapestries, antiques, rare books, fine art, many of which were bought sight unseen and remained that way for the entirety of his ownership—that he required a block-long collection of warehouses five storeys high to contain them all. So much stuff over so large an area required a full-time staff of thirty just to keep track of it all. "How could one man buy all these things?" asked Hearst's wife, Millicent, when she visited the site. Upon reflection, she added: "I think he went out and bought things whenever he was worried." (See shopology, and shopititis.)

Shoparrhea is also what ailed Lucy Magda, an extreme autoshopper (and contrashopper). Magda was a classified-advertising accounts manager making $47,000 a year at the *St. Catharines Standard*, a daily newspaper in Ontario. In 2004, a court found that Magda, sixty-one, had stolen more than $2 million from her employer between 1992 and 1997, and spent the bulk of it in a years-long orgy of mindless autoshopping. When police went to search her modest home in nearby Thorold for evidence, they couldn't open the door for all the consumer items. When they finally gained entry, they discovered an "Aladdin's Cave" where "stuff was packed from the floor to the light fixtures," according to a news report in the *Hamilton Spectator*. Stacked on couches and stuffed into cupboards was more than $1 million worth of items, many still in boxes and shopping bags, some moth-eaten with price tags still attached: a $3,900 raincoat in the garage, a $2,900 cashmere sweater nearby, a $2,600 gold bracelet on a stand in the bedroom. Magda, who most colleagues described as a "kind-hearted woman," had stashed numerous products from clothes to cosmetics to cold, hard cash: six hundred pairs of shoes, many still in their boxes, seventy-two Tupperware containers of jewelry, fifty diamond rings, ten fur coats, multiple handbags and $430,000 in cash stored in paper bags, including thousands that seemed misplaced or concealed under piles of stuff. "I have never seen another house loaded with so much property that was not a retail outlet," said acting police inspector Murray Macleod.

The car collection of Hassanal Bolkiah, the sultan of Brunei, a tiny country on the north coast of Borneo, and his brother Jefri, indicates a particularly expensive case of shoparrhea. Bolkiah was once believed to be the richest man in the world as a result of oil reserves in the tiny Southeast Asian nation. Jefri was labelled the Playboy Prince, who, according to *Vanity Fair* magazine in 2011, "has probably gone through more cash than any other human being on Earth." The two had a collection of opulent homes, planes, jewels, art, chandeliers, yachts (Jefri named his Tits, which came with two tenders: Nipple 1 and Nipple 2) but it is the cars that are famous. The family collection numbered in the thousands. Michael Sheehan, an exotic car broker who visited the collection in 2002, found the vehicles—Rolls-Royces, Ferraris, Porsches, McLarens—all slowly decaying and literally melting in a series of buildings without air-conditioning in the Southeast Asian jungle. "Only a few hundred cars in total were commercially viable. All had minimal mileage, but all were poster children for deferred maintenance. None had been started in five years and so over two thousand lesser cars were simply beyond saving."

Automobile-related shoparrhea also afflicted Roger Baillon, a French business owner who collected one hundred vehicles from the 1950s and '60s but never quite got around to organizing them. By the 1970s, Baillon had fallen on hard times and was forced to unshop or deshop several dozen of the vehicles. For better or worse, he never got around to unshopping the rest, and the remaining fifty-nine vehicles sat untouched and virtually unknown for decades, languishing in barns, garages and ramshackle outbuildings at a rural property in western France, some covered in dust and debris, others entwined in ivy and weeds. Baillon died in the early years of the twenty-first century, but the collection didn't come to public notice until his son died in 2013. That's when his heirs decided to deshop (or unshop, as it turned out) the entire kit and caboodle, little knowing perhaps that it would fetch a fortune. One dilapidated car, a 1961 Ferrari 250 GT SWB California Spider, sold for $18 million, perhaps partly because it was once owned by right-wing French sex symbol Alain Delon, who had been photographed in it with left-wing American sex symbol and activist Jane Fonda. Another, a forsaken 1956 Maserati A6G, sold for $2.2 million. Both vehicles had sat decaying side-by-side in a broken-down shed for decades, strewn with stacks of decaying books and magazines. The collection generated $28 million at auction.

Shoparrhea can be deadly. That is illustrated nowhere more tragically than in the story of the infamous brothers Collyer in New York in the 1940s. They liked stuff more than most. A half-century before hoarding became a prime-time television obsession, Homer and Langley Collyer were living in a rundown brownstone in Harlem, paranoid of being robbed and reluctant to venture out except to shop for food, or to scout for urban detritus after midnight (see cryptoshop and pseudoshop). One day in 1947, a neighbour complained about the smell of rotting flesh, and authorities arrived to investigate. When they finally broke down the door, police faced an avalanche of stuff, including five pianos, dressmaker's dummies, solid walls of newspapers, folding beds, chairs, half a sewing machine, parts of a wine press, assorted machinery and a disassembled Model-T Ford, much of it inherited, some overshopped, and despite the brothers' considerable wealth, most of it scavenged and hoarded. Finally, after hours of excavation, investigators discovered the body of Homer, who had been frail, blind and in the care of his brother.

But there was no sign of Langley. There was speculation he had skipped town. Investigators continued the deshopathon for two more weeks, removing three thousand books, a horse's jawbone, an X-ray machine and more newspapers. More than one hundred tons of junk was removed from the house before they discovered Langley's decaying and rat-eaten body covered in debris, only ten feet from where they found Homer's. Langley, terrified of burglars, had been killed by one of his own booby traps and was buried by his own stuff. Homer, blind and unable to move, starved to death without his brother to deliver food.

SHOPITITIS

This is what some folks refer to as "all shopped out."

It's an admitted rarity in today's world, but often prevalent among the bankrupt or near-bankrupt, those whose houses are overrun with stuff, and perhaps some random overshoppers. More and more, it describes entire nations, whose governments have spent too much, usually on high-tech instruments of death and other war toys, so they can no longer afford health care, education, public transportation or clean water for their people.

Shopititis is what finally happened to multimedia entertainer Erika Girardi, the free-spending star of TV's *The Real Housewives of Beverly Hills*. She told readers of her 2018 memoir that she embarked on a music career, a highlight of which is the song "XXpen$ive," because "there was nothing more I could buy." Alas, she may now be better known for a scandal that played out on her own reality TV show and in the courts: her lawyer husband (whom she was divorcing during the show) is alleged to have misappropriated millions and she was named by the bankruptcy trustee as a co-defendant (see also contrashop).

Shopititis can be both mental and physical—it can describe people tuckered out from walking the malls or genuinely exhausted from working to pay for all that stuff. It describes Felice Campbell, a woman made famous by billionaire media queen Oprah Winfrey in 2007, herself an overshopper of some consequence. Featured on Oprah's talk show, taking television cameras on a tour of her house, Felice exclaimed: "This furniture is old to me 'cause I've had it for like three years now." Pointing to two couches, she said, "at my next garage sale, I was planning on selling both these items. The silk plants, I've probably got five, $6,000, $7,000 invested in plants." She told Oprah on national TV that she spent so much on stuff she had nothing left for her kids' health insurance.

Usually shopititis is little more than a temporary malaise, but occasionally it is more serious. In 2018, writer and former shopaholic Carla Sosenko reported in *Cosmopolitan* that she spent "$98,000 on shoes, clothes, furniture and other stuff I can barely remember now" during the first six months of the year. She writes of a "manic state" and "anxiety" about shopping, reshopping and overshopping: "It's not about the buy, it's about the buying." Finally, as the stuff piled up in her home ("windowsills stacked with sunglasses, chairs piled with clothes, and a closet full of new outfits"), she recalled, "I pictured myself old and alone struggling to survive financially, because I'd wasted all my money on stuff. I've never been suicidal, but I sometimes found it comforting to think, *Maybe I'll get hit by a bus and won't have to worry about it.*"

She recovered, but others, tragically, have not been so lucky. James Hammond, a nineteen-year-old British resident, killed himself in 2014 after stealing money from his mother to feed a shopping addiction he developed after his father died. His mother, Elizabeth Hammond, told an inquest into the death: "He displayed obsessive behaviour—cleaning and often throwing things away having recently bought them. The £6,000 he got in inheritance, he just blew the lot." Such addictions are well-documented, variously called compulsive buying disorder, oniomania, shopaholism . . .

At some point, it all becomes too much. In 2010, the ubiquitous British composer and impresario Andrew Lloyd Webber was forced to take to the airwaves to unload hundreds of bottles of wine—a small portion of his "precious wine collection." Sotheby's, which described Lloyd Webber as a "committed and knowledgeable collector of both art and wine," organized the auction of his French wines in Hong Kong and explained that, "as with all collecting, the magpie instinct can get the upper hand and there comes a time when there is no more space on the walls nor in the cellar." The auction raised £3.5 million.

It doesn't seem to matter who we are—rich or poor, old or young, male or female—the desire to acquire often seems unstoppable. I am often intrigued by a homeless man who inhabits an empty lot near my house. Some of us know his name, but he keeps mostly to himself and is largely unobtrusive. His stuff, however, is another matter. The detritus generated from his committed scavenging invariably accumulates to a point where it becomes an imposing urban sculpture. City officials arrive to politely remove most of it, this gentleman sets out quietly to build back better, and the cycle begins anew. People want stuff.

Increasingly, shopititis describes the malady afflicting the entire planet. In his book *The Day the World Stops Shopping*, author J.B. MacKinnon points out that since the turn of the current century, overconsumption, not overpopulation, has become the biggest environmental threat to the planet. We're devouring and excreting a lot of stuff. As a result, our rivers, lakes and oceans are so polluted they are becoming incapable of supporting the life that once thrived in them. Our air is ever more unbreathable, the smog thicker and respiratory diseases more common. Our land is progressively stripped of minerals, cleared of trees, deluged with artificial fertilizers, paved with asphalt and swaddled in landfill sites. Our carbon footprint is ever deeper. And our climate is changing. The planet has shopititis. Everyone agrees it must stop, as long as the stopping doesn't start with them.

PROXYSHOPPER

A shopper shopping for someone else.

Proxyshoppers include purchasing agents, military procurement officers, officials for almost any government and many private companies, personal shoppers, personal assistants, stylists, money managers, servants and thieves. Sometimes, they are those mysterious no-name bidders you see in movies taking place at high-end art auctions. Sometimes, it's the unsupervised IT guy at your company, mindlessly buying the best computer software or hardware because, well, it's the best, or supposed to be the best, even though most staff will never use the fancy bells and whistles because they are too complicated. Sometimes it's the military, with all its billions, somehow purchasing toilet seats and hammers for prices that make them sound gold-plated, or buying problem-plagued aircraft, leaky submarines or boats that won't float. They have no skin in the game. Sometimes it's just the office manager buying enough staples or paper clips to fill a storage locker. Any time someone is shopping with someone else's money, it's likely to lead to disaster (see overshop).

Sometimes it's a professional personal shopper, a growing industry in a world of consumerism. These folks shop for people who don't have the time, energy or wherewithal to shop, or are too famous to be seen in the shops, but they still want stuff. Todd Klein, a New York decorator, once told the *New York Times* he had a client who "authorized him to spend 10 hours looking for the perfect trash bin. 'It didn't matter if I eventually found one at Gracious Home for $13—the client would still pay me for 10 hours.'" Los Angeles–based personal shopper Nicole Pollard said in a 2016 interview that her clients included "heads of state, royal families, celebrities and studio heads." At the time, she charged $400 an hour or a percentage of the price tag for her proxy-shopping. "I've cultivated a strong network of dealers to help me find everything from Kanye West Yeezy sneakers (now selling for upwards of $500 on secondary markets) to really rare gifts, like the Hermès Birkin with diamonds and crocodile skin that is pure white because [the crocodile has] never seen sunlight," Pollard told *Vanity Fair*. "No matter what it is, we find it. That's our job. I've had to work with auction houses and dealers from around the world to find those bags, which might sell at a store for $250,000. If it's not available in the store, we have to go to a secondary market, where that might go for $1 million. I have clients buying rare watches from brands like Audemars Piguet and Patek Philippe that cost as much as a house in the suburbs of Los Angeles."

Adventure writer Brandon Presser described working as a proxy-shopper at the now-defunct luxury department store Barneys New York on Madison Avenue: "Busy shopaholics with reliable sizing can have Barneys stylists messenger fashion picks to try on at home, as part of the store's consignment program. For one loyal customer I worked with, that meant $75,000 worth of clothing every week, sent out on Wednesdays, as a means to stay on top of the latest looks. Several stylists have clients that are needier and ask for full-on house calls. These requests are often driven by special needs: say, a total closet overhaul, or packing help for an upcoming holiday."

One of the most famous proxyshoppers in the world is the renowned and beloved Betty Halbreich, the personal shopper at Bergdorf Goodman in New York City for as long as anyone can remember. It would seem she has helped anyone who was once someone find just the right outfit: Candice Bergen, Meryl Streep, Stockard Channing, Joan Rivers, Liza Minnelli and Mia Farrow, who was one of the few who balked at a dress, according to Halbreich. It was "a little hundred-dollar Adele Simpson number, so that dates the story. She said it would have fed a village in Biafra." (See undershop.) Not surprisingly, Halbreich was no slouch at shopping for herself. She has a series of closets "with high ceilings, sturdy poles along both sides, and, above them, shelving. The larger stalls might accommodate a Lipizzaner, with its tack," writes Judith Thurman. "The heavy doors are fitted with custom-made wooden shoe racks that open like a steamer trunk. Halbreich organizes her wardrobe the way Bergdorf does its merchandise: by the season, function and style. Vintage evening wear has its own closet; sweaters are arranged by weight and colour. Her summer day clothes were in the hall outside her bedroom, and every padded hanger had breathing room."

Proxyshoppers don't always enlist; sometimes they are drafted. Consider Millan Hupp, director of scheduling and advance for Scott Pruitt, the ethically challenged former administrator of the US Environmental Protection Agency who was finally terminated halfway through the administration of US president and fake university founder Donald Trump. For reasons which are peculiarly unclear, Pruitt was interested in "securing an old mattress from the Trump Hotel" in Washington, DC. Why Pruitt might have been interested in a used hotel mattress is anyone's guess, but shoppers are not always known for making smart decisions. Hupp testified she presumed it was for personal use. Pruitt was obviously not anxious to have the world know about his personal bedding choices, perhaps because this particular bit of proxyshopping was unethical, or maybe because it was just plain odd. Maybe not so personal (although it's also not clear) were the purchases by Hupp, at Pruitt's request, of twelve fountain pens for about $1,560. That's $130 a pen, which qualifies it as ultrashopping and perhaps as contrashopping, especially in a "drain-the-swamp" administration. (Fountain pens are somehow a growing ultrashopped item, for reasons only users can explain. Trump's ridiculous personal lawyer Rudy Giuliani spent $7,131 on them, according to his estranged wife during divorce proceedings, amid other expenses, including more than $12,000 on cigars, at a time when the couple was spending $230,000 a month.)

Finally, there are the rest of us, proxyshoppers all in some form or another. Picture yourself as a hapless spouse, parent or kid: There's been some kind of once-a-year catastrophe in your household, which means a family member can't make it to the store. He or she gives you the list of multiple items, or even just a single item of necessity, and forces you out into the great unknown, where you wander the aisles, trying to decipher the handwriting in the note and the specific instruc- tions, and in the end, making your best guess (and also tossing into the cart some of those as-seen-on-TV products you've always wanted). You buy the jumbo-sized jar of pickled capers rather than the medium one—not knowing that for some reason the medium is a better deal— or the one-inch nails rather than the one-and-a-quarter-inch nails, or the wrong style of jeans, or the wrong brand of sneakers, and the next thing you know you're in the doghouse again for bad shopping (see misshop), a hopeless proxyshopper who should never have agreed to the task in the first place. In a modern world, there is really no excuse for not being a good shopper.

SHOPACADEMY

Any place or organization that helps
grow, cultivate or educate shoppers.

It could be an advertising agency. It could be a marketing and communications firm. Or perhaps a magazine publisher or social media platform. An operation that connects manufacturers to consumers is a shopacademy. Storied advertising firms such as New York's J. Walter Thompson and Ogilvy & Mather were among the legendary shopacademies of the twentieth century, as was London's Saatchi & Saatchi. Today's big firms, such as the WPP Group in London, the Omnicom Group in New York and the Publicis Groupe in Paris continue the work, employing hundreds of thousands of people around the world who work to persuade people to buy more stuff, nurturing shoppers and holding our collective hands while we waffle over big shopping decisions. Advertising is a $550-billion business worldwide. Without shopacademies, shoppable items wouldn't be nearly as shoppable. Without shopacademies, we simply wouldn't know what stuff to buy. Shopacademies are the reason someone like me, a lifelong non-smoker, is somehow acutely aware of dozens of brands of cigarettes, from Marlboro to Craven "A," from Benson & Hedges to Camels, Rothman's to Lucky Strike.

Perhaps the best early example of a wildly successful shopacademy is the diamond producer De Beers. It pretty much invented the idea that a betrothal wasn't a betrothal without a diamond engagement ring, a bended-knee proposal wasn't worth considering if it wasn't accompanied by bling, and love wasn't true if it didn't sparkle in multiple carats—the more the better. After all, without constant reminders that diamonds are not only a sign of your commitment but also an excellent investment, people might suddenly wake up and realize they were paying all that money for useless rocks.

But while De Beers is famous for manipulating demand, choreographing supply was its raison d'être. Before the dazzling diamond discoveries in South Africa in the late nineteenth century, diamonds had been rare indeed, found only in pockets of India and later Brazil, and available mostly to royalty and the richest of the rich. After the South African discoveries, not surprisingly, supplies swelled and prices withered. Business executives quickly realized they'd need to promote the illusion that these rocks were still rare despite the recent bonanza if they were to make any money out of the enterprise. By the 1920s, De Beers cornered the market and tried to maintain the ruse by controlling supply. It worked, but only temporarily.

By the 1930s, they were obliged to turn their attentions not only to supply, but also to demand. The glittering rock had lost some of its lustre by then, and it needed a little spit and polish to catch the eye of the masses. So De Beers enlisted the services of New York's NW Ayer advertising agency, a shopacademy, to sell more. Subtly, or perhaps not-so-subtly, the company presented media outlets with stories about glamourous celebrities who wore diamonds—big ones— and promoted the idea that true love could only be expressed with a glittering rock, a tactic that many fashion designers and other merchandizers use to this day. In a 1948 strategy paper, NW Ayer stated: "We spread the word of diamonds worn by stars of screen and stage, by wives and daughters of political leaders, by any woman who can make the grocer's wife and the mechanic's sweetheart say 'I wish I had what she has.'" It was, in fact, an NW Ayer copywriter, Mary Frances Gerety, who came up with "A Diamond is Forever," a phrase that *Advertising Age* magazine claimed was the best slogan of the twentieth century.

The duplicitous enterprise was wildly successful. De Beer's has never looked back: wholesale diamond sales went through the roof, rocketing from $23 million in 1939 to $2.1 billion in 1979. And the advertising budget? It went from $200,000 to $10 million annually.

Marketing classes at distinguished universities still study the slogan to learn its secrets. It was featured in the titles of books and movies and songs. And why not? De Beers, according to one observer, had succeeded in "converting tiny crystals of carbon into universally recognized tokens of wealth, power and romance."

People want diamonds. Some people want lots of them, and most are under the illusion they are a good way to preserve a fortune. "Diamonds are not an investment," says Ira Weissman, a diamond industry expert who has travelled the world buying and selling the shiny rocks. "They are a retail product like any other. People explain away spending thousands of dollars on a little stone because they mistakenly believe that the diamond is a solid investment." The diamond business, he says, is a "shark tank" and "the greatest scam in history."

The shopacademy won't tell us that, of course. The shopacademy is not interested in recommending we save our money. Its sole purpose is to get us to part with it. Without a shopacademy, how would people know what stuff to buy? They arrange for shopaganda on television commercials, in newspapers and on news sites, in elevators and at bus stops. A shopacademy is there to keep a brand's existence front and centre—beneath the ice at a hockey game, on a car at the racetrack, on a blimp above a baseball game—or subtly place the idea, or even the hint of it, into our brains without us even knowing it. They pay millions to top athletes to wear logos, an endeavor that often delivers more to a sports professional's bank account than playing the game ever could.

Modern shopacademies are as voracious as they are prevalent. Everything, everywhere is available for purchase, and increasingly it doesn't have a price tag or a "sale" sign on it. Every event, every moment, every opportunity is leveraged to promote a brand, place it in the public consciousness and make us comfortable with it. Modern shopacedemies create interactive art exhibitions, plan social media campaigns and stage flash mobs. They hire shopostles to write blogs or go to events and parties. They disguise publicity stunts as intriguing incidents worthy of sharing on social media. A shopacademy is both overt and covert, obvious and insidious, in total control and simply along for the ride. Anything that gets their name in the consciousness of the shopper.

And somehow it all works miraculously. People buy stuff, especially stuff they recognize. This was demonstrated by vapid former tennis champion Andre Agassi following the 1992 Davis Cup. As Agassi explains in his highly acclaimed autobiography, *Open*, he wore a pair of Oakley sunglasses to "conceal my bloodshot eyes" after a night of hard partying with ill-tempered tennis legend John McEnroe and his wife, former child actor Tatum O'Neal. The result was an unintended fashion statement highlighted a week later on the cover of *Tennis* magazine. Jim Jannard, the astonishingly rich founder of Oakley, was so delighted he promptly delivered—unannounced and unsolicited—a red Dodge Viper automobile to Agassi's Las Vegas home, a gift for wearing the glasses and unwittingly promoting the brand. Reflected Agassi: "Nice to know that, even if I've lost my game, I can still move product." (See shopostle.)

In the twenty-first century, an intuitive shopacademy goes with the flow. It recognizes that modern technology and social shifts now mean it doesn't necessarily control the brand; the consumers do. A modern shopacademy doesn't lament the fact; it embraces and leverages it. It understands that brands can go viral, even if owners and shopacademies cannot determine exactly how. It is what author Rob Walker, in his book *Buying In*, calls murketing—or murky marketing: "'Murketing' served as my shorthand description of the practices of certain brand managers who aimed to blur the rules of the traditional sales pitch—to make marketing more murky."

SHOPPING SHEEP

People who do what marketers and influencers tell them to do.

This includes most of us. As shoppers, we tend to do what we're told by advertisers. Let's say you have a white refrigerator. You like the refrigerator. It fits perfectly in your kitchen, it's reliable, it's quiet and it's reasonably efficient. It keeps things cold. It has a built-in icemaker and other bells and whistles. And it is paid for. But one day you realize it is white. Everyone else seems to have a black refrigerator, a slate gray refrigerator, a stainless-steel refrigerator, a harvest gold, an avocado green, or whatever colour of refrigerator happens to be in vogue this year—fire-engine red, turquoise?—and you say to yourself and your spouse, "we need a new refrigerator." The same goes for kitchen countertops, window blinds, sinks, bathtubs and faucets. Carpets are out, so you must get rid of your carpets and install hardwood floors. When hardwood goes out of fashion, you'll need to cover them all again with carpet.

Fashion enslaves us all. Three-button versus four-button jackets. Wide ties versus narrow ties or lapels. Rounded or pointy shoes. Vests. Shoulder pads. Mini, midi, maxi skirts, elephant pants, hot pants, Hammer pants, capris, khakis, bell-bottoms, new jeans, faded jeans, ripped jeans . . .

Hush Puppies, a decades-old shoe brand that saw a sudden uptick in sales in the mid-1990s, is a good example. As outlined by Malcolm Gladwell in his groundbreaking book *The Tipping Point*, sales of the shoe had dwindled to thirty thousand pairs a year in 1994. In 1995, it sold 430,000 pairs, and sales over the next several years continued to increase exponentially "until Hush Puppies were once again a staple of the wardrobe of the young American male." Gladwell mounts a fascinating and convincing explanation for the sudden success of Hush Puppies in his book, but we could simply chalk it up to the fact we are all shopping sheep. When something is popular, we all flock like sheep to buy it—what Gladwell calls "contagious behaviour." When something becomes less-than-fashionable, we gather as one to rid ourselves of it and travel en masse to the dump or have someone else do that so we don't have to think about it. We are all victims of fashion. We are all shopping sheep.

Luxury consumption in particular is influenced by the human need to forever belong to a better "class"—or at least a wealthier group—of people. It is about self-esteem. Once again, we are—or at least we think we are—what we buy; and we must keep up with the in-crowd. Bergdorf Goodman personal shopper Betty Halbreich once lamented the reality: "I mean, once everybody gets on a trend, then everybody has to wear them? Everyone has to carry the same handbag? Wear the same white jeans? Wear the same puffer coat? Are we a nation of sheep?"

The answer, clearly, is yes: we are all shopping sheep.

SHOPPING SHERPA

Someone to help carry your recent purchases.

Shopping is not easy. A few shopping bags might be manageable, but what about those boxes? And all that packaging. And you couldn't find a parking spot for your pickup truck close enough to the door at the mall. Or you can't carry all your shopping bags on the train or on public transit. Or it's all just too heavy, and you need help. You could ask a friend or your kids, or a spouse. If so, they become shopping sherpas. The term gained some currency (and may even have been coined) in 2006 when Leanne Domi, the estranged wife of former National Hockey League tough guy Tie Domi, labelled her allegedly cheating husband a "shopping sherpa" for billionaire business owner and former opportunistic Canadian politician Belinda Stronach. But shopping sherpas come in many forms: wives and husbands, children and parents, personal shoppers, personal assistants, valets, butlers, chauffeurs, retailing assistants, the bagger at the grocery store. Supershoppers can't do it alone. They need help. They need shopping sherpas. Engineers, of course, have already invented a machine that will do that for you. Two-wheeled mechanical shopping sherpas, basically high-tech, self-driving shopping carts (think R2-D2 from *Star Wars*), connected wirelessly to our phones, are already available, ready to follow ultrashoppers around the mall at a discreet distance. And then there are all those hundreds of thousands employed by Amazon and other organizations to deliver your stuff directly to your door.

SHOPOPOLIS

A city devoted to shopping.

Originally, communities were born and thrived because they had easy access to water and food: good fishing, plenty of game and rich soil for agriculture. Later, they grew because of a strategic location: a sheltered harbour, a defensible site on the crest of a hill, a busy place near the fork in a river. Others thrived because of a religious temple or monument. But the most successful communities—then and now—were along trade routes, those that attracted travellers or rural inhabitants to stop and shop, stock up and spend: the shopopolis. Early trade routes—the Amber Road, the Silk Road, the spice routes, the Incense Route—were often built because of things people wanted rather than needed. One of the oldest, the Amber Road, supplied people living along the Mediterranean Sea with a useless gemstone made from fossilized tree resin that came from as far away as the Baltic Sea. They lugged it across rivers and mountains, through snowy forests and parched deserts because they knew far-away strangers would go crazy for shiny stuff. Humans have collected amber for jewelry for at least thirteen thousand years and continue doing so today. The Indus Valley in modern-day Pakistan, home to one of the world's earliest civilizations from about 5500 BCE to 1300 BCE, reached greatness because it was a complex network of trading communities, famous for making beads for necklaces, bangles, trinkets and other knick-knacks from, among other things, carnelian and lapis lazuli. They of course made more useful things, but the entire economy seems to have been dependent mostly on commerce, with traders coming from as far away as Mesopotamia and even Crete.

Trade routes once made cities such as Lisbon, Istanbul and Mumbai the places to be. The better the shopping, the more likely people were to visit; the more ideas that gained currency, the more able the communities were to thrive and adapt. All global cities, past and present—from Carthage, Babylon and Samarkand; to Venice, Barcelona and Malacca; to Hamburg, Timbuktu and Amsterdam— thrived because of trade. At least until some other trade centre became more interesting.

In a modern world, the sign of a thriving city is the number of shopportunities it offers visitors, whether those visitors are landing at the airport, arriving at a central railway station or coming off the highway through the predictable gauntlet of fast-food joints and sprawling shopitoriums. When a city is no longer a shopopolis, it ceases to exist in the minds of most people, even if it retains a welcome sign on the outskirts of town. If there's no shopping, people will pass by. The list of the planet's abandoned communities is boundless: Petra in Jordan or Taxila in Pakistan, or just a one-horse town like Cooper's Falls in Canada. Some withered away for reasons of war, environmental disaster or, often, a lack of employment. But many disappeared because people went somewhere else to shop, leaving nothing but an aging church, a windswept graveyard and a few forlorn homes. And nobody but non-shopping hermits like that.

Today, the internet is chockablock with lists of the best shopping cities in the world, which include all the usual suspects—New York, London, Paris, Milan, Istanbul, Tokyo. Cities such as Singapore, Orlando and Las Vegas have invented or reinvented themselves as places for people with time and money to buy stuff, but it is perhaps Dubai that best personifies the modern shopopolis. It has been around for centuries, once famous for its pearling industry, which lasted five hundred years, later for its deep-water port, but in recent decades mostly for its oil and its shopping. It is one of the world's fastest-growing economies and is one of the most visited cities on the planet (and climbing), mostly based on shopping. Marked by opulence and decadence, the city has more than seventy shopping centres amid the many mosques, including the world's largest, the Dubai Mall. It has a world-famous Dubai Shopping Festival every January and February. It has the world's tallest building, a theme park bigger than Disney World, an underwater hotel, a Global Village entertainment and shopping centre, and an archipelago of several hundred fake islands with a "Floating Venice." And Dubai has a domed ski resort. With snow. And penguins. All in the middle of the desert.

Dubai is the capital of brands, and perhaps the capital of brand influencers, so it's no surprise it has a carefully nurtured brand of its own built over years by its developers, its retailers, its influencers and its overseer, Mohammed al-Maktoum, the emir of Dubai, whose vision has made it the place to be for conspicuous consumers. It is a land where swimming pools are refrigerated, where islands are manufactured, where communities are gated, where the yachts loom large and the lines between shopping, culture and entertainment are blurred by the sheer excess of it all. Aquariums and ski hills, art and architecture, culture and food are intertwined with shopping. It is where anything seems possible and nothing is too much. Like the rest of the world, Dubai has connected shopping to everything, except on a far grander, glitzier, excessive scale. Every activity—cultural, culinary, musical, physical, social, theological—has been intertwined with the real adventure, shopping. And to celebrate it all, a quarter of a century ago it invented a shopping festival, which operates each winter for one month, attracting shoppers from far and wide to experience overindulgence on a grand scale.

SHOPWARD

The direction of shops.

Since there are shops almost everywhere on the planet, almost every direction is shopward. Shopward is the direction of the mall, the market or Main Street. If you are north of the Arctic Circle, shopward is probably not north, but don't count on it. If you are on a commercial jetliner, it is possible that shopward is only downward, but for years, many airlines did a brisk business in "duty free onboard sales," and some still promote it, so shopward is basically any direction, even way up there. Shopward on a boat is probably not downward, unless you are on the upper decks of a cruise liner, in which case there are lots of shops below decks, and above for that matter. "Shopward" is a catchall or a safe answer whenever anyone asks "which way are you headed?"

AEROSHOP

To shop in the sky or in the airport.

For many people—even those beautiful people in first class—commercial air travel is the height of misery. No pretty or handsome flight attendants, no Denzel Washington or Charlize Theron movies, no Beluga caviar and Veuve Clicquot champagne served at your seat, no Nora Roberts novel or Maya Angelou book can do much to mitigate the wretchedness of being crammed into a tin cylinder travelling at high speed through turbulence, accompanied by hundreds of grumpy, sniffling, smelly, impatient travellers. Nor does the anticipation that you will soon be on your way to another carefree vacation in some international capital, or on an exotic island with lots of happy, fun-loving, fit-looking people, do much to lessen the torment of baggage check-ins, customs interviews and security inspections.

But the in-flight duty-free catalogue? Or the Prada store in the departures area?

Well, now we're talking.

The in-flight duty-free catalogue is a purported bargain-hunter's paradise right at your seat on some airlines. All that stuff to buy and nothing else to distract you except a lineup for the lavatory and the snoring passenger drooling on the seat next to you. A few airlines, ever mindful of your comfort and their bottom line, will remind you of this opportunity, via a commercial before your in-flight movie: "And now it's time for an important part of your flight—shopping," grins the perky flight attendant on the screen in front of you. Were you rushed at the airport? Couldn't spend enough time in the duty-free shop? Weren't able to acquire that certain something that's completely useless but oh-so-necessary for your spouse? Don't lose out on this exciting opportunity to fill your suitcase with even more stuff. And it's all delivered to you personally on your way out the door!

Aeroshopping is even more rampant at the airport. Before the pandemic cleared them out, shoppers worldwide were expected to spend $49 billion in airports by 2021. Meanwhile, the aggressive airports are building more retail and recreation space to lessen the misery and extract more cash from weary travellers. How else to explain the fantastic number of Hermès and Gucci stores, tourist boutiques and bookshops, magazine booths and tie stands? Singapore's Changi Airport had more than two hundred retail outlets before the pandemic. LAX had almost one hundred. As the airport security chief said to the Tom Hanks character trapped in an airport in the 2004 Steven Spielberg movie *The Terminal*: "There's only one thing you can do here, Mr. Navorski: Shop."

After all, there may be a reason for all the delays, the bad lighting, the uncomfortable chairs, the crowds forced to bumble over your outstretched legs, the airwaves resounding with repeated announcements about Passenger Smith or Passenger Gupta or warnings about unattended baggage. They don't want you to feel relaxed; they don't want you to sit there and read a book; they don't want you to pore over your laptop—they want you in the shops, buying booze, jewelry, perfume, scarves, luggage, cameras, bad food, little tiny Eiffel Towers, Empire State Buildings and other things you'd never have the time or inclination to purchase otherwise. In fact, aeroshoppers are often business travellers who never have any time otherwise to get stuff. Dad or Mom, rushing home from the fifth business trip this month—guilty at having left their kids at home alone with the spouse for most of the last three weeks and missing both the school play and three soccer games—tears through the airport curio emporium, willing to pay any amount for the something they're not even sure the kids will use, waits in line while eyeballing their watch, then jams their purchase into a shopping bag and rushes for the departure gate. For airport shoperators, these people are sitting ducks.

AQUASHOP

To shop on water.

This is more common than you may think. Aquashopping, like aero-shopping, is often associated with vacations. It's shopping on cruise ships, on a beach, on a bridge, by a waterfall. Anywhere adjacent to or actually in water is a prime location for retailers, including almost any developed and public beach in warm climates around the world. Secluded beaches with still blue waters, pristine white sand and low-hanging palm trees may beckon us in advertising and posters, but such places are a) increasingly few and far between and b) not really that much fun anyway because there is no shopping there—no cold drinks, no T-shirt shacks, no sunglasses racks, no French fries, no annoying hawkers of kitschy local crafts. A beach that is not shoppable is no beach at all. That beach in your mind's eye, the remote one with white sand and lush palm trees, as yet unsullied by tiki bars, buzzing personal watercraft and broiling tourists? At first glance it may seem a true paradise, but sooner or later, likely sooner, most of us will get bored and start looking for a shop.

In the past, bridges were among the most popular aquashopping destinations in much of Europe. London Bridge, long since fallen down and rebuilt without shops, was the most famous, but Bath's Pulteney Bridge survives, attracting trinket-loving tourists from far and wide to its shops-upon-Avon. The German city of Erfurt features the Krämerbrüke, or merchants' bridge, which has stood since 1510, and still features shops today. Florence's storied Ponte Vecchio over the Arno River, upon which merchants have hawked their goods for one thousand years, also endures, as does Venice's Rialto Bridge. In fact, the entire old city of Venice is an aquashopping centre, and more so every day in an era of rising tides and climate change. So is much of Bangkok. Niagara Falls might be mistaken by tourists on both sides of the United States–Canada border as an awe-inspiring natural wonder of the world. But residents and visitors know the thundering water and iridescent mists are simply the foundation for a kitschy aquashopping centre. Any cruise ship worth vacationing on has shops (shipshops) with fine jewelry, Swiss watches, leather goods and luxury brands, as if there weren't enough shopportunities at each daily port of call. The downside to aquashopping, unfortunately, is that while it may often be fun, it is never cheap, as there are virtually no bona fide bargains at most aquashopping establishments. They've got you in the deep end.

SHOP THERAPY

Shopping to alleviate depression.

Sometimes known as retail therapy, this is a treatment for people feeling down, a balm for what ails you. Buying stuff always makes us feel better, no matter how sorry the state of our finances or mental health. As Elton John says, "there's nothing more relaxing than an afternoon of shopping." Unfortunately, it's a bit like sex and drugs. It's fun while it lasts—but then, not so long afterward, we get depressed and want to do it again.

Problem:	Solution:
My back hurts	We need a new mattress
My neck hurts	We need new pillows
My muscles ache	We need a hot tub
I'm fat	We need an exercise machine
I've lost weight	I need a new wardrobe
I'm depressed	Let's go to the mall
I've got the flu	We need a new furnace
I'm cold	We need a gas fireplace
I'm hot	Let's get a pool
I have allergies	We need new carpets

Shop therapy may be responsible for the miserable fate of repair shops everywhere. While repairing old stuff is troublesome and boring, shopping for new stuff is exciting and fun. This is why tailors, seamstresses, cobblers, mechanics and all manner of fixers are a dying breed. Electricians, carpenters and plumbers are too busy building new houses to even bother answering your call about a minor repair to your aging toaster, back door or old sink.

Problem:	Solution:
The sink is clogged	We need to renovate the kitchen
The sole of my shoe is worn	Let's hit the outlet store
This shower is grimy	Let's get an insert
This knife is dull	We need a food processor
This pot is black	Walmart is having a Paderno sale
This house is old	It's a tear-down

Shoe repair is still possible, if you look hard enough, but good luck with your toaster; you should have bought a better one to begin with. Automobiles are progressively more difficult to repair the way our grandparents did. There is hope: the so-called right-to-repair movement has gathered steam across North America and in Europe in the new millennium and has lobbied governments to introduce laws to stop the madness.

SHOPPORTUNITY

An opportunity to shop.

A shopportunity, or shop-op for short, is a random chance to buy stuff. Your meeting is cancelled. Your luncheon guest bailed at the last minute. Your plane is late. The weather is too cold/hot/rainy. Your spouse is sick in bed. These shopportunities present themselves to us daily, hourly, almost by the minute.

You're free on Saturday morning during your kid's two-hour dance class. What do you do? Shop.

You're on a couples' weekend in Philly, and the boys decide it's time for a cool one at the local sports bar. That's a shop-op.

You're on holiday? It's one big shop-op.

All sales are shop-ops. They cannot and should not be passed up. Eddie Bauer Canada sometimes has a Memorial Day sale, even though Memorial Day doesn't exist in Canada. That is a shop-op, and you can honour the fallen while you're at it.

Someone's sick? Shop-op.

A friend is having a baby? Shop-op.

Your folks are having an anniversary? Shop-op.

Your sister's getting a divorce? Shop-op.

You got fired? Shop-op.

A new house? Huuuuge shop-op. ("That banister is all wrong.")

You're on a lunch break but not hungry? Shop-op.

Wake up in the middle of the night and can't sleep? Shop-op.

Bored? Shop-op.

Not surprisingly, many shopportunities occur while you are already shopping. For example, you go to the hardware store to get a box of nails, but while there you are presented with the latest in pots and pans. After you have found the box of nails, you proceed to the cashier, where you are presented with items for purchase while you wait to pay: a tiny flashlight, perhaps a jackknife or a stuffed animal? The grocery stores pioneered this kind of in-line shopping decades ago by peppering the checkout line with celebrity magazines and candy, and now modern retailers are setting up shops within their shops faster than you can say "one moment please." Shopping occupies shoppers while they're waiting to pay for their shopping, which thereby a) diffuses complaints that the shops aren't hiring enough shopkeepers and b) sells more stuff that people don't really need. Today, it seems most savvy retailers force customers to wait in queues that are lined with hampers of stuff, trinkets, gadgets and fancy chocolate that would otherwise be ignored but are now hard to resist.

DESHOPPING CENTRE

The last stop.

A deshopping centre is a place for stuff people don't want. The consignment store. The recycling centre. The dump. And they don't want to see it either; it is a reminder of overshopping excess. Deshopping centres are on the other side of the tracks: resale operations in industrial areas; a rusting donation box at the far corner of the mall parking lot; the promised safe waste disposal centre on the outskirts of town. Or a sprawling landfill site a world away in a developing country, where rich countries export their troublesome waste, like plastics or electronics. When China decided in 2018 that it no longer wanted to be the world's garbage dump and stopped accepting *yang laji*, or foreign garbage, the world had to look elsewhere. Garbage exports to Africa quadrupled the following year. Places such as Canada, Australia, Argentina, Saudi Arabia and many European countries sent plastic waste to Malaysia instead. In 2018, the United States sent 157,000 shipping containers of plastic waste to poor countries that were already overwhelmed by stuff from foreign shores.

In 2019, ninety-six different countries accepted more than one billion pounds of plastic waste from the US. It's supposed to be recycled, but much of it finds its way into rivers and oceans, washing up against beaches in rolling waves of trash. Many landfills are so big and poorly managed that disasters are inevitable: they smell, they leak toxic waste, they combust spontaneously. It's still unclear how many creatures, human or otherwise, are dying nearby, and from what? Sometimes the trash is piled so high that deshopping centres suffer garbage landslides, burying the legions of poor people who pick through the trash for miserable treasure, and anyone else nearby. These incidents are tragically common: one in the Philippines in 2000 killed at least two hundred people. Another in the Philippines in 2011 buried twenty houses. In Indonesia in 2005, 143 people were killed in a garbage landslide; in Shenzhen, China in 2015, seventy-three were killed. In Addis Ababa, Ethiopia, 2017, 115 were killed.

After organic material—food, yard waste, wood—packaging tops the list of stuff destined for the dump, not a surprise to any Westerner who sorts their trash before the weekly collection. That is followed closely by plastics, metals and glass—the stuff that most stuff is made of. After that, it's clothing. As any shopper knows, clothing stores dominate Main Street, the mall and the internet. In a developed world ruled by fast fashion, humans are shopping and deshopping clothing at a distressing rate: the average North American buys about seventy-five or eighty pieces of clothing each year, most of which lands in a deshopping centre sooner rather than later.

But while humans get poor marks on the first of the three Rs (reducing) there are glimmers we are at least improving on the second and third (reusing and recycling) when it comes to clothing. The global apparel resale market is increasing by roughly $2 billion a year, and some socially conscious rich people seem to have bravely decided that once is not enough to wear an outfit in public. Eco-friendly actor Cate Blanchett, for example, wore the same black Armani dress to the 2018 Cannes Film Festival that she wore to the 2014 Golden Globes, turning the heads of gasping spectators and journalists. "From couture to T-shirts, landfills are full of garments that have been unnecessarily discarded," Blanchett declared. "Particularly in today's climate, it seems wilful and ridiculous that such garments are not cherished and reworn for a lifetime." She credited producer, activist and celebrity wife Livia Firth and "the Green Carpet Challenge" for inspiring her decision to be seen in public twice in the same outfit. Inspired by Firth or not, others who have been caught proudly wearing the same thing twice include royal spouse Kate Middleton, fashion maven Anna Wintour and acclaimed actor and naturist Helen Mirren. Actor and environmentalist Keira Knightley reportedly wore the same dress to her own wedding that she had worn several years earlier to an after party at the British Academy of Film and Television Arts Awards. And magnificently resilient actor Rita Moreno attended the 2018 Academy Awards in the same gown in which she won an Oscar more than a half-century earlier—in 1962.

ECO-SHOPPING

Shopping only for stuff you need.

Given human nature, few of us are doing much eco-shopping. We buy organic stuff, artisanal stuff, green stuff, eco-friendly stuff, fair-trade stuff and local stuff. It makes us feel good and could somehow be called eco-shopping, but we still buy too much stuff, which does not exactly make us champions of the planet. People in remote jungles, and perhaps a few on the African savanna, are likely better candidates. But leaving a small environmental footprint in a world that offers so much temptation is difficult for the rest of us. We are buying more food, clothing and shelter than ever. We believe outrageous "green" claims by manufacturers (see shopaganda) because we want to feel good about buying stuff, even though we know in our heart of hearts we probably don't need it. Environmentalists, ecologists, conservationists, nature-lovers, eco-activists and tree huggers all talk a good line, but we do not expect them to actually put words into action. Model-dating bachelor Leonardo DiCaprio, for example, may be among the planet's most high-profile environmentalists. He's donated millions to various causes, and when he won an Oscar in 2016, he used the opportunity to spread an eco-message to the world: "Climate change is real, it is happening right now. It is the most urgent threat facing our entire species, and we need to work collectively together and stop procrastinating." He may buy electric cars and heat his home with solar panels, but he is buying them nonetheless. Finally, as a regular user of private jets, an occasional user of superyachts and an owner of several houses plus a Caribbean Island, he's a shopper like the rest of us, and likely a great deal more than that, a point many of his critics take glee in pointing out.

SHOP-O-EROTIC

A sexually charged shopping experience.

Some purchasing experiences are so enjoyable they are better than sex, and in some cases so good they make you want to have sex. Shopping is so ubiquitous, so widespread, so easily accessed, that it is today often little more than a pleasant diversion. For most of us it is a common everyday occurrence we rarely stop to contemplate. It can be fun, it can be exciting even, but it isn't exactly sensual, no matter how much money and time you have. But acquiring something really special, something you've coveted for years (or at least days) and getting a bargain—a real bargain—to boot? Well, that can be orgasmic. We're not talking about everyday sales. We're not talking about 50 per cent off. We're talking about 50 per cent off the 50 per cent sale price. And it *fits!* We're talking about a steal. A deal so good that you might need to take a moment just to collect yourself. You might need a rest and a cigarette after leaving the store. You might mistake it for winning the lottery. And you are certainly going to need to talk about it with others, boast about it to colleagues and share the experience with friends like it was a holiday in the Poconos or a blissful first date. That's shop-o-erotic.

Anyone who has ever got a deal on something they always wanted is well aware of this, but in case there was any doubt about the nature of shop-o-eroticism, science as usual has stepped in to confirm it for retailers. In a study conducted in 2010 at the University of Westminster in London, sixty shoppers were shown a variety of images: men and women having sex, as well as familiar British products with special offers. The conclusion: both the bargains and the pornography provoked a similar response. The study used eye-tracking software to measure the responses, which indicated pretty clearly that getting a deal while shopping may be as exciting as sex. In another British study in 2017, neuroscientists partnered with officials at MyndPlay, a company that does "academically backed research campaigns and experiments . . . aimed at using brain science and physiological emotional response to help a company, organization or brand gain a deeper insight into the minds and emotional response of their core audience." They analyzed gamma brainwaves and concluded that many shoppers experience "prolonged highs in the brain comparable to sexual intercourse."

SHOPORNOGRAPHY

Sexual images intended to stimulate purchases.

Marketers recognized the connection between sex and sales centuries ago, and despite questionable research, it has long been taken for granted that it works. But advertisers didn't really dive in until the latter part of the nineteenth century, with such products as soap and cigarettes. In 1947, sultry actor Lauren Bacall, during a promotional moment on *The Jack Benny Program*, said this about Lucky Strikes: "They're so round, so firm, so fully packed, so free and easy on the draw."

By the 1960s, manufacturers were using sex to subtly or unsubtly sell almost anything, usually to men. Countless products from Pepsi soft drinks to Calvin Klein jeans have raised eyebrows and offended sensibilities, simply by transmitting the idea that buying their products will improve our sex lives. Companies making underwear, cologne, even hamburgers, have used sexually suggestive images to attract buyers. One of many clumsy and blatant attempts came in the 1960s from the makers of Hai Karate cologne, who told men to "be careful how you use it" or they'd have to defend themselves against sex-hungry women.

Car manufacturers, tire makers and related industries have done the same, regularly and incongruously draping bikini-clad women over the hoods of otherwise dreary automobiles and automotive products, a practice that continues with appalling frequency today. Given that women today are said to buy the majority of cars on the road and have influence over as much as 80 per cent of all vehicle purchases, it seems risky at best. "The companies that don't recognize this are giving their competitors the upper hand," writes Bridget Brennan in her book *Why She Buys*.

Some shopornography is sophisticated; some not so much. Some ads are creepy; some are just plain crass. Until recently, television advertising for Hardee's hamburgers in America featured the likes of Paris Hilton and Kim Kardashian "lustily devouring drippy hamburgers," and other fast food, according to USA Today. "We believe in putting hot models in our commercials, because ugly ones don't sell burgers," the company once said in a press release. The chief executive was later nominated by lecherous adulterer US president Donald Trump as his labour secretary—at about the same time, the Hardee's marketing strategy was deep-sixed in favour of something more "upscale."

Other brands seem to bask in controversy. Commercials for beer, soft drinks and jeans continue to raise eyebrows and make the news, for better or worse. Former juvenile delinquent, rapper and box-office star Mark Wahlberg became internationally famous for showing off his impressive physique while modelling Calvin Klein underwear, a stunt repeated a generation later by convicted vandal and recording star Justin Bieber. Provocative images often get headlines, and even make careers, but experts are divided on whether sex actually sells or shopornography works, especially in a #MeToo era. Despite considerable research showing that such material can be as offensive as it is attractive, many modern ads continue to drip with sex.

In his book Buyology, Martin Lindstrom predicts that soon, due to the ubiquity of sex in media, "most of us will have become so desensitized to sex in advertising we won't even notice it anymore." Lindstrom conducted a neuromarketing study that "peered inside the brains" of volunteers to see how they reacted to shopaganda, shopornography, ads, brands, logos and the like and further concluded, "sexual ads in the future will get sneakier, subtler. They'll suggest, but they won't complete. They'll flirt, but take it no further than that. They'll propose, then leave the rest up to our imaginations."

SHOPETERIA

A store that forces you to shop in one-way corridors.

Like an old-fashioned high-school or hospital cafeteria, where you line up at one end with an empty tray and emerge at the other end with a hot turkey sandwich and a fruit cocktail and a cashier tallies it up. This was perfected by IKEA, the ubiquitous Swedish retailing giant and the world's largest furniture retailer. Call it the Scandinavian retailing way—a lobster trap, a maze, a retailing labyrinth. You enter through one door, and even if you want a single item, say a crib for your newborn, or a couple of candles for the table, there's no going back. You're stuck in the place, wandering through each department like you're in the drive-thru line at the Coffee Time or a ride at Disney World, drawn deeper and deeper into the store's depths—unable to reverse course or you'll be hopelessly lost—and forced to survey every department from bedroom textiles to office products, unconsciously falling prey to impulse items along the way until you finally escape into the cashier line with a cart full of items, including the crib, another crappy bookcase, a lamp, a package of cheap placemats, two candles, three pillows and a stomach full of Swedish meatballs.

The modern checkout lines in many sophisticated stores mimic the shopeteria. Shoppers are herded into a funnel-shaped cashier line that seems unnaturally slow. Once there, we are forced to run a gauntlet of items we had earlier ignored and had no interest in acquiring, but which we are now reconsidering because, well, we can't escape and there's nothing else to do but look at our phones.

What IKEA staffers call "the long natural path" exists more subtly in almost every department store, and has since its earliest days. You may want to buy a pair of gloves or a bathing suit, but you must first navigate the labyrinthine maze through the high-end (and high-profit) makeup, jewelry and perfume areas in order to reach the bargains, a reality credited to Harry Selfridge, a Chicago retailer who established the famous Selfridge's in London in 1909. Selfridge is often credited with promoting the idea that shopping could be more than just a necessity, but a pleasure as well, although it's hard to believe humans hadn't already discovered this without help several millennia earlier.

SHOPITORIUM

The modern big-box store.

Walmart. Costco. The outlet mall. The shopitorium is a relatively new phenomenon. Dull, inward-looking garages, with no windows to distract or remind you that another pleasant summer afternoon is slipping away. Like casinos, once they have you, they want to keep you. With only one entrance and one exit, they are designed for acquisition, lit for maximum consumption, surrounded by an ocean of parking and spread across an expansive sea of asphalt.

Shopitoriums didn't set out to be ugly, nor in the beginning were they even strictly business. Like the architectural wonders in Europe, the early North American department stores were bright, airy landmarks lined with plenty of windows, design flourishes (see shopararium) and panache. Macy's, Marshall Field's, Eaton's and even discount stores such as Woolworth's took their street presence seriously, and they had to—shoppers had to be enticed inside. Their transition to the monolithic boxes of modern times coincided with the move to the suburbs.

When smooth-talking Austrian-born architect Victor Gruen built the first enclosed US shopping mall in Edina, Minnesota, in 1956, Southdale Center was meant to herald a new era of not just retailing, but modern living, where people would abandon their cars and stroll amid the plant jungles, sit and enjoy the indoor fountains, and eat at "open air" restaurants under towering glass roofs (see shopararriums). They were meant to mingle as one would on Main Street. Gruen's vision of a socially vibrant gathering space was never fully realized, perhaps because visitors were not as interested in mingling socially as they were in shopping for bargains. From a commercial standpoint, however, the mall was a raging success. Hundreds like it were built across the continent, grandiose monuments to the glory of retailing. Many attempted to be more elaborate than their predecessors, adding higher glass ceilings and better attractions such as merry-go-rounds, but from the sprawling parking lots that surrounded them, each one looked the same: a concrete bunker closed off to the outside world with a tiny door at the front to get in and get out. There was no way to look inside. Even those built to "revitalize" downtown cores in the 1970s paid little if any heed to their surroundings. The whole idea was to look inward. Few malls could ever be described as architecturally pleasing.

Several decades later, the mall had become, as Gruen later sadly reflected, little more than "a giant shopping machine." But the twisted economics and friendly tax incentives of mall-building meant they couldn't be stopped. These places were multiplying across the planet, swallowing communities whole and steamrolling over traditional downtown shops, making easy millions for their developers if not necessarily their retailers. Even in communities where the population was sliding or stagnant, developers were building not just one mall, but multiple malls the population couldn't hope to support. Later in life, Gruen, who built as many as fifty malls across North America, expressed extreme disappointment about the North American mall in general—"I refuse to pay alimony for those bastard developments"— and spent his remaining years working to create pedestrian-friendly downtown environments.

As the new century dawned, economics finally caught up with many of the enclosed shopping malls in North America. The original developers had long ago cashed out, and they started closing by the hundreds, shoved aside by changes in society, improvements in technology and the introduction of the car-centric outlet malls that Gruen had tried to eradicate in his early years. The strolling, the mingling, the meeting, the relaxing? It was always secondary to the acquisition of goods, and now even more so—the true shopitorium was born. The big-box store has no fountains, no plant jungles and certainly no windows.

There are few places to sit, relax or mingle. If you want to escape shopping for a moment, you need to head to the in-store fast-food joint or the cafeteria. People are there mostly to get stuff and get out.

And all those malls, built one after another to great fanfare over the latter part of the twentieth century? Experts say many, perhaps most, are doomed, leaving the modern phenomenon of so-called "ghost malls" in their wake. Even in a throw-away society, it's an untimely death.

SHOPARARIUM

A glassed-in shopping area.

Windows were not exactly the defining feature of the early North American shopping mall. When they were conceived, some had a few skylights and a glass door or two. But many in the 1950s, as now, were happy to have shoppers bathe in fluorescent light and focus on the merchandise. By the end of the twentieth century, in part to push back against their reputations as shopitoriums, an increasing number of malls rebranded themselves "gallerias" to imply glass palaces, even if they delivered only a few errant rays through a skylight. To shed their growing reputations as shopitoriums, and to bring natural light into the drab premises, some modern malls have built edifices of glass in an attempt to recreate the original glass palaces of the early days of department stores. It is as if they have come full circle.

London's Crystal Palace, built for the Great Exhibition in 1851 as an enormous glass showcase for consumer goods from around the world, was nothing if not a shopararium, but the fragile structure didn't last. Nevertheless, the world's original department stores were architectural wonders, with plenty of windows that announced "welcome" to those on the street. Indeed, the early department stores of the nineteenth century were often lavish monuments to art and architecture of the era. Art nouveau and art deco in Paris, beaux arts classicism and Edwardian baroque in Britain and America, innovative ultra-modern design in Germany. Across Europe and America they were fun, airy, beautiful structures, trumpeted as downtown landmarks, written up in magazines and visited by tourists far and wide. Among the oldest, Paris's Le Bon Marché was ahead of its time with skylighted interior courts designed by, among others, Gustave Eiffel of Eiffel Tower fame, and remains an architectural prize and commercial success to this day. On the inside, Le Bon Marché, and many other department stores like it, mixed art and sculpture, reading rooms and children's play areas among the merchandise. On the outside, they were grandiose reminders of the role of art and architecture in adding texture, character and significance to a modern city.

That was just as important in America, perhaps even more so. In 1887, Henry Hobson Richardson designed the seven-storey landmark that was Marshall Field's Wholesale Store in Chicago. Only five years later, and not so far away, legendary architect Daniel Burnham was commissioned to build the company's famous retail store at State and Washington streets. Burnham, known for designing much of the 1893 Chicago World's Fair, also helped with the initial design for Selfridge's magnificent and classical beaux arts palace fronted by a wall of plate glass in Oxford Street, London. The idea was to make shopping fun and exciting, and the store a cultural landmark, a place to be—a gleaming, sparkling, shimmering shopararium.

Selfridge's stores in Britain are still known for their architecture— and for being not just buildings to house merchandise, but also tourist destinations to delight and amuse shoppers. Despite the darkness of the decade before the Second World War, the Peter Jones department store, a modern triumph celebrated for its bright, airy interior, opened in London's Sloane Square in 1935. In those days, a department store, inside and out, was an architectural wonder to behold. Somewhere along the line, about the time of the suburban mall, the shopararium evolved into a shopitorium. In recent years, some have attempted to help the department store recapture the architectural brightness of an earlier age, but many retailers, including the mighty Walmart and Costco, resist any such sentiments.

There is hope for a return to the excitement of the old days, of course, but mall malaise, at least across North America, is making revitalization a challenge. Such was the excitement around a project in New Jersey called American Dream that the developer said the term "mall" didn't do it justice. Just over the bridge from Manhattan, it is meant to be bigger, better and more exciting than the gargantuan Mall of America in Minnesota and the West Edmonton Mall in Alberta, with amusements such as a DreamWorks water park, an Angry Birds mini golf, a Legoland and an indoor ski slope mixed amongst the shops. Its March 2020 opening was postponed amid the coronavirus pandemic, and a skyrocketing number of loyal mall shoppers are turning instead to teleshopping and cybershopping.

ANTI-SHOPPER

A person who is against shopping.

Contrary to all appearances, there are some anti-shoppers, and there always have been. It is likely such party-poopers emerged the day an early human first picked up a shiny rock of no obvious use. Lugging around such material and slowing down a hunting party tasked with finding food might not have gone over well with those focused on basic survival. And then there are modern anti-shoppers who are fed up with the consumerism (see shopophobia and shopititis). Plato was not likely the first to commit such thoughts to paper (or papyrus), but in 375 BCE or thereabouts, he wrote *The Republic*, his best-known work, in which he opined presciently that the luxurious state would lead to injustices: "For I suspect that many will not be satisfied with the simpler way of life. They will be for adding sofas, and tables, and other furniture; also dainties, and perfumes, and incense, and courtesans, and cakes, all these not of one sort only, but in every variety; we must go beyond the necessaries of which I was at first speaking, such as houses, and clothes, and shoes: the arts of the painter and the embroiderer will have to be set in motion, and gold and ivory and all sorts of materials must be procured."

Jesus of Nazareth took up the mantle several centuries later; the Bible is full of anti-consumerist preaching: "Take care, and be on your guard against all covetousness, for one's life does not consist in the abundance of his possessions" (Luke, 12:15). Indeed, could it be argued that his anti-shopping tendencies led directly to his arrest, when, according to Matthew (21:12–13), "Jesus went into the temple of God, and cast out all them that sold and bought in the temple, and overthrew the tables of the money changers, and the seats of them that sold doves, and said unto them, It is written, My house shall be called the house of prayer; but ye have made it a den of thieves"? His official crime may have been sedition or treason for being called "the King of the Jews," but it was causing a disturbance—and upsetting those who wanted to buy stuff—that was the beginning of the famous end.

Hispano-Roman Stoic philosopher Lucius Annaeus Seneca said, "You ask what is the proper limit to a person's wealth? First, having what is essential, and second, having what is enough." Greek Stoic philosopher Epictetus is famous for this: "Curb your desire. Don't set your heart on so many things and you will get what you need."

A thousand years later, Italian philosopher Thomas Aquinas reminded the few who would listen: "If the citizens themselves devote their life to matters of trade, the way will be opened to many vices. Since the foremost tendency of tradesmen is to make money, greed is awakened in the hearts of the citizens through the pursuit of trade. The result is that everything in the city will become venal; good faith will be destroyed, and the way opened to all kinds of trickery; each one will work only for his own profit, despising the public good; the cultivation of virtue will fail since honor, virtue's reward, will be bestowed upon the rich. Thus, in such a city, civic life will necessarily be corrupted."

Saint Francis of Assisi, who loved nature, shunned material possessions and promoted the simple life, might be appalled today to see modern tourists from around the world flock to his hometown in Italy to buy little Saint Francis statuettes, mugs shaped like friars and religious souvenirs in the stores that line the streets.

Finally, there is the committed minimalist Henry David Thoreau, author of *Walden*, who wrote famously in 1854 that "my greatest skill has been to want but little."

Genuine anti-shoppers have been joined by legions of hypocrites over the centuries: philosophers and popes, authors and environmentalists, "impoverished" spouses and family members, many neglecting to actually practise what they preach. But it is politicians, with perhaps less noble intent, who have turned cheap talk into creative action over several millennia, with a variety of infamous anti-shopping or so-called sumptuary laws. Ancient Greece forbade some women from wearing gold in the seventh century BCE. In ancient Rome, men were forbidden from wearing silk. In Renaissance Italy, in sixteenth century Europe, in Colonial America and beyond, attempts were made, often successfully if temporarily, to prevent some people, usually common people, from shopping for stuff that until then only rich people could afford.

In his all-encompassing book *Empire of Things*, author Frank Trentmann discusses the hundreds of anti-shopping ordinances passed in German-speaking central Europe between 1244 and 1816: "The laws' fixation on clothing is simple to explain. These were the most visible markers of one's place in the social order, denoting status, rank, age and gender . . . most European sumptuary laws were instruments of inequality, seeking to preserve a finely graded hierarchy." It wasn't enough to be able to afford an item of clothing; you had to be the right class and profession also.

Revolutionary Chinese leader and famous anti-shopper Mao Zedong banned ownership of gold (among other things) in the 1950s, and the shiny metal remained off limits until the turn of the century. Today, the Chinese are the world's biggest hoarders of the stuff. Kings, emperors, popes and politicians have all taken a stab at deciding what others can buy, railing against excess and the social ills that come from shopping for things that they themselves have already shopped for with impunity and stockpiled in excess.

Economist, philosopher and author Adam Smith explained it in *The Wealth of Nations*: "It is the highest impertinence and presumption, therefore, in kings and ministers, to pretend to watch over the economy of private people, and to restrain their expense, either by sumptuary laws, or by prohibiting the importation of foreign luxuries. They are themselves always, and without any exception, the greatest spendthrifts in the society. Let them look well after their own expense, and they may safely trust private people with theirs. If their own

extravagance does not ruin the state, that of their subjects never will."
Despite the exploding consumerism of the late twentieth and early-
twenty-first centuries, anti-shopping movements persist. Yet given
human nature, it's likely that current practises will continue—until
they can no longer continue.

PSEUDOSHOP

To shop without buying.

The pseudoshopper likes to look but not buy: window shoppers, browsers, mall wanderers. They look, they touch, they examine, they consider, they hem and they haw. And they walk away. They figure they simply can't afford all that stuff, or it won't fit in their houses. But they enjoy looking. Merchants hate them. Shouldn't they be out in the mall sitting on a bench, waiting for their spouses?

Some pseudoshoppers test-drive cars for mere entertainment. "It's really easy," says one Reddit user. If you like driving exotic cars for fifteen minutes at a time and pretending you're a player, "dress well but informally," he advises. "Learn about the car you want to drive. ACT LIKE YOU BELONG." And: "Don't crash."

More common perhaps are wannabe house hunters and upshopping homeowners. Once, this meant spending weekend afternoons touring realtor open houses in the neighbourhood, pretending to be shopping but really just snooping. Today, it means surfing real estate sites for hours on end, perusing overpriced homes, audibly lamenting renovation disasters and forlorn decorating mistakes, with no intention of ever setting foot in the place.

SHOPAPALOOZA

Shopping at an ostensible cultural event, or because of one.

From time to time, you may find yourself in a museum shop. Or a store at Disney World. Perhaps perusing T-shirts at the AC/DC concert. Or hockey jerseys at the game. The Lassie lunch box. Scooby-Doo pyjamas. Van Gogh neckties at the gallery store. The mug from Niagara Falls. The ball cap emblazed with the name of the Shakespeare play you just sat through. Various estimates on the actual value are unreliable, but it's safe to say merchandise associated with the *Star Wars* movie franchise has generated tens of billions in retail sales. Billions too can be attributed to *Toy Story*–related material, *Winnie the Pooh* paraphernalia, *Peanuts* knick-knacks and *Star Trek* stuff. *Thomas the Tank Engine*, *Angry Birds*, James Bond all sell stuff. J.K. Rowling's Harry Potter generated billions in book sales, a stunning feat in a modern era, but even more at the box office, and more still in merchandizing. Marty Brochstein, senior VP of industry relations and information for the Licensing Industry Merchandisers' Association, explained the desire: "People want to own a piece of what they just saw."

The 1970s rock band KISS got into the merchandizing act early and often with action figures, board games, pocket knives, wine and a KISS casket (see necroshop). The merch table at rock concerts is a regular stop for fans. The online store for country music superstar and former drug addict Keith Urban, for example, sells T-shirts, knapsacks, key chains, PopSockets, baseball caps, water bottles, tote bags, enamel pins, guitar picks, gift cards, and yes, music—all branded appropriately for Keith Urban fans. Not so long ago, you could have purchased a Michelle Obama bobblehead doll at the White House gift shop, along with Barack Obama's autobiography. At the George W. Bush

Presidential Center, you can get a President Bush Camp David Bomber Jacket or a Barbara Bush three-row pearl necklace.

Ever since Mickey Mouse first appeared on a writing tablet in 1929, and on a lunch box a few years later, it has been obvious to merchandizers that people will buy stuff they recognize, no matter how bad the reproduction, how poor the quality of the item or how dumb the design, to remind themselves and others of their television viewing habits, their attendance at a concert or their recent exotic vacation— or just to impress people with the illusion that they are "cultured."

Today, the museum store is a highlight for visitors. But it is more than that. It is the final exhibit, explains writer Karen Chernick, the place that elevates mass-produced curios to objects of cultural significance. It is where museum staff put cool stuff you can't find in other stores and certify it as worthy of purchase or simply an intelligent choice.

Even those who don't attend an event often want a piece of it— how else to explain the brisk business in sports and entertainment memorabilia? In 2021, for example, rich overshoppers paid $5.2 million for a LeBron James basketball card and $308,000 for the "Wilson" volleyball from the Tom Hanks movie *Cast Away*. The online shops are full of used jerseys, baseball bats, boxing gloves and hockey sticks, all selling a piece of nostalgia. Sometimes, such investments pay off handsomely. Other times, not so much. In 1998, Canadian comic book artist Todd McFarlane spent $3 million on the baseball that was Mark McGwire's seventieth home run. Today, the ball may not be worth even $500,000 (see misshop).

SHOPTOMETRY

*Measuring what we buy, when we buy
it, where we buy it—and how.*

If merchandisers and manufacturers are going to sell us ever more stuff, they need to know more about how we shop. A long time ago, this meant reviewing receipts and examining remaining inventory at the end of the day to help shopkeepers know what to make or order more of. Then it became more sophisticated: managers watched how people interacted with merchandise, moved around the store and lingered over certain shelves while ignoring others. Then it became a science, with sophisticated organizations lurking around corners, sometimes spying on us, sometimes interviewing us, always with the same things in mind: How do we get these folks to buy more? How do we determine what will be hot?

Shoppers may not understand how they shop, but experts do. Among the most famous is Paco Underhill, an environmental psychologist from New York whose popular books include *Why We Buy* and *Call of the Mall.* His teams have loitered around stores and malls for decades, watching and learning, tracking shoppers' behaviour, interviewing them and assessing processes, then telling retailers how to act accordingly. Underhill will tell you what now seems obvious: the best way to get people to buy more is to keep them in the store longer. "If we went into the stores only when we needed to buy something, and if once there we bought only what we needed, the economy would collapse, boom."

So shoptometrists such as Underhill tell merchandisers the world over how to design stores, which aisles to make wider and which to make narrower, where to put merchandise and how exactly to display it, how to draw in customers and how to keep them exploring every nook and cranny of the place. Why do we turn right upon entering a grocery store, as most of us do, rather than left? Why do we move away from one table of clothing but linger at another, even if the selection of goods is identical? Why do some people look but not buy? How do we react to different attendants? After they've watched long enough, they stop spying and interview us, putting the whole thing on camera for dissection later. Needless to say, retailers spend lots of time and money understanding such behaviour, and when they do, leveraging it so that we'll buy more stuff.

So-called rewards cards, points cards or loyalty cards may or may not deliver bona fide discounts to consumers, but they do provide retailers—pharmacies, department stores, airlines, movie theatres—with enormous amounts of consumer information that shoptometrists use to better market and advertise goods and services. That raises the ire of privacy advocates who wonder exactly what the information is being used for. The business of shoptometry unleashes apocalyptic visions of a world where shoptometrists control our lives in ways we can't even imagine, but this state of affairs existed long before the invention of the internet. Indeed, people may not like the fact that shoptometrists want personal information, but when faced with a choice between keeping their personal information private or acquiring stuff and getting a bargain, shoppers inevitably choose the latter. We rail on about privacy, but we keep buying.

As retailers make it even easier for us to shop, they make it easier for themselves to gather information. In 2022, Amazon introduced what it calls Just Walk Out technology to some Whole Foods stores. It allows customers to scan their palms, link them to their Amazon account and fill their baskets to their heart's content—all under the watchful electronic eyes in the ceiling. No need for a checkout line; Amazon technology knows what you bought and will bill you later.

Online shoppers have long left a digital footprint in their wake. The internet opened up a rich vein of information for advertisers, and they've been mining it since people were using dial-up. That's why clumsy ads follow us around the internet, often trying to sell us more of the item we've just bought, even as more sophisticated advertising methods permeate cyberspace. That's why media companies, for example, are information companies, gathering data about the people who visit and selling it to advertisers.

Shoptometrists use algorithms to understand our shopping desires, dislikes and tolerances. Laura Antonini, policy director at the Consumer Education Foundation in California, reminds us that if we are shopping online, someone is watching. She raised the alarm with colleague Harvey Rosenfield, president of the foundation, in a report in June 2019 to the US Federal Trade Commission. "A shadowy group of privacy-busting firms" are compiling "secret surveillance scores" to enable them to "charge some people higher prices for the same product than others, to provide some people with better customer service than others, to deny some consumers the right to purchase services or buy or return products while allowing others to do so."

Your shopping history is translated into a number by an algorithm and "transmitted to corporate clients looking for ways to take advantage of, or even avoid, the consumer." The modern shoptometrist is an algorithm, deciding, for example, what caller gets answered sooner, regardless of how long they've been waiting in an electronic queue. The report names Home Depot, Walmart and Expedia among the companies that use secret surveillance scores to charge different prices. Much of it is done in the name of fraud detection and prevention, but the big question is what other information is being collected during the process, and why? As Antonini says, "it's creepy."

SHOPOLOGY

The study of shopping. Why we shop.

The innate human desire to collect stuff is rare among the planet's eight-and-a-half million species. Humans are almost alone in their desire for material not directly related to their survival. Most of God's creatures stockpile only things they need—food, nesting material— and leave the useless stuff where it lies. Even the few creatures that use tools do not harbour or worship them. The vast majority of animals do not require any possessions to enrich their lives, signal social status or attract a mate.

A few do have an eye for decoration. Pack rats, also known as woodrats, are collectors with a particular fondness for shiny objects, often those discarded by humans, which they use to adorn their nests. Perhaps, like humans, they appreciate "art." And they are shoppers of a sort, often abandoning something they're transporting home for something they encounter along the way that looks better, a familiar human trait (see deshop and reshop).

Some observers speculate that birds such as crows and magpies also like to collect shiny things, but there is no real evidence of that. The bowerbird of Australia and Papua New Guinea, however, is famous for using eye-catching objects to attract a mate. First, the male builds a bower—a structure whose sole purpose is to impress the opposite sex. It's not a nest; simply an architectural monument to himself that announces his manliness. Then, he sets out to decorate it with colourful objects—once fresh flowers, feathers or colourful leaves, and today often scraps of shiny human litter—in order to better dazzle a female, an activity most humans should recognize (see shop-o-erotic). Even with all the shiny stuff he has collected, the male bowerbird must still enact an elaborate and exhausting dance that shows off his physical prowess to close the deal.

Humans, too, collect all manner of shiny objects to impress a mate and, well, everyone else. But it is not only because, like Victoria Beckham, we "don't know how to resist it" or, like Bill Koch, we "just had to have them." Unlike any other animal, humans are capable of abstract thought—we can see beauty in *everything*. And therefore, despite what aristocratic curators, self-obsessed sculptors, egocentric painters, self-important dancers, pretentious performers and various other snotty artists may say, everything is art: a Monet, a Calder, a Basquiat. A Limoges dinner plate, a Porsche car, a Rolex watch, a Frank Lloyd Wright house. A rock, a piece of wood, a ripple of water.

When two people agree that something is beautiful, they immediately label it "art" and start collecting it, telling others they simply must get one too. Out of a need to belong, we follow suit, believing we become important not because of who we are or how we think or what we do, but because of our stuff. People are somehow impressed by possessions. Other animals understand social status, and many try to control territories, but accumulating items to bolster our presumed importance is uniquely human and demonstrates the ability to understand concepts and think beyond the physical. It may explain why we have been decorating our bodies with bones, shells, pebbles, ochre and other detritus for tens of thousands of years.

For millennia, humans have often gone without other more useful luxuries or even necessities to acquire and possess symbolic items. How long exactly is unclear, but there is evidence that Neanderthals had an eye for such impractical things as far back as 130,000 years ago—a site in Croatia indicates that Neanderthals collected, polished and assembled eagle talons, perhaps for jewelry. Another extinct human species, the Denisovans, might also have created jewelry fifty thousand years ago in Siberia. Beads found in caves at the southern tip of Africa, meanwhile, indicate jewelry-making by humans seventy-five thousand years ago. And there is some suggestion that even *Homo erectus* may have produced jewelry as early as 500,000 years ago, as indicated by an engraved shell on the island of Java. Amid hunting, gathering and barely surviving, these early humans collected shiny rocks with no clear purpose beyond the aesthetic or symbolic—and probably status—and may even have buried their dead with them. While there is no evidence this diversion from acquiring the necessities of life led to the extinction of Neanderthals or Denisovans, it may not have been the best use of their energy way back then, when life was tough, malnutrition rampant and even the survival of their species was in question.

Homo sapiens, too, have been intrigued by such matter since their earliest days in Europe, and likely earlier. During the Upper Paleolithic era, about forty thousand years ago (and perhaps longer), humans made art from stones and shells and collected shiny rocks. Like the Neanderthals, our appreciation of art would have been a factor, as was social status. It's likely, too, that religion played a role. The famous Venus of Willendorf, a feminine figurine carved from limestone and found in Austria in 1908, is estimated to have been made about thirty thousand years ago. Germany's Löwenmensch or lion-man figurine may be thirty-five thousand or forty thousand years old. Some of these things were quite possibly important religious icons, revered and shared by a community. But nomadic life could not have lent itself easily to the accumulation of this stuff. After all, one could haul around only so much detritus, and rocks are heavy. In the end, like all stuff, they were abandoned by their owners.

As soon as humans gave up hunting and gathering and instead began farming and building permanent communities about twelve thousand years ago, the collection of knick-knacks, already underway, gained considerable steam. Not only did we have extra time to make this stuff, we now had a permanent home in which to keep it reasonably safe, display it proudly and lord it over visitors. Of course, not all these items were completely useless. In addition to being attracted to things of no obvious practical value, humans have always been intent on improving themselves and their surroundings. We can't help ourselves. It's why we moved from caves to grass huts to brick houses. It's how we went from spears to bows to firearms, from chamber pots to toilets, from campfires to electric stoves. From the stone tablet to the abacus to the computer. Somewhere along the way it got out of hand. The family homestead, originally designed to shelter its inhabitants from the elements and protect them from hungry animals and trespassing human neighbours, began to serve increasingly as a storage facility for stuff and a monument to its owner's status, good taste and decorating skills. These structures began filling up with the silt of daily life. Successful farmers, meanwhile, realized that not only could they sell their excess crops, they now had the time to make stuff that others would buy, so they in turn could buy stuff others made, just like you and your neighbours at the street-wide garage sale (see deshopathon). Subsistence farming graduated rather quickly to all-out commercialization and spread rapidly as the development of land- and water-vehicles and pack animals made transport over distances easier. Civilization was born, the global economy had begun to simmer, and trade—shopping—spread rapidly across the planet.

The so-called cradles of civilization, from the Euphrates River to the Indus Valley and many places in between, are rife with evidence that people liked stuff, and lots of it, from the moment it became available. Humans have been shopping ever since. The less practical the item, the more loudly we display it. Top of the list has always been jewelry—mostly rocks, sometimes artfully but usually ostentatiously created and displayed—which may have impressed humans since our ancestors learned to talk. Second on the list are even less practical items that have no purpose other than to amuse us: knick-knacks. Keepsakes. Gewgaws, trinkets, tchotchkes. Baubles, bric-a-brac, curios, mementos, memorabilia. Souvenirs, sundries, doodads, doohickeys, bits and bobs, odds and ends. No wonder the English language has so many words for this stuff—there's a lot of it.

Like almost everyone else, I am not immune to the pull of such items. For decades, I have displayed just such an article on my desk. Acquired from a hotel I once lodged at in India, it was a sign at a checkout counter in Jaipur that said simply: Wait. It is one of those triangular things with a brass plaque you might find on the desk of a company vice-president or school superintendent in the 1960s, identifying them by name and title. This one presented me with information that was not only self-evident, as I had already waited thirty minutes to check out, but it delivered a message with which everyone in India, visitors and residents alike, was painfully familiar. Of the many obsessions in India, "waiting" was among the most common, so the sign seemed endlessly hilarious to me, and I decided I must have it:

"How much for this sign?" I asked the attendant when the waiting had stopped.

"No sir, it is not for sale."

"I'll give you 10 rupees," I said.

"No sir," she shook her head.

"Fifty rupees," I said, determined.

"No sir, you cannot have it."

"One hundred rupees," I insisted, offering the equivalent of $10, a small fortune to me at the time, and an even larger one to her.

She looked at me, then at the sign, and then glanced furtively both ways.

"Here," she said, handing it over. "Take it."

I doubt its absence affected customer service.

From time immemorial, people have gathered keepsakes. Tradable or shoppable "art" becomes more prominent in the archeological record twelve thousand years ago, when the world economy—what we call civilization—began to expand in earnest. And such items, then as now, inevitably became insufficiently impressive and needed to be replaced with something bigger, better, shinier, rarer or more numerous. With each passing decade, the rich got richer, and upshopping stepped up a notch. It became a cycle. You upshopped for one like the neighbours', so they upshopped a bigger and better one than you, and therefore you needed to upshop a bigger and better one than them, and so on. "It is because mankind are disposed to sympathize more entirely with our joy than with our sorrow, that we make a parade of our riches, and conceal our poverty," wrote economist Adam Smith more than two centuries ago.

Many marketers prey on this simple age-old human weakness, but as primatologist Frans de Waal has famously demonstrated, other animals may have similar desires. He videotaped an experiment, which is popular on YouTube: Two capuchin monkeys are perfectly happy performing a trick and being rewarded with a piece of cucumber. They do this happily and repeatedly until one of them gets a grape instead. When the other is given a cucumber as usual, it is tossed back with clear outrage. It's one of the more hilarious animal videos among the millions available, and a revealing experiment about what de Waal explains is one of the "pillars of morality": fairness. But could it also be possible that capuchin monkeys, dogs and other animals are upshoppers like the rest of us? If someone near you has something, you probably want one like it too: the latest phone, window covering, car, shoe, handbag, countertop appliance, golf club, boat . . .

You might think that after several millennia of unbridled consumption, the most intelligent species on Earth would get bored of shopping, of collecting, of signalling status with stuff. And perhaps there is hope. As the writer Douglas Coupland noted, "*Star Trek* characters never go shopping." But *Star Trek* is fiction. There is, after all, no single reason why we shop, though libraries and industry journals are full of learned studies on the subject.

We shop because we need something. Or we simply want it. We all need shelter, for example, but do we need something like the $1.3-billion palace allegedly built by murderous and despotic Russian President Vladimir Putin on the Black Sea? Or "The One," a 100,000-square-foot mansion in Los Angeles that sold in 2022 for $126 million, slightly less than the $500 million the developer was originally asking. Does the owner really need a thirty-car "auto gallery," five swimming pools, a twenty-four-seat theatre, forty-two bathrooms and a bowling alley?

We shop to stay busy; we shop because we are bored. Like watching television or snacking on popcorn, we do it automatically and without an agenda, not to amuse ourselves or feed ourselves but simply because it is there. We find ourselves in the malls, Main Streets, markets or online, shopping for the sake of shopping (see autoshop). In a 2020 headline during the coronavirus pandemic, *Bloomberg News* reported that "Bored Rich People Are Shopping Online For $500,000 Bracelets." People were buying jewels "as a sort of pick-me-up," the article reported, quoting Catharine Becket, a specialist at Sotheby's. "Clients are sequestering at home and, generally speaking, leading relatively dreary lives . . . they're wearing their big diamonds inside their homes because it brings joy."

We shop to stay socially relevant, to be involved in what everyone else seems to be involved in. In their book, *Gen BuY*, Kit Yarrow and Jayne O'Donnell explain that shopping helps connect people to others. Shopping makes them feel like they belong.

Our desire to acquire stuff is often motivated by what economist Harvey Leibenstein in 1950 called the "bandwagon effect" or "the extent to which the demand for a commodity is increased due to the fact that others are also consuming the same commodity. It represents the desire of people to purchase a commodity in order to get into 'the swim of things'; in order to conform with the people they wish to be associated with." If everyone has an iPhone, we want one too. If everyone is wearing designer jeans, we assume they won't mingle socially with us if we don't wear designer jeans too.

We also shop to impress ourselves and others. This is what Leibenstein called "the snob effect." Or "the extent to which the demand for a consumers' good is decreased owing to the fact that others are also consuming the same commodity (or that others are increasing their consumption of that commodity). This represents the desire of people to be exclusive; to be different; to dissociate themselves from 'the common herd.'" In other words, if the gang seems to have migrated to drinking Grey Goose vodka or Patrón tequila, the snob will move on to an obscure but expensive gin. The snob will eschew $400 designer jeans for $500 ripped and faded jeans, until everyone else is wearing ripped and faded jeans, at which point they will refuse to wear such leg coverings and go back to wearing plain old Levi's, as long as they are far more expensive than the plain old Levi's you might find at Walmart—and certainly more expensive than ripped and faded designer jeans. Leibenstein differentiates his snob effect ("a function of the consumption of others") from the so-called Veblen effect ("a function of price"). The Veblen effect explains that rich shoppers don't mind the high price of goods as long as others know it, since that happens to be the point.

We shop because we are deluged by the cacophony from shopostles, shopacademies, shopocrats and shopaganda telling us to shop every moment of every day. We can't stop shopping because we're brainwashed to do it. "Own it now"; "The only brand you'll ever need"; "Because you're worth it"; "It's finger lickin' good"; "Don't leave home without it"; "The ultimate driving machine"; "Does she or doesn't she?"; "Good to the last drop"; "Think different"; "Takes a licking and keeps on ticking"; "Just do it." Not only are we deluged by perpetual messages to consume, we are also surrounded by the consumables: in stores everywhere and at the touch of a button or two at home. Contrary to some opinions, we live in a world that is not necessarily governed by demand, but by supply. Remember Say's law, which holds that production is itself the source of demand, or as economist John Maynard Keynes later observed: "Supply creates its own demand." In other words, people like stuff: the more that exists, the more they'll buy.

We shop to improve ourselves. Innovating and wanting better things is the essence of being human. Getting better stuff, no matter how useful or useless, also helps us transform into the people we think we are or would like to be. That shirt, that handbag, that car, that watch—it's part of the disguise, part of the equipment that helps us believe—and others believe—we are more than we think we appear. Such things liberate us. They help lift our spirits, make us feel better; they make us seem—at least to ourselves—like more alluring, more attractive, more interesting human beings. They demonstrate to others that we are cool, chic, smart, woke, artsy, funky, bohemian, rich, erudite, liberal, conservative, progressive, alternative . . .

We shop because we are defined, remembered and perhaps immortalized by our stuff. Death is the only certainty in life, but our stuff? Well, some of it may live on for generations. Our stuff can tell our stories after we're gone, as author Karen von Hahn explains in her hilariously tragic and eloquent book, *What Remains: Object Lessons in Love and Loss*: "Each thing has a story. And the story is ultimately about us. Hence the 'back story' of every brand and label eager to form a bond with its target market with all the intimacy and loyalty of a true friendship; the dedication of the collector to both the expansion of their personal assemblage and the art of its display; and the enduring power and significance of the souvenir."

Bestselling author Yuval Noah Harari says modern consumerism is linked to "the imagined order" that allows humanity to co-operate. We believe some stuff, no matter how obviously useless, is of value because others believe it is of value. Without such myths and the co-operation it renders, Harari writes in his book *Sapiens*, organization would be difficult and nothing would get done. "Like the elite of ancient Egypt, most people in most cultures dedicate their lives to building pyramids. Only the names, shapes and sizes of these pyramids change from one culture to the other. They may take the form, for example, of a suburban cottage with a swimming pool and an evergreen lawn, or a gleaming penthouse with an enviable view. Few question the myths that cause us to desire the pyramid in the first place."

We shop because we are happy and we shop because we are sad. We shop because we have too much money or not enough. We shop to give our lives purpose. We shop for recognition. As a species, it may be our defining characteristic, but as individuals it doesn't necessarily improve our lives. Indeed, while it is obvious to many that shopping and acquisition make life better and more fun, some studies and more than one adage have concluded shopping does not make us happy. Much has been written about people who shop not to acquire stuff but to assuage anxiety, boredom, heartache, illness or imminent death. In his book *Affluenza*, Oliver James describes what he calls the virus: Shopping fills a void left by a lack of human interaction, he writes. The more we shop, the more unhappy we become; the more unhappy we become, the more we shop.

Two good examples were provided at the outset of the Great Depression, when the world was introduced to Barbara Hutton, heir to the Woolworth fortune, for whom the term "poor little rich girl" was originally coined, and her lifelong rival, Doris Duke, heir to a tobacco fortune, often described as the "world's richest girl." The two future socialites were born within weeks of each other and came of age during the 1930s, inheriting huge sums at a time when most of their compatriots could barely feed themselves.

Duke, the owner of expansive homes in New Jersey, Rhode Island, Hawaii and California, plus two apartments in Manhattan, owned her own Boeing 737 and collected thousand-dollar bottles of wine, expensive art and a staggering array of jewels. She gave her second husband several sports cars, a bevy of polo ponies, a luxuriously refitted B-25 bomber and a coffee plantation during their brief marriage, plus a house in Paris upon their divorce. Once suicidal, in later years she became a reclusive drug and alcohol addict.

Hutton, whose father made a fortune by collecting nickels and dimes at Woolworth's, was even more imprudent. The free-spending overshopper married seven times, shedding part of her fortune during each liaison, buying homes in exotic locations around the world and spending constantly on the usual array of yachts and jewelry. One oft-told story has it that drug-abusing kinky voyeur and actor Errol Flynn, upon seeing a chandelier while visiting Duke's home, joked: "Doris, what are you doing with one of Barbara's earrings?"

The two women had been friendly in their teenage years, but refused to speak to each other for much of their adult lives, a standoff gleefully documented by the era's gossip columnists. And both were miserable and alone in later years. Hutton, too, was addicted to drugs and alcohol, and died while living in a Beverly Hills hotel, on the verge of bankruptcy. When Duke died, estranged from close friends and lacking family, she left most of her wealth to charity and a nephew, Walker Inman II, a gun-loving drug addict who liked to blow things up, and whose horrendously abused and traumatized children would eventually inherit the fortune.

In his book *Vanderbilt*, which details the history of his mother's famously rich family, CNN anchor Anderson Cooper notes it is a story of "the greatest American fortune ever squandered." Most family members, he writes, "churned through their fortune not in the cause of making lasting change, but on massive outlets for conspicuous consumption. Vanderbilt millions bought palatial houses, astonishing yachts, cars in the hundreds, and jewels both magnificent and rare." Ultimately, he reflects, *Vanderbilt* is an account of how "a family story about wealth and triumph becomes, in some respects, a story about sadness and isolation."

There is an enduring interest in the role money plays in our happiness, and experts in psychology and economics continue to debate it. An oft-discussed study done in the late 1970s asked lottery winners and catastrophic accident victims about their relative happiness. The conclusion? The lottery winners were no happier a year after their big win, but those rendered paraplegic and quadriplegic were not as unhappy as we might expect a year after the accident. Predictably, other studies—and the first-hand experiences of many—draw a direct connection between money and happiness.

Regardless of the studies, it's fair to say that while money may not buy happiness, it often helps. As the saying goes, "I'd rather be rich and unhappy than poor and unhappy." Indeed, if you are rich and unhappy, at least you can go shopping. The use of shopping as a balm for depression has been well recognized for centuries, and nowhere is it more acute than in the quest for clothes. "The lust for clothes is a brilliant defence mechanism (particularly if you are a person of means)," says personal shopper Betty Halbreich. "The displacement of love, affection and attention onto a pair of shoes or a dress has built an entire industry."

But everyone, rich and poor, knows shopping can make you happy only temporarily. Does being happy mean being content? A new pair of shoes, a new suit, a new car or a new kitchen appliance can cheer us up, but for how long? Not long at all, say scientists who study dopamine, a neural transmitter in our brain connected to pleasure. Dopamine, it turns out, is released in anticipation of pleasure, not as a result of the reward itself. By the time we receive a treat—ice cream, sex, a shopped item—the pleasure has already dissipated. So the *idea* of shopping is the fun part, not the acquisition itself, and getting stuff is probably not the best formula for happiness, especially if stuff weighs you down. Many insist that happiness is achieved through relationships, accomplishments, exploration or charitable works. And as fashion designer Christian Dior reminded us, no amount of beautiful things (jewels, clothing, ornaments) will make you beautiful if you are not happy: "Happiness is the secret to all beauty."

The ancient Greek philosopher Epicurus believed true happiness could only be realized through modesty and simplicity—by eliminating pain and fear from one's life. Some mistakenly believe Epicureans are focused on sensual pleasures—good food or drink—and often confuse it with hedonism. Epicureans do indeed seek only pleasure, but it is not the fleeting pleasures such as sex, drugs and shopping that hedonists desire. Epicureans do not pursue pleasure in a modern sense, but pleasure defined by the absence of pain and fear, a state of grace that can only be achieved through modest living. Everyone who has owned a vehicle—bicycle, car, boat or plane—or any number of other complicated items, including a house, a computer or a smartphone, knows that with all that fun comes a considerable amount of frustration and responsibility: the house needs repair and renovation, the car rusts, the boat leaks, the plane requires constant maintenance, the computer needs an upgrade and the ongoing costs and headaches never end. As Thoreau wrote in *Walden*, "the cost of a thing is the amount of what I will call life which is required to be exchanged for it, immediately or in the long run." Hillel the Elder, a Jewish religious leader in the first century BCE, summed it up more concisely: "With more property comes more anxiety."

In his splendid 1926 essay, "My Wood," the writer E.M. Forster contemplated the burden that property ownership placed on him: "In the first place, it makes me feel heavy. Property does have this effect," Forster wrote. "In the second place, it makes me feel it ought to be larger." Hoarders and collectors (and any of us really) may recognize these sentiments: one may be too much; but some is never enough.

And as any good shopper knows, one shopped item usually leads to another, as described more than a century ago by the French philosopher Denis Diderot. Once you buy a stainless-steel fridge, for example, you inevitably want a stainless-steel stove and dishwasher to match. Once you renovate the kitchen, the dining room immediately looks shabby and needs refinishing. Once the porch has been rebuilt, the front yard needs re-landscaping, and really, that driveway pavement should be removed and replaced by interlocking brick. Consumer experts call this never-ending cycle of consumerism the Diderot Effect.

Ultimately, the infinite quest for more can end only one way, as Leo Tolstoy demonstrated in his celebrated 1886 short story "How Much Land Does a Man Need?" His greedy protagonist Pahom, who wants more and more land to create more and more wealth, never truly learns the answer before he keels over and dies of exhaustion and avarice. But readers do: just enough for a shallow grave. Wrote Tolstoy: "Six feet from his head to his heels was all he needed."

NECROSHOP

To shop in preparation for, or as a result of, a death.

Some of us prefer to ignore the inevitable. We'd just as soon leave such unpleasantness to survivors, and we don't really care if they toss us out with the trash or cram what's left of us into a cardboard box and burn us in a crematorium or on a discreet pyre. But many insist on planning years ahead of time, necroshopping for a nice gravesite near the dell or the church, a carved granite tombstone and a ridiculously expensive, polished-wood coffin with brass handles, years in advance of any indication that we're on our way to a better place. Or they leave detailed and expensive instructions regarding their disposal to survivors so that, even in death, they can regale friends, relatives and strangers with their greatness. Relatives and friends are even bigger necroshoppers, fond of burying loved ones in needlessly brand-new suits, placing perfectly good bottles of whiskey with the dearly departed, or including in the coffin a favourite keepsake, a wristwatch say, a musical instrument perhaps, or some other useful item that will not see the light of day for several centuries.

Others are somewhat more elaborate in their planning, necroshopping for family crypts and vaults so everyone can be dead together, with many of them still clinging to their most prized possessions in the growing number of environmentally suspect graveyards across the world. The cost to dispose of "King of Pop" peculiarity Michael Jackson included $35,000 spent on clothes for the body, and more than half a million dollars for his crypt at Forest Lawn's Great Mausoleum in Los Angeles, where famous dead neighbours include the original blonde bombshell Jean Harlow and Hollywood machoman Clark Gable. Jazz great and drug-abusing wife-beater Miles Davis was buried with at least one of his horns; unlucky fabulist Wild Bill Hickok was buried with his rifle; ganja-smoking reggae pioneer Bob Marley was buried with his Gibson Les Paul guitar, along with some marijuana. Frank Sinatra was buried with a bottle of Jack Daniel's whiskey and a dollar's worth of dimes, in case he needed to make a phone call from beyond the grave.

It is all an improvement (or a letdown, depending on your point of view) over some of the excessive necroshopping of the past. In our very earliest days as a species, of course, humans simply walked away and left family and friends to rot when they fell, where they were promptly disposed of without fuss or environmental cost by local wildlife and the elements, perhaps feeding a pack of hungry wolves and doing something useful in death. But it wasn't long—as early as 100,000 years ago—before we decided these folks had to be buried, and, sometime thereafter, that they had to be buried with various keepsakes, a practice that has pretty much continued, to greater and lesser extents, ever since.

The earliest evidence of excessive necroshopping can be found at the Varna Necropolis in modern-day Bulgaria. Discovered in the early 1970s and known as the oldest gold treasure in the world, it goes back 6,500 years, predating the pyramids by more than four millennia. A few of the graves at Varna were chock full of gold, copper, masks, pottery, beads, bracelets, earrings and other mostly useless trinkets in life, let alone death. One clearly important community member was buried with several pounds of gold, including a gold penis sheath, while other graves hold only a few beads and knick-knacks. Varna is proof, some scholars say, that the stratification of society began early in civilization, and an upper class—an ancient 1 per cent—recognized by their possession of useless stuff, existed even 6,500 years ago.

The most prominent necroshopper of all time may well be the Egyptian pharaoh Khufu, the builder of the Great Pyramid at Giza, a tomb that took him twenty years to erect. It remained the world's tallest structure for 4,500 years thereafter. Egyptian tombs were once constructed by the dozens across the land, often stuffed to the stone rafters with all manner of ostensible riches—bejeweled statues, gold coffins, face masks, thrones—along with other material that might be somewhat more practical, like underwear and bedclothes, if only these people weren't dead. Most of it was looted by successive generations of people who wanted stuff but were unwilling or unable to pay for it (see contrashop). A temporary exception was King Tutankhamun's tomb, which stood untouched for almost three thousand years before it was discovered in 1922 and found to contain more than five thousand items, all of which were officially removed after Egyptians decided three millennia was time enough for the late boy king to enjoy them in the afterlife.

A thousand years after the reign of King Tut, Emperor Qin built what is now known as the Terracotta Army in 246 BCE, an over-the-top example of funerary art buried in what is today Shaanxi province in China and not discovered until the 1970s. The entire site takes up as much as ninety-eight square kilometres, almost twice the size of Manhattan. The idea, presumably, was that this army, an estimated eight thousand life-sized, carefully constructed and expensively decorated soldiers, and their attendant chariots, horses, weapons and other detritus, would serve and protect the emperor in the afterlife, or perhaps just remind the gods how important he was. Definitely an impressive bit of necroshopping.

Construction of India's Taj Mahal, meanwhile, began in 1643 by Shah Jahan after the death of his beloved wife Mumtaz Mahal, and was completed more than twenty years later. Today, the tomb, like so many others, is a World Heritage Site, popular tourist destination and reputed modern "wonder of the world." It was once decorated with precious gemstones and other necroshopping splendours, some of which were predictably looted by invaders in subsequent years.

The planet is littered with such places. The famous Tomb of Mausolus at Halicarnassus, Turkey, from which came the word "mausoleum," was—before it was destroyed by successive earthquakes—one of the Seven Wonders of the Ancient World, along with the Great Pyramid. The Sutton Hoo in Suffolk, England, is protected as a national treasure because it contains a ship burial dating back to the early seventh century.

Alas, cemeteries around the world, whether they contain ancient Britons or modern Hollywood stars, are filling up with bodies and other debris faster than we can afford to build new ones. Some cities are reintroducing the catacomb or massive crypt, not dissimilar to those famous places beneath Rome, Paris, Palermo, Alexandria, Vienna or Rabat, Malta, where tourists can mingle among the macabre mementos. The city of Jerusalem has recently taken a page from the past, boring a big hole under the Har HaMenuchot cemetery and creating a necropolis that will hold twenty-two thousand crypts, their human occupants and likely a lot of other stuff. While the inane practice of burying bodies is clearly unsustainable (and fortunately there is a growing trend toward alternatives worldwide), the deluge of rotting corpses stuffed with oceans of embalming fluid continues, even as some cemetery operators stack them up two and three deep. It's all accompanied by enough wood, steel and concrete to build dozens of vast cities. People want stuff, even when they are dead.

SHOPOCALYPSE

The end of shopping.

Imagine a world with no shopping. It's difficult, isn't it? Even in times of war and pestilence, humans find a way to shop, and in a digital world, it's getting easier. The COVID-19 pandemic may have seemed like a shopocalypse for many, and it was indeed pretty bleak. From Wuhan to Milan to Lima, workers went home and people were told to avoid crowds. Stores closed. Malls were abandoned. Streets were empty. Many shoppers went without and retailers were devastated; J.Crew, Neiman Marcus, Lord & Taylor, JC Penney and Brooks Brothers all filed for bankruptcy. If ever there were a modern shopocalypse, the coronavirus pandemic appeared to be it, but shoppers soon found a way to get stuff, scoping out deals on Amazon or eBay or Alibaba or Etsy in record numbers, engaging proxyshoppers to deliver things to their doorsteps, fighting over toilet paper at local grocery stores (see shopomania) and bravely venturing into Walmart for "necessities."

In short order, Amazon hired more than 400,000 people, a staggering number that doesn't include another half-million drivers who help deliver things to your door. I am clearly not representative of the wider population, but for an entire year in 2020–21, I didn't enter a single store—whether it be for groceries, drugs, clothing, hardware or books. But that didn't mean I didn't shop. I simply had all that stuff delivered to my door.

Human ingenuity and our desire to shop have allowed us to weather various shopocalypses in the past. The Great Depression of the 1930s was a shopocalypse on a monumental scale, lasting almost a decade. Nobody made anything because nobody could afford to buy it.

Nobody bought anything because nobody paid them to make it. It was a vicious circle that required another horrific world war to snap us all out of it. Assembling armies and making weapons is always a good way to reduce unemployment, and destroying stuff means someone has to get to work rebuilding it all. And while it is difficult to shop when you are trying to stay alive dodging bombs, many manage that too. Much of Syria became virtually non-shoppable after civil war broke out there in 2011, on account of the complete destruction of many cities and the many shops that populated them. But within months of the conflict's outbreak, Asma al-Assad, wife of the country's brutal dictator, was not discouraged from doing a little cybershopping. As her nation crumbled around her, she found time to search for deals online, according to hacked emails acquired by the *Guardian* newspaper: "The emails appear to show how tens of thousands of dollars were spent in internet shopping sprees on handmade furniture from Chelsea boutiques. Tens of thousands more were lavished on gold- and gem-encrusted jewelry, chandeliers, expensive curtains and paintings to be shipped to the Middle East."

Sometimes a shopocalypse is a temporary inconvenience. Religious holidays are never good for shoppers. Gods, whoever they may be and wherever they are, are apparently anti-shoppers, a fact that has somehow been lost on many religious leaders and the bulk of their followers. Some God-fearing Christians continue to insist all stores be closed on Sundays so people can go to church or hang out with their families or friends, or give those overburdened retail workers a day off on weekends like everyone else. But shoppers everywhere, and especially in North America, have long opposed such draconian measures, sometimes claiming the restrictions are anti-democratic, inefficient, unenforceable—or just plain dumb. Shoppers don't want governments or religious leaders telling them when they can't shop (see shopocracy). The endless debate seems to be losing steam in a digital world, where people can shop for anything they want, wherever they want, any day of the year or any time of the night.

So the spectre of a shopocalypse raises two questions:

1. Is such a thing possible in a modern world?
2. And is it even *desirable* in a dynamic society?

We must surely ask ourselves how much is too much—but we must also discover how much is not enough. After all, we cannot simply stop shopping. A true shopocalypse of any length will benefit no one.

Despite the environmental damage being visited on the planet from the ongoing shopathon of modern human life, consumerism is necessary. Shopping not only defines individuals—it has defined our species. It has made us who we are and what we are: the most successful creatures on Earth. (It's worth remembering that the derisive use of the term "dinosaur" refers to a group of animals that roamed the planet for 150 million years and left only their bones and a few footprints as evidence, while humans have been around just five million years, and we've already created an indelible mark.) Without shopping, our desire to innovate, the ability that makes humans so adaptable, would wither.

Shopping—or trade—has been responsible over millennia for the transfer of information and ideas across our species. Those communities that embraced shopping were also those most likely to be progressive and open to new ideas and change. Those open to change were best able to adapt and survive. Indeed, some anthropologists insist that shopping—superior trading habits—may have been a deciding factor that allowed *Homo sapiens* to thrive in Europe forty thousand years ago when Neanderthals could not. That's right, it is quite possible that a lack of shopping doomed the Neanderthals. There is no reason to believe that shopping won't serve us well in the future, as long as we're smart about it.

But while we can't live without shopping, we can't keep up this pace either. We're going to need to find a middle ground. The reasons for the collapse of a civilization are always complex: war, social strife, environmental degradation, climate change, natural disasters. But overspending, excess, decadence and a widening gap between rich and poor have simmered underneath each one, from ancient Egypt in the seventh century BCE to Rome in the fifth century to the Kingdom of France in the eighteenth century. Today, there is really only one civilization—and it is global. We are wrecking the place together, and shopping is mostly to blame. The very thing that has made humanity so successful could well be the end of us.

Shopping in one form or another has existed for millennia, but (aside from a few slumps) each generation has outdone the previous one. The current one is no exception: shopping has grown exponentially over the past five decades. A United Nations annual "emissions gap" report in 2020 stated that the rich will have to slash their carbon footprint by 30 per cent to battle climate change. It's going to be a tough challenge.

As Western extravagance has gained steam, Russia, China and India have climbed aboard, embracing capitalist consumption with a pent-up vengeance. Either we slow the train down or it will run itself off the rails. But how? We can't stop making stuff, selling stuff and buying stuff.

Economic stagnation would lead to social strife. We can't stop being employed, innovative, progressive, curious; but maybe, just maybe, we can contemplate what it is all for. We can live more modestly and reassess how we occupy ourselves. We can try to leave a lighter footprint. We can consider needs—and alternatives. We can question conventional wisdom. We can mitigate the damage done to the Earth and those we share it with, human or otherwise. We can occupy ourselves and fulfil our destinies and still rejuvenate a polluted planet. We cannot stop shopping, but we can at least stop engaging in so much deshopping. Clearly, we can ease up. "I also have in my mind that seemingly wealthy, but most terribly impoverished class of all," wrote Thoreau in *Walden*, "who have accumulated dross, but know not how to use it, or get rid of it, and thus have forged their own golden or silver fetters."

Is more restraint required? Do we need to work so hard and so long to make so much stuff so *we* can buy so much stuff (only to deshop it months or years later)? Do the spoils of wealth justify the costs? Are the stress and the mental health issues and the misery worth it? Is stuff more meaningful than friendship? Must we idolize wealth and possessions in every conversation, television show, movie and social media channel? Do our lives need resetting? Are our lifestyles healthy? Do the forces of globalization, free trade and tax laws conspire to split the world into not just haves and have-nots, but the needlessly rich and the appallingly poor, those with far too much and those with not nearly enough?

SHOPTOPIA

A place where the shopping is very, very good.

Once upon a time, Shoptopia was a crossroads on a trail or a port of call on a trade route. In ancient Greece, they called it the agora. In ancient Rome, the forum. Elsewhere Shoptopia was an emporium, a souk, a bazaar. Later, it was Bloor Street in Toronto, Fifth Avenue in New York, the Ginza district in Tokyo; your favourite department store or shopitized mall or shopified Main Street; Walmart. Today, it's the entire freaking internet. But of course, many apparent shoptopias were not sustainable. Some of them were destructive. Some even ended in shopocalypse.

What might a *truly* good, truly sustainable Shoptopia look like in the future? Will it resemble my neighbourhood tool library, which for years allowed me, for an annual fee, to borrow shovels, rakes, power saws and lawnmowers? After all, who really needs a lawnmower that may be used no more than twenty-five days out of 365? Or a shovel that sees even less service? Or will Shoptopia be a consignment store? The resale sector is rapidly growing, and thrift shopping is increasingly a badge of honour. Clothing swap and resale websites are multiplying. Some experts estimate shoppers will spend more on second-hand clothes in the next five years than in any other clothing sector. Now worth an estimated $28 billion, reworn clothing sales are expected to balloon to $64 billion by 2024. Some savvy luxury shoppers research which brands of clothing, like cars, have the best resale value. When Kardashian Kloset, a luxury designer resale site brought to us by the ubiquitous star overshoppers, launched in 2019, it was another indicator of the growing market for resale. Anna Wintour, the powerful editor of *Vogue* magazine, said recently it's time to spend less on "disposable clothes" and think more about how garments could have a longer life. "I think for all of us it means an attention more on craft, on creativity, and less on the idea of clothes that are instantly disposable, things that you will throw away just after one reading." Fashion icon Gwyneth Paltrow made approving headlines when she wore vintage Valentino from 1963 to the 2019 Emmy Awards. And activist actor Jane Fonda announced in 2019 that she was done with shopping for clothes: "We've got to cut back on consumerism," she said. And then, in reference to a signature red coat she was often seen in at climate-change demonstrations: "That red coat I bought on sale. I've said it's the last piece of clothing I'll ever buy. Sorry Saks."

In tomorrow's Shoptopia, will motorists still possess cars that are driven only five per cent of the time and remain parked for the other 95 per cent, as they do today, or will drive-share programs expand? In fact, self-driving vehicles will soon be available to us at the press of a few buttons on our phones, negating both the need for so many parking lots and the continued widening of highways.

Or will we still want to "own" stuff with impunity? Will unburdened consumption be little more than a memory in coming decades? Will the cost of disposing of things outweigh their usefulness? Will we be more socially and environmentally conscious of the things we buy, their origins, the lives we affect and the footprint we leave? Will divorcing couples fight over what must go rather than what must stay?

Humanity is given to excess, but in future it is likely to pale in comparison to the voraciousness of the current era. It must. Even by today's excessive standards, and despite many indications to the contrary, many of us consume more responsibly than we did only decades ago. Cars are cleaner and safer and last longer. Travel by rail is on the rise. Energy is increasingly renewable. Coal-burning for energy continues to drop. Houses are better insulated. Bicycles are multiplying—and increasingly shared. Decades ago, if you didn't want to listen to the radio and couldn't attend live concerts, consuming music meant buying vinyl LPs, eight-track or cassette tapes or compact discs, most of which ended up in dumps and deshopping centres. Bulky and problematic stereo systems have been replaced by something small enough to fit in a handbag. Movies are no longer on film or tapes or discs. Items are still being deshopped, plastics remain omnipresent, the dumps continue to fill with toxic wastes, and more people than ever are consuming, but there is hope. Shoptopia in future should be guilt-free, a place where shopping is not only fun but sustainable, where stuff improves and enhances life rather than cluttering and burdening it.

We can do this because we are, after all, the planet's most intelligent species. If we invented shopping and deshopping, we can invent something to replace it. We can do a better job of making the cycle of stuff truly circular rather than linear. We can stop wasting water. And we can stop polluting it. We can reduce our carbon emissions. We can cease denuding forests and paving fields, and poisoning valleys without mitigation. We can be more environmentally, socially and politically conscious of what we buy and how it comes to us—and where it will go after we are finished with it.

A species that has made shopping so pervasive can figure all these things out with little more than co-operation and creativity, the two traits that define humanity and have made us so successful. After all, humans are pretty good at fixing stuff we've broken. We've still got a long way to go, but we're learning to be better stewards of the planet. For all the animals we've forced into extinction, we have brought others back from the brink. For all the nuclear accidents we've created, we are more aware today that nothing is without cost. For all the mistakes we've made, we've had many triumphs that have helped the world become a better place. For all the excesses we've succumbed to, we've shown much restraint. For all the arguments, disagreements, debates, battles and stupid wars, we communicate and co-operate as well or better than the most successful creatures on the planet. In the end, we face three simple questions:

- *What do we really need?* Food, shelter, clothing.
- *What do we really want?* Mental and physical fitness and social interaction? (And yes, some stuff is nice too.)
- *How do we achieve these things?* By recognizing that while shopping is a solution for many needs and a cure for many ills, it is the cause of others. And by asking if it is really necessary to "own it now" as we have been told—endlessly—since childhood. Must we possess everything to enjoy it? Do we really need all that stuff? Do we need to replace useful things just because they no longer look fashionable? Can we not use our stuff better, share it more widely, deshop it more responsibly? Can we break the cycle of shop, unshop, reshop and deshop?

These are questions humans have asked themselves for centuries, and we still don't agree on the answers. But soon there will be no choice. Many federal governments are putting a price on carbon, which will make excessive consuming more expensive—and responsible consuming more attractive. It will force us to be more thoughtful about shopping, if only because humans always, always look for the best deal—and the cost of deshopping will be part of the calculation. Municipalities, meanwhile, are increasingly putting a limit on how much trash we can take to the curb each week without financial penalty. Being consumers, we hate taxes on shopping, but it's obvious we'll see more in future. Excessive packaging is universal and unavoidable, and deshopping is cheap and easy, but lawmakers everywhere will inevitably be forced by economics alone to make garbage disposal more expensive and more difficult.

After all, why do we recycle so much when what is really needed is more reusing and more reducing? The answer: because it is still too easy to deshop. Laws will soon (but not soon enough) force us to consider each purchase because it will cost more to get rid of both the thing itself and its excessive packaging. Littering, dumping and illegal disposal of garbage will become a bigger crime—legally and socially. So we'll stop buying the packaging we can't afford to throw away, or we'll leave it at the stores for retailers to deal with. And, lo and behold, corporations will come up with better, friendlier, cheaper and more ecologically sustainable ways to package. When governments finally stop spending all our money building roads, and charge users per kilometre to drive on them, people will fall out of love with cars and look for alternatives.

When heating and air-conditioning costs rise ever higher, people will spend more on insulation, better windows and more renewable fuels. When consumption taxes get ever higher, we'll think twice about yet another pair of shoes. When buying cheap stuff becomes too expensive financially, socially, politically, environmentally, we'll think more about the durability of the things we buy, and we'll insist that corporations make stuff that can last longer and be more easily repaired.

If we're not thinking hard enough, activists will assist, as they always have, organizing boycotts of materials that are not produced fairly or sustainably. Many such efforts are failures (people want stuff, after all), but there are enough successes to ensure boycotts will continue or even increase. Just ask brands such as Nike, Mitsubishi and Firestone, all of which felt the wrath of consumers' displeasure for a variety of reasons and improved their methods as a result. Right-to-repair movements, zero-waste organizations, post-materialism groups, Earth Day and Buy Nothing Day are well established. Sustainable consumption, ethical consumerism, simple living and ecological economics are here to stay. Former overshoppers Joshua Fields Millburn and Ryan Nicodemus have made a career out of using less: writing books, making podcasts and filming Netflix documentaries about the joys of minimalism. Described as "the embodiment of upwardly mobile, busy, fashionable, unhealthy, wasteful, young professionals," the two friends have now branded themselves as *The Minimalists* and insist they are happier with less.

In tomorrow's Shoptopia, things will be different. More of us will be employed repairing stuff rather than manufacturing it anew. We won't have as much stuff, perhaps, but what we do have we'll keep for longer. We may have only one watch or handbag or coffeemaker, but it will be *used*. And we'll be able to locate it all easily. Our stuff will not be lost amid the flotsam and jetsam of endless drawers, closets, attics, basements, garages and predeshopping centres. All this stuff will have more meaning and our lives will have more purpose. Entrepreneurs, innovators, scientists, teachers, engineers, politicians and creators everywhere will focus on sustainable pursuits. They are doing it already. The question is: are we moving fast enough? Are we doing enough, or will we simply shop, unshop, reshop and deshop ourselves to death?

EPILOGUE

The telephone rang in the kitchen and my sister handed me the receiver.

"Mr. Berton?"

"Um," I replied. Nobody had ever called me that before. After all, I was only seven.

"Paul Berton?"

"Yes."

"It's the IGA calling. You've won our contest."

I started jumping up and down. I yelled out in triumph to my mother and older sister: "I've won, I've won, I've won!"

A week earlier, my father had taken my brother and me to the IGA grocery store, and in the meat department was a salami that stretched the entire length of the counter. Customers were asked to guess its length.

In my memory, the salami was as long as a school bus, but at the time, I really had no concept of feet and inches, so after my dad and my brother filled out a form with their guesses and placed them in the contest box, I handed mine to my dad and he filled it out for me.

Now, on the phone, I pictured the salami and I imagined what riches would come my way. I was grinning from ear to ear. I had trouble catching my breath. I couldn't think straight.

My sister was excited for me, and she asked: "What did you win?"

I stopped jumping and calmed down for a moment and asked the IGA man on the phone: "What did I win?"

"A ham," he said. "You've won a ham."

"A ham, a ham, I've won a ham!" I yelled to my sister and anyone who would listen, and started jumping up and down again.

My sister was grinning. I imagined she was happy for me. My mother approached and took the phone to facilitate the important work of acquiring my treasure.

I was delirious, already dreaming of the new life we'd have, the things I'd buy, now that I'd won the salami contest. We'd have a ham and a mansion and a yacht! And I would be responsible for all of it. I would be the hero! Maybe I'd be on TV!

When my dad came home, I rushed to tell him, and the next day at school, I told my friends. I couldn't wait for my new life to start.

That afternoon, I accompanied my mother to the IGA. We were going to have the ham for dinner that night. I imagined tickertape and triumphant music and cheering crowds.

At the meat counter, my mother introduced me to the butcher: "This is Paul Berton. He won the ham." The big moment had finally arrived.

The butcher wiped his hands on his white apron, smiled at me kindly, reached into the refrigerator and pulled out one of those perfectly round half-hams wrapped in plastic. Not even the size of a grapefruit, it was the type that in those days might be served with a ring of pineapple and a maraschino cherry. He passed it to my mother. She gave it to me. I looked at it, stunned. It's a ham, I thought, staring in disbelief, just a ham, and not a very nice one at that.

Is that it?

I tossed it in the shopping cart with the carrots and apples.

"Where's the salami?" I demanded.

It had already been sliced into cold cuts, I was told.

My mom and I did the rest of the shopping in silence and drove home. No cheering crowds, no tickertape, no yacht. We ate the ham for dinner that night, but I knew that neither my mother nor my father nor even my siblings were particularly fond of that kind of ham, and frankly, neither was I.

It was all an illusion. I had won, but what had I won? The thrill of winning, to be sure. A fleeting moment in which I gained some stature, if only in my own mind, because of an imagined possession. A twinkling chapter of my life in which I acquired something that made me special, only to realize it wasn't special at all, and that nobody really cared anyway.

Stuff is like that. Whether it's a Barbie doll or a bicycle or a baseball bat. Or a toy car that seems, for a brief and shining moment, like the most important thing in the world. A stereo set, a watch, a desk lamp, a new automobile or a renovated kitchen may seem the centre of the universe for the first few days or weeks or even years of its existence. Such things help us forget, perhaps, the other challenges and shortcomings, but not for long. They inevitably begin to fade in our esteem almost as soon as they are acquired. The useful stuff becomes worn out or obsolete. The art and the clothes and the collections sometimes grow on us and take on outsize importance, but more often they get taken for granted or go out of fashion. They are not the things we'd rescue in a fire. Everything, eventually, gets passed down or put away or thrown out or simply lost—recycled, crushed, shredded, burned or reduced to dust—often without our even missing it.

Only a few manufactured items have lasted as long as humanity itself. These early objects continue to mystify archeologists and museum curators; those created in the last two thousand years are desired for their stories and their rarity and their clues to a bygone era. But most of the stuff we collect today does not survive even a single lifetime. Each thing has a moment of glory, making us feel special and transmitting to others that we are more than we may seem. Of those items we do manage to cling to throughout life, a few are curiously taken to the grave, but most become an unwelcome burden for the next generation and the planet itself, and are quickly lost to time. Like a prized Dinky Toy buried in a forgotten sandbox, almost everything ends up where it came from.

ACKNOWLEDGEMENTS

A great deal of research has been done on consumerism, very little of it by me. This book stands on the shoulders of that work, much of it conducted by industry insiders, academics and consultants, often on behalf of retailers and manufacturers to help them sell us more stuff. I am also indebted to the many economists, sociologists, psychologists, environmentalists, authors and others who study how and why we shop. Also, this book would not have been possible without the reporting done by journalists and writers who have documented the acquisitive habits of humans, and—above all—those who have publicly shared (voluntarily or otherwise) their stories about stuff.

I am grateful to various friends and relatives who read early versions of the manuscript and gave frank observations and suggestions, including David Dauphinee, Ian Gillespie and George Sinclair, who offered detailed critiques, as well as Christine Diemert, Signy Eaton, Jeff Shier, Teresa Evans, Patsy Berton and Peter Berton, many of whom also tolerated my rants on the topic over the years.

Patricia Hluchy provided an early copyedit as well as encouragement and guidance on tone, structure, content and propriety. Anne Bokma offered many suggestions, insights and commentary on both process and content. Peter Norman improved pace, wording, flow and structure and helped rid the book of a lot of stuff, including entire chapters, to which I was irrationally (and ironically) attached. Caroline Skelton went through the manuscript with fine-toothed comb, sharpening the language and saving me from endless embarrassments, inaccuracies and trespasses. Finally, I am grateful to Anna Comfort O'Keeffe, publisher at Douglas & McIntyre, who had faith in this book from the beginning. I am beholden to all of them.

NOTES

INTRODUCTION

the term "shop": You can find an exhaustive list of various shop rootwords—there are dozens—used over the centuries in the *Compact Edition of the Oxford English Dictionary* (Oxford University Press, 1971, 2 volumes).

humans may never have invented writing: Stephen Brown and Hope Jensen Schau, "Writing Russell Belk: excess all areas," *Marketing Theory* 8, no. 2 (June 1, 2008): 143–65.

UNSHOP

one in five Britons is a chronic unshopper: Sirin Kale, "One in five of us do it, but is 'wardrobing' ever acceptable?" *Guardian*, September 18, 2019.

bulky plastic tags: Eun Kyung Kim, "Bloomingdale's new b-tags block used clothing returns," *Today*, September 19, 2013, https://www.today.com/money/bloomingdales -new-b-tags-block-used-clothing-returns-4b11199683.

a 1961 Rolls-Royce Silver Cloud II Drophead Coupe, once owned by jewel-loving and serial-marrying actor Elizabeth Taylor: James Barron, "Elizabeth Taylor's 'Green Goddess' Rolls-Royce on the Auction Block," *New York Times*, July 31, 2019.

In 2019, . . . it sold for more than a half a million dollars: "Liz Taylor's 'Green Goddess' 1961 Rolls Royce goes for $520K in auction," *Fox Business*, August 7, 2019, https://www .foxbusiness.com/markets/liz-taylor-rolls-royce-sells-auction-520000.

$400 billion is returned: Jeff Chen, "How Retail Brands Can Work To Reduce Returns," *Forbes*, September 14, 2021.

the case of a once-ordinary comic book: It is a famous story, well known among the comic-book crowd, but here's one that covers it from beginning to end:

Andy Lewis, "Nicolas Cage's Superman Comic Nets Record $2.1 Million at Auction," *Hollywood Reporter*, November 30, 2011.

Rob Ford managed to unshop the otherwise ordinary tie: Canadian Press, "Rob Ford's crack-confession tie sells on eBay, again," CBC *News*, April 15, 2021, https://www.cbc.ca /news/canada/toronto/rob-ford-s-crack-confession-tie-sells-on-ebay-again-1.3042710.

the remarkable story of the so-called "Paul Newman" wristwatch: Much has been written about this insane tale, but two worth reading include:
Hyla Ames Bauer, "Paul Newman's 'Paul Newman' Rolex Daytona Sells for $17.8 Million, A Record for a Wristwatch at Auction," *Forbes*, October 26, 2017.
Matt Stevens, "Paul Newman Rolex Sells at Auction for Record $17.8 million," *New York Times*, October 27, 2017.

RESHOP

Donald Trump did this in 1991, when he was forced to deshop his personal Boeing 727: Peter Grant and Alexandra Berson, "Trump and His Debts: A Narrow Escape," *Wall Street Journal*, January 4, 2016.
Mark Singer, "Trump Solo," *New Yorker*, May 19, 1997.
Howard Kurtz, "Donald Trump: A tycoon with a towering ambition," *Washington Post*, *Toronto Star*, December 26, 1987.

Alanis Morissette, who once described: Simon Houpt, "Alanis uncluttered," *Globe and Mail*, April 3, 2004.
Samantha Battistone, "Celeb Home Tour: Alanis Morissette's serene sanctuary in Canada's capital," *Style at Home*, August 9, 2016.
Chloe Best, "Alanis Morissette has sold her £4 million mansion – take a look inside," *Hello!*, October 27, 2017.

Kim Kardashian and her now ex-husband: Mayer Rus, "Step Inside Kim Kardashian West and Kanye West's Boundary-Defying Home," *Architectural Digest*, February 3, 2020.

there may be no better unshopper and reshopper than . . . Ellen DeGeneres: Steven Kurutz, "The Unsettling Thing about Ellen," *New York Times*, April 23, 2014.

DeGeneres also has/had a Royère couch: Hannah Martin, "The Story Behind Jean Royère's Iconic Design," *Architectural Digest*, July 14, 2017.

A scant seven months later: Lauren Beale, "Ellen DeGeneres sells trophy home to tech billionaire Sean Parker," *Los Angeles Times*, July 12, 2014.

There are always a few losers: Hannah Ferrett, "This is the trashed mansion Lotto lout Mickey Carroll sold at a £600K loss," *Sun* (London), July 12, 2016.

DESHOP

Basinger . . . sold the town of Braselton: Carol Marie Cropper, "Even in bankruptcy, Basinger lives well while town does not," *Baltimore Sun*, January 3, 1995. Associated Press, "Actress Pays $20 million for town," *Toronto Star*, March 29, 1989. Dan Chapman, "Town for sale: $2.5 million," Dan Chapman, *Atlanta Journal-Constitution, Toronto Star*, June 9, 2012.

billionaire Elon Musk: Elon Musk, "#1470 – Elon Musk," interview by Joe Rogan, *The Joe Rogan Experience*, podcast, May 8, 2020, https://www.rev.com/blog/transcripts/joe -rogan-elon-musk-podcast-transcript-may-7-2020.

Elon Musk (@elonmusk), "I am selling almost all physical possessions. Will own no house," Twitter, May 1, 2020, https://twitter.com/elonmusk/status /1256239554148724737.

Paris Hilton indulged in some serious deshopping after she announced: "Hilton's Charitable Gesture," *Contactmusic* (website), September 20, 2007. (Article no longer available on website.)
Hilton was quoted again several years later in *CelebsNow*, saying mostly the same thing: "I never wear an outfit more than once unless it's like, a really cool pair of jeans or a leather jacket. I have so many clothes in my closets that still have the labels on. I see them so often I think I've worn them, but then I realise I haven't." (Article no longer available on website.)

Mary Tyler Moore did the same thing when she unloaded: Mary Tyler Moore, *After All* (New York: G. P. Putnam's Sons), 28–9.

Deshopping is what questionable deal-maker Donald Trump: Julie Satow, "That Time Trump Sold the Plaza Hotel at an $83 Million Loss," *Bloomberg Business*, May 23, 2019.

lunatic overshopper and evil mastermind Osama Bin Laden: Peter L. Bergen, *The Osama bin Laden I Know: An Oral History of al Qaeda's Leader* (New York: Free Press, 2006), 12.

London mayor Sadiq Khan was forced in 2017 to deshop a trio of water cannons: Matthew Weaver, "Boris Johnson's unused water cannon sold for scrap at £300,000 loss," *Guardian*, November 19, 2018.

Wright lost his home: Robert C. Twombly, *Frank Lloyd Wright: His Life and His Architecture* (New Jersey: John Wiley & Sons, 1991), 189–92.

Bank of Wisconsin, which deshopped thousands of his expensive prints for a dollar apiece: Holland Cotter, "Art Review; Seeking Japan's Prints, Out of Love and Need," *New York Times*, April 6, 2001.

In 2010, cash-strapped eccentric Nicolas Cage: Lauren Beale, "Nicolas Cage's Bel-Air home goes to new owner for just $10.5 million," *Los Angeles Times*, November 11, 2010.

NON-SHOPPER

natives in 2018 speared to death: Kai Schultz, Hari Kumar and Jeffrey Gettleman, "Sentinelese Tribe That Killed American Has a History of Guarding Its Isolation," *New York Times*, November 22, 2018.

Leonard Cohen, for example, did not accumulate much: Sylvie Simmons, *I'm Your Man: The Life of Leonard Cohen* (Toronto: McClelland & Stewart, 2021), 324–5.

And he once wrote an earlier lover: Ibid., 152.

Nor did Cohen's aversion to consumerism: Brian D. Johnson, "Leonard Cohen wore earplugs to a Dylan show?" *Maclean's*, June 8, 2009.

Hughes checked into Las Vegas's Desert Inn: Laura Wolff Scanlan, "Vegas's Revolutionary Recluse," *Humanities*, March/April 2010.

he bought the CBS affiliate KLAS: George Knapp, "How KLAS-TV became a part of Howard Hughes' empire," *8 News Now Las Vegas*, July 18, 2018.

Ice Station Zebra: Geoff Schumacher, *Sun, Sin & Suburbia, An Essential History of Modern Las Vegas* (Las Vegas: Stephens Press, 2010), 100.

Apple Inc. perfectionist and former deadbeat dad Steve Jobs: Leander Kahney, "John Sculley on Steve Jobs, The Full Interview Transcript," *Cult of Mac*, October 14, 2010,

https://www.cultofmac.com/63295/john-sculley-on-steve-jobs-the-full-interview
-transcript/63295/.

he appeared to shop for very few clothes: Ryan Tate, "Steve Jobs on Why He Wore
Turtlenecks," *Gawker*, October 11, 2011, https://www.gawker.com/5848754/steve-jobs
-on-why-he-wore-turtlenecks.

J. Paul Getty: Agustino Fontevecchia, "The Tragedy Of The Gettys: Billions, Affairs,
Severed Ears, Drug Overdoses, And Oil," *Forbes*, July 11, 2014.
Alden Whitman, "J. Paul Getty Dead at 83; Amassed Billions From Oil," *New York
Times*, July 6, 1976.

Levine's description of the last item: Judith Levine, *Not Buying It: My Year Without
Shopping* (New York: Free Press, 2006), 10.

SHOPOPHOBIA

Elton John, who admitted to dispersing: Paul Kelso, "Elton John tells of his epic
spending sprees," *Guardian*, November 16, 2000.

Seventies movie star and wise-cracking nightclub owner Burt Reynolds: Ned Zeman, "Burt
Reynolds Isn't Broke, but He's Got a Few Regrets," *Vanity Fair*, December 2015.

SHOPIFICATION

officials now worry that too many rich visitors shopping: Ivana Kottasová, "These
European cities are fed up with tourists," *CNN Business*, August 25, 2017, https://
money.cnn.com/2017/08/25/news/economy/tourism-backlash-europe/index.html.

SHOPITIZATION

One of the first suburban (or rural) shopping centres: The urban Market Square (1916)
and the suburban Country Club Plaza (1922) are certainly among the first shopping
centres in the United States, but both are predated in a smaller way by Baltimore's
Roland Park in 1907. Michael H. Ebner, *Creating Chicago's North Shore, A Suburban
History* (Chicago: University of Chicago Press, 1988), 206.
For more about Country Club Plaza see:

William S. Worley, *J.C. Nichols and the Shaping of Kansas City: Innovation in Planned Residential Communities* (Columbia: University of Missouri Press, 1990).

Sara Stevens, "J.C. Nichols and the Country Club District: Suburban aesthetics and property values," The Pendergast Years (website), Kansas City Public Library, https://pendergastkc.org/article/jc-nichols-and-country-club-district-suburban-aesthetics-and-property-values.

For more about Market Square see:

Susan Dart, *Market Square, Lake Forest, Illinois* (Lake Forest: Lake Forest-Lake Bluff Historical Society, 1985).

Perhaps the best example is Detroit's Renaissance Center: Colin Marshall, "The Renaissance Center: Henry Ford II's grand design to revive Detroit – a history of cities in 50 buildings, day 42," *Guardian*, May 22, 2015.

Singapore committed the sin of shopitization: Philip Shenon, "Singapore Journal; Back to Somerset Maugham and Life's Seamy Side," *New York Times*, October 10, 1991.

SHOPPABLE

Pitcairn Island: Pitcairn Islands Tourism (website): https://www.visitpitcairn.pn/.

Deutsche Bank does an annual cost-of-living survey: "Mapping the World's Prices, 2019," *Deutsche Bank Research*, May 16, 2019, https://www.dbresearch.com/PROD/RPS_EN-PROD/PROD0000000000494405/Mapping_the_world%27s_prices_2019.PDF.

translate such information into listicles: Jessica Mendoza, "The best and worst places to shop in the world," *Christian Science Monitor*, April 16, 2015.

an advertising writer named Gary Dahl: Margalit Fox, "Gary Dahl, Inventor of the Pet Rock, Dies at 78," *New York Times*, March 31, 2015.

The one distinguishing feature of vodka, after all, is its utter lack of any discernible favour: Canadian Law: Canada, *Food and Drugs Act*, SOR/2019-217, s. 1, https://laws.justice.gc.ca/eng/regulations/C.R.C.,_c._870/page-20.html#h-569931.

Seth Stevenson, "The Cocktail Creationist," *New York*, December 30, 2004.

Sidney Frank as told to Stephanie Clifford, "How I did it: Sidney Frank, founder, Sidney Frank Importing," *Inc.*, September 1, 2005.

Dan Pashman, "Is There Really A Difference Between Expensive Vodka And Cheap Vodka?" *All Things Considered, Planet Money*, NPR, March 1, 2018, https://www.npr.org

/2018/03/01/590022606/is-there-really-a-difference-between-expensive-vodka-and
-cheap-vodka.

by 2017, water had become so shoppable: Business Research Company, "The Global
Bottled Water Market: Expert Insights & Statistics," *Market Research* (blog),
February 28, 2018, https://blog.marketresearch.com/the-global-bottled-water-market
-expert-insights-statistics.
International Bottled Water Association, "Consumers reaffirm bottled water is
America's favorite drink," May 31, 2018, news release, https://bottledwater.org/nr/
consumers-reaffirm-bottled-water-is-america-s-favorite-drink/.
Rachel Arthur, "'Bottled water is America's favorite drink!' Bottled water takes top
spot in US," *Beverage Daily*, June 1, 2018, https://www.beveragedaily.com/Article
/2018/06/01/Bottled-water-takes-top-spot-in-US-in-2017.
Trevor Nace, "We're now at A Million Plastic Bottles Per Minute – 91% of Which Are
Not Recycled," *Forbes*, July 26, 2017.
P H Bleick and H S Cooley, "Energy Implications of bottled water," *Environmental
Research Letters* 4, no. 1, February 19, 2009, http://iopscience.iop.org/article/10.1088
/1748-9326/4/1/014009/fulltext/.

"... one of the greatest marketing coups...": Elizabeth Royte, *Bottlemania: How Water
Went on Sale and Why We Bought It* (New York: Bloomsbury, 2009), 40–1.

or Kabbalah water, made famous by: Peter H Gleick, *Bottled & Sold: The Story Behind Our
Obsession with Bottled Water* (Washington, DC: Island Press, 2010), 133–4.

swimming pool with the stuff: Urmee Khan, "Guy Ritchie cancels Madonna's order to fill
swimming pool with Kabbalah water," *Telegraph*, October 28, 2008.

Water sommeliers help thirsty customers: Jeanette Settembre, "LA restaurant unveils
45-page bottled water menu," *New York Daily News*, August 9, 2013.

Sommeliers join bottlers: Fine Water Sommeliers (website): http://www.finewaters.com
/premium-bottled-water/finewaters-summits/fine-water-summit-2017.

MEGASHOPERATOR

Sam Walton started out: "History," Walmart (website), https://corporate.walmart.com
/our-story/our-history.

"Sam's Truck," Walmart Digital Museum (website), https://www.walmartmuseum.com /content/walmartmuseum/en_us/timeline/decades/1970/artifact/2580.html.

Various family members: Mary Hanbury, "Meet the Waltons: How America's wealthiest family spends its Walmart fortune," *Business Insider*, August 16, 2018.

Ingvar Kamprad: Emmie Martin, "4 unusual ways self-made billionaire IKEA founder Ingvar Kamprad insisted on saving money," CNBC, January 29, 2018, https://www .cnbc.com/2018/01/29/money-habits-of-self-made-billionaire-ikea-founder-ingvar -kamprad.html.
Robert D. McFadden, "Ingvar Kamprad, Founder of Ikea and Creator of a Global Empire, Dies at 91," *New York Times*, January 28, 2018.

Stefan Persson: Damien Pearse, "H&M billionaire Stefan Persson buys Hampshire village for £25m," *Guardian*, May 25, 2009.

Leslie Wexner: Steve Eder and Emily Steel, "Leslie Wexner Accuses Jeffrey Epstein of Misappropriating 'Vast Sums of Money,'" *New York Times*, August 7, 2019.
Ben Widdicombe, "The Secret History of Jeffrey Epstein's New York Townhouse," *Town & Country*, May 27, 2020.

Bernard Arnault: Vanessa Friedman, "Bernard Arnault Just Bought Tiffany. Who Is He?" *New York Times*, November 25, 2019.

UPSHOP

Thorstein Veblen: Thorstein Veblen, *The Theory of the Leisure Class* (New York: The Macmillan Company), 12.

keeping up with the Joneses: The *Times* says James Duesenberry introduced the fictional family in *Income, Saving, and the Theory of Consumer Behavior* in 1952: The Times, "Questions Answered," *Sunday Times*, April 1, 2004, https://www.thetimes. co.uk/article/questions-answered-m79nqnfdxgj.
William Safire, "On Language; Up the Down Ladder," *New York Times*, November 15, 1998.

The quandary: Minas N. Kastanakis and George Balabanis, "Between the mass and the class: Antecedents of the 'bandwagon' luxury consumption behavior," *Journal of Business Research* 65, no. 10 (October 24, 2011): 1399–1407.

Larry Ellison: Barry Pickthall, "Allen Vs. Ellison: Two of America's richest men keep building bigger and bigger yachts in the race to have the largest of them all," *Yachting Magazine*, October 4, 2007.
Tim Thomas, "Mark Cuban's, Larry Ellison's New Yachts on New Ranking of 100 Biggest Yachts," *Forbes*, January 25, 2013.

Trump bought the vessel originally built by the notorious arms dealer Adnan Khashoggi: Roxanne Roberts, "Inside the fabulous world of Donald Trump, where money is no problem," *Washington Post*, October 9, 2015.
Michael Kilian, "Going Overboard: Donald Trump Ballyhoos his hand-me-down boat. But has anyone ever seen him swim?" *Chicago Tribune*, July 27, 1988.

a few years later: Sara Kamouni, "Inside Trump's Superyacht," *Scottish Sun*, February 11, 2017.
For a pretty good history of the *Trump Princess*, you could do worse than an article first published in 1989 in *Boat International*:
John Taylor, "Trump Princess: Inside Donald Trump's lavish 86m superyacht," *Boat International*, https://www.boatinternational.com/yachts/editorial-features/trump-princess-inside-donald-trumps-lavish-86m-superyacht--34381.

Frank Stronach, the free-spending Austrian-born Canadian: Leah McLaren, "The $500-million family feud," *Toronto Life*, June 17, 2019.

DOWNSHOP

Lev Parnas, the mysterious Ukrainian-born American: Rosalind S. Helderman and Paul Sonne, "'Once this is over, we'll be kings': How Lev Parnas worked his way into Trump's world – and is now rattling it," *Washington Post*, January 18, 2020.

Fearless performer Nicolas Cage: "Nic Cage spent too much: Ex-manager says," CNN *Money*, November 17, 2009, https://money.cnn.com/2009/11/17/pf/Nicolas_Cage_lawsuit_manager.cnnw/index.htm.

Overindulgent '80s hip-hop artist MC Hammer: Cynthia Robins and *San Francisco Examiner*, "Hammered," *Chicago Tribune*, May 10, 1997.

British *"lotto lout" and former garbage collector Michael Carroll*: Hannah Ferrett, "'This is the trashed mansion Lotto lout Mickey Carroll sold at a £600K loss," *Sun* (London), July 12, 2016.
"Who wants to be a millionaire?" *Independent* (London), October 22, 2006.

Canadian single mom Sharon Tirabassi: Molly Hayes, "Hamilton's penniless millionaire," *Hamilton Spectator*, March 21, 2013.

MISSHOP

former drug-addled domestic abuser Charlie Sheen: Joyce Chen, "Charlie Sheen Sells Beverly Hills Mansion for $6.6 Million," *Architectural Digest*, January 9, 2020.
Nancy A. Ruhling, "Charlie Sheen's L.A. Mansion Relists at a Discount," *Mansion Global*, January 30, 2019, https://www.mansionglobal.com/articles/charlie-sheen-s-l -a-mansion-relists-at-a-discount-120579.

bought art purportedly by Mark Rothko: M. H. Miller, "'The Big Fake: Behind the Scenes of Knoedler Gallery's Downfall," *ARTnews*, April 25, 2016, https://www.artnews.com/ art-news/artists/the-big-fake-behind-the-scenes-of-knoedler-gallerys-downfall-6179/. Patricia Cohen, "Possible Forging of Modern Art Is Investigated," *New York Times*, December 2, 2011.

billionaire collector and competitive sailor Bill Koch: Peter Hellman, "Wine Counterfeiter Rudy Kurniawan's Sentencing Is Delayed," *Wine Spectator*, May 29, 2014.
Megan Chuchmach and Brian Ross, "What Makes a Billionaire Cry? Bill Koch Duped by Wine Fakes," *ABC News*, June 12, 2014, https://abcnews.go.com/Blotter/makes -billionaire-cry-bill-koch-duped-wine-fakes/story?id=24111774.
Bianca Bosker, "A True-Crime Documentary about the Con that Shook the World of Wine," *New Yorker*, October 14, 2016.

evangelical Christian and American business tycoon Steve Green: Scott Neuman, "Museum's Collection Of Purported Dead Sea Scroll Fragments Are Fakes, Experts Say," *NPR*, March 17, 2020, https://www.npr.org/2020/03/17/817018416/museums -collection-of-purported-dead-sea-scroll-fragments-are-fakes-experts-say.
"A Journey for the Truth: Investigating the Recent Dead Sea Scrolls Fragments," Museum of the Bible (website), https://museumofthebible.org/dead-sea-scroll -fragments.

rose in price to ten thousand guilders: Mike Dash, *Tulipomania: The Story of the World's Most Coveted Flower & the Extraordinary Passions It Aroused* (New York: Three Rivers Press), 108–9.

also hot commodities: Ibid., 125.

Beanie Babies to finance his sons' university educations: You can see Chris Robinson's delightfully horrifying eight-minute documentary at:
Chris Robinson, "Bankrupt by Beanies," YouTube video, 8:28, May 15, 2009, https:// www.youtube.com/watch?v=PgDsyj5eLmo.

John Rae: John Rae, *The Sociological Theory of Capital: Being a Complete Reprint of the New Principles of Political Economy, 1834* (New York: Macmillan Company), 53–4.

In 1940, light bulb manufacturers: Much of the information about planned obsolescence here comes from an excellent documentary film:
Cosima Dannoritzer (writer/director), Joan Úbeda and Patrice Barrat (executive producers), "The Light Bulb Conspiracy," YouTube video, 52:52, June 7, 2017, https:// www.youtube.com/watch?v=e9xmn228HMo.

realtor named Bernard London: Bernard London, "Ending the Depression through Planned Obsolescence," 1932, https://www.semanticscholar.org/paper/Ending-the -Depression-through-Planned-Obsolescence-London/622892147cfe3c4567d0d92d5283 94423d93e5a4.

CRYPTOSHOP

". . . even if the billionaire is in a T-shirt . . .": Chrystia Freeland, *Plutocrats: The Rise of the New Global Super-Rich and the Fall of Everyone Else* (Toronto: Anchor Canada, 2012), 235.

"The art of being rich . . .": Richard Conniff, *Natural History of the Rich* (New York: W. W. Norton & Company, 2003), 182.

Abdullah II bin Al-Hussein, the king of Jordan: Greg Miller, "While His Country Struggles, Jordan's King Abdullah Secretly Splurges," *Washington Post*, October 3, 2021.

sex trafficker and monstrous predator Jeffrey Epstein: Leena Kim, "Everything We Know About Jeffrey Epstein's Vast Real Estate Portfolio," *Town & Country*, May 28, 2020.

OVERSHOP

environmentalist Annie Leonard: The Story of Stuff Project (website), https://www
.storyofstuff.org/.

celebrated personal shopper Betty Halbreich: Betty Halbreich with Sally Wadyka, *Secrets of a Fashion Therapist* (New York: HarperCollins, 2011), 11.

UNDERSHOP

like Warren Buffett, choose to live: Hillary Hoffower and Taylor Nicole Rogers, "Here's how the notoriously frugal billionaire spends his $67.6 billion fortune," *Business Insider*, March 23, 2020.

the "comic frugality" of telegenic US politician Mitt Romney: Michael Barbaro and Ashley Parker, "Two Romneys: Wealthy Man, Thrifty Habits," *New York Times*, December 10, 2011.

Jeff Bezos, the nerdy founder of Amazon: Bob Simon, "The Jeff Bezos of 1999: Nerd of the Amazon," CBS *60 Minutes*, December 1, 2013, https://www.cbsnews.com/news/the
-jeff-bezos-of-1999-nerd-of-the-amazon/.
Nancy Keates, "The Many Places Amazon CEO Jeff Bezos Calls Home," *Wall Street Journal*, January 9, 2019.
Katy McLaughlin and Katherine Clarke, "Jeff Bezos Buys David Geffen's Los Angeles Mansion for a Record $165 Million," *Wall Street Journal*, February 12, 2020.

right-wing News Corp. heir Lachlan Murdoch: Joyce Chen, "Rupert Murdoch's Son Lachlan Breaks Records With the Purchase of a $150 Million Property," *Architectural Digest*, December 12, 2019.

ULTRASHOP

Disco-dancing actor John Travolta: Anastasia Dagaeva, "The full story behind Travolta's private jet fleet," *Beam Aviation*, February 11, 2018.

Southern preacher Jesse Duplantis . . . telegenic Texan Kenneth Copeland: Lisa Guerrero, "Why Do These Televangelists Need Expensive Jets?" *Inside Edition*, May 3, 2019, https://www.youtube.com/watch?v=FZmGmGnkBVM.

fraudster Jim Bakker and his raccoon-eyed wife, Tammy Faye: Art Harris, "Jim Bakker, Driven By Money or Miracles?" *Washington Post*, August 29, 1989.
"Televangelists Jim and Tammy Faye Bakker build a multi-million dollar empire," ABC *News*, January 18, 2019.

Ostentatious jewel-bedecked or gilded items:
There are many "reports" about celebrity ultrashopping, but some are difficult to nail down:
Mike Tyson likely did spend $2 million on a bathtub, although reports of "solid gold" or "jewel-encrusted" cannot be verified. That said, the price is an indicator of expensive material. See:
Geoffrey Grey, "Tyson's Last Match," *New York Observer*, December 22, 2003.
or
Mark Schlabach, "The Punch Line? A Knockout Debt; After squandering $400 Million, Tyson Returns to the Ring," *Washington Post*, July 24, 2004.

Less easy to verify is Ben Affleck's widely reported purchase of a jewel-encrusted toilet seat for Jennifer Lopez. The reports appear to have originated with the *National Enquirer*, not exactly a reliable purveyor of news, but while some of their reports are highly questionable, others turn out to be true. One news service said Lopez later explained the purchase wasn't exactly as reported.

David Beckham likely did buy an expensive diamond-encrusted handbag for Victoria Beckham. See:
Leah Ginsberg, "You know you're rich when you buy this—a $379,261 handbag is the most expensive ever sold at auction," CNBC, June 21, 2017.
or
Ingrid Schmidt, "Luxury Handbag Reseller Rebag Simultaneously Opens Two Stores in Los Angeles," *Hollywood Reporter*, November 8, 2018.

It's unclear if Beyoncé Knowles actually bought the shoes. The *Birmingham Mail* reported it after an interview with Chris Shellis, owner of House of Borgezie:
Mike Lockley, "Beyonce buys £200,000 pair of shoes from Jewellery Quarter company," *Birmingham Mail*, August 2, 2015.
but Beyoncé denied it:
Barnali Pal Sinha, "Beyonce Denies Splurging For $312,000 on Shoes," *International Business Times*, August 7, 2015.

Jennifer Aniston's purchase of the gold-plated motorcycle was reported by MSN.com and others, but it can't be verified.

Tamara Ecclestone actually admitted to Britain's *Daily Mail* that she spent £1 million on the bathtub because "I spend a lot of time in the bath so it's worth it." Caroline Graham, "'I'm spending £1m on a crystal bath but it's worth it': Billionaire's daughter Tamara Ecclestone lifts the lid on her extravagant lifestyle in revealing interview," *Daily Mail*, September 13, 2011.

Barbara Amiel Black: Barbara Amiel Black made the "extravagance that knows no bounds" comment during an interview with *Vogue* magazine in 2002, but it's not clear if she was merely being ironic. The comments about jewelry, hers and others', came from a 2003 interview with *GQ* magazine. These quotes are simply too juicy to ignore, but they are also frighteningly perceptive, especially given they were made twenty years ago, when general extravagance by rich people around the world had not yet pushed the bounds we recognize today.

ultrashopping rapper Drake: The Unknown Vlogs, "How Much is Your Outfit?" YouTube video, 5:33, April 3, 2019, https://www.youtube.com/watch?v=7pWCYUiU7zM.

another rap star, 50 Cent: Simon Hattenstone, "50 Cent on love, cash and bankruptcy: 'When there are setbacks, there will be get-backs,'" *Guardian*, May 4, 2020. Katy Stech, "50 Cent Bankruptcy: By the Numbers," *Wall Street Journal*, August 2, 2015.

Wang Sicong: Robert Frank, "Rich Chinese man buys 2 gold Apple watches for dog," *CNBC*, May 27, 2015, https://www.cnbc.com/2015/05/27/rich-chinese-man-buys-2-gold-apple-watches-for-dog-.html. Kenneth Tan, "Wang Jianlin's son shows off dog's 2 Apple Watches on Weibo," *Shanghaiist*, May 5, 2018 (website discontinued).

Manuel Franco, who won an almost unfathomable jackpot: "Manuel Franco: Powerball jackpot winner says he'll use his $768 million wisely," *TMJ4 News*, April 23, 2019, https://www.youtube.com/watch?v=MMC3DHoGhP8.

John and Lisa Robinson: Kristin Leigh, "Where are they now? Munford lottery winners living lavishly," *Fox13 Memphis*, July 8, 2016, https://www.fox13memphis.com/news/where-are-they-now-munford-lottery-winners-living-lavishly/393232343/.

Take Stephen Hung: Fred Barbash, "The world's biggest spender: Stephen Hung just bought 30 custom-made Rolls-Royce Phantoms for $20 million," *Washington Post*, September 17, 2014. Pierre Delannoy, "The extravagant Mr. Hung," *Paris Match*, January 27, 2014.

Indian business tycoon Mukesh Ambani: "Inside Antilia, Muskesh Ambani's $2 billion Mumbai mansion," *Architectural Digest*, April 19, 2019.

single-family dwelling known as Versailles: Jessica Pressler, "177 Minutes with Jackie Siegel," *New York*, April 26, 2013.
Hal Boedeker, "'Queen of Versailles' Jackie Siegel: 'We're sorry we ever started' house," *Orlando Sentinel*, November 2, 2019.

Imelda's shoe collection is notorious: The number of shoes Imelda Marcos left behind when she fled the Philippines with her husband in 1986 is unclear: figures include 1,060, 1,200, 1,220, 2,700 and the infamous 3,000. As recently as 2019, the *New Republic* and *Esquire* quoted the 3,000 figure.
See:
Seth Mydans, "A Recount: 1060 pairs, not 3,000," *New York Times*, February 9, 1987.
Shirley Escalante, "Imelda Marcos shoe museum: the excess of a regime that still haunts the Philippines," *ABC News* (Australia), October 1, 2016, https://www.abc.net.au/news/2016-10-02/imelda-marcos-shoe-museum:-the-excess-of-a-regime/7877098.
Associated Press, "Imelda Marcos's shoe collection gathers mould after years of neglect," *Guardian*, September 23, 2012.

Imelda once spent $3.3 million during: Jane Perlez, "Marcos Linked to Four Manhattan Sites," *New York Times*, March 21, 1986.
Peter York, *Dictator Style: Lifestyles of the World's Most Colorful Despots* (San Francisco: Chronicle Books, 2006), 69.

despotic footwear, Grace Mugabe: Guy Martin, "Zimbabwe's Grace Mugabe: How Her Addiction to Luxury Caused Her Fall From Power," *Forbes*, November 18, 2017.

assemblage of furs gathered by contrashopper Elena Ceausescu: Kate Connolly, "Ceausescu sale: Everything must go," *Guardian*, August 6, 1999.

Iraq's late unlamented ruler Saddam Hussein: It is unclear how many palaces the Iraqi leader had or how even to define them: 20, 50, 80 or more.
Neil MacFarquhar, "Saddam Hussein, Defiant Dictator Who Ruled Iraq With Violence and Fear, Dies," *New York Times*, December 30, 2006.
Colin Freeman, "Saddam Hussein's palaces," *Sunday Telegraph*, July 16, 2009.
Brendan Koerner, "How Many Palaces Hath Saddam," *Slate*, October 3, 2002, https://slate.com/news-and-politics/2002/10/how-many-palaces-hath-saddam.html.
Adel Darwish, "Saddam Hussein builds palaces to rival Versailles," *Independent*, March 19, 1995.

Editorial Board, "Saddam Hussein's Guest List," *New York Times*, November 29, 1997.

His son Uday: The much-quoted story of Saddam burning his son's famous car collection is from Chapter 21 in Will Bardenwerper, *The Prisoner in His Palace: Saddam Hussein, His American Guards, and What History Leaves Unsaid* (New York: Scribner, 2017), Chapter 21.

legitimately paranoid North Korean dictator Kim Jong-un: Maria Tadeo, "Kim Jong-un 'spent over $600m in a year' while North Korean citizens starved to death," *Independent*, February 21, 2014.
Soo Kim, "Inside the luxury world of Kim Jong-un," *Telegraph*, August 25, 2015.
Miranda Prynne, "North Korea uncovered: Palaces, labour camps and mass graves," *Independent*, June 21, 2009.

the Mexican drug lord El Chapo: Alan Feuer, "El Chapo's Narco Spoils: A Beach House, a Zoo and a Fleet of Cash-Filled Jets," *New York Times*, November 27, 2018.

Loathsome former Italian prime minister: Emma Glanfield, "Berlusconi sells his 68-room Sardinia mansion to Saudi royals for a whopping £350m (bunga bunga girls not included)," *Daily Mail*, August 10, 2015.
Simone Filippetti, "Party's rise puts Berlusconi's mansion back in spotlight," *National*, February 17, 2020.

former WorldCom chief executive Bernard Ebbers: Peter Kennedy, "Buyer found for Ebbers ranch," *Globe and Mail*, May 31, 2003.

CNN pioneer and philanthropist Ted Turner: Turner Enterprises, Inc. (website) https://www.tedturner.com/turner-ranches/.

Canadian Business tycoon Paul Desmarais: James Deacon, "The fairest of fairways: luxury golf," *Canadian Business*, May 22, 2006.

songwriting timber baron Tim Blixeth: Larry Bohannan, "Porcupine Creek, site of Trump's upcoming fundraiser, one of the desert's most intriguing golf properties," *Desert Sun*, February 13, 2020.

once spent $3.3 million during: Jane Perlez, "Marcos Linked to Four Manhattan Sites," *New York Times*, March 21, 1986.

AUTOSHOP (SHOPOMATIC)

Ryan Cassata, a twentysomething singer-songwriter: "'We Are All Accumulating Mountains of Things,'" by Alana Semuels, *Atlantic*, August 21, 2018.

Lauren Bowling, a personal finance and self-help blogger: Lauren Bowling, "How I overcame a shopping addiction," *Financial Best Life* (blog), May 28, 2021, https://financialbestlife.com/how-i-knew-i-had-a-shopping-addiction/.

pop idol and alleged child-molester Michael Jackson: You can see this distressing behaviour in the documentary film *Living with Michael Jackson*, directed by Julie Shaw and presented by Martin Bashir (Manchester, England: Granada Television).

In her book Overdressed: Elizabeth L. Cline, *Overdressed: The Shockingly High Cost of Cheap Fashion* (Toronto: Portfolio/Penguin, 2013), 99.

PREDESHOP

Construction costs on self-storage outlets: Colton Gardner, "Four Predictions about the Self-Storage Industry," *Forbes*, November 25, 2019.
Alexander Harris, "U.S. Self-Storage Industry Statistics," *Sparefoot*, March 7, 2020, https://www.sparefoot.com/self-storage/news/1432-self-storage-industry-statistics/.
Nicholas Kohler, "How the self-storage business is evolving for Canada's urban future," *Canadian Business*, July 24, 2017.

there is now more than 1.7 billion square feet of rentable self-storage: Alexander Harris, "U.S. Self-Storage Industry Statistics," *Sparefoot*, March 7, 2020, https://www.sparefoot.com/self-storage/news/1432-self-storage-industry-statistics/.

Provocative musician and Sex *author Madonna*: "Madonna blocks sale of intimate items at auction," BBC, July 19, 2017, https://www.bbc.com/news/world-us-canada-40656485.
Sarah Grant, "NY Court Keeps Order Halting Sale of Madonna, Tupac Prison Letter," *Rolling Stone*, July 21, 2017.

a storage locker belonging to celebrity party girl Paris Hilton: Robert Welkos, "Treasures of Paris (Hilton) Offered for $20 Million," *Los Angeles Times*, February 3, 2006.

drug-addicted music superstar Whitney Houston: CBC Arts, "Whitney Houston's gear sold to cover storage fees," CBC News, January 9, 2007, https://www.cbc.ca/news/entertainment/whitney-houston-s-gear-sold-to-cover-storage-fees-1.635779.

'90s TV star Tori Spelling: True Tori, Episode 2, Season 2, aired October 28, 2014.

SHOPATHON

"No one man grasped": Lindy Woodhead, Shopping, Seduction & Mr. Selfridge (New York: Penguin, 2013), 2.

$25 billion on Valentine's Day gifts: J. Craig Shearman, "Confident consumers and broader buying lead to record Valentine's Day spending plans," National Retail Federation (website), January 30, 2020, https://nrf.com/media-center/press-releases/confident-consumers-and-broader-buying-lead-record-valentines-day.

sultry actor and quirky humanitarian Angelina Jolie: Christopher Dilella, "Angelina Jolie Gives Brad Pitt an Olive Tree for Valentine's Day," CBS News, February 9, 2011, https://www.cbsnews.com/news/angelina-jolie-gives-brad-pitt-an-olive-tree-for-valentines-day/.

Or headline-grabbing rapper Kanye West: Anya Leon, "Kim Kardashian Receives 1,000 Roses on Valentine's Day: See the Pic," People, February 15, 2014.

Kathy Mason, a resident of the Toronto area: Amy Kenny, "Class or crass? Wedding gift spat spirals out of control," Hamilton Spectator, June 19, 2013.

Americans spent $9 billion on costumes: "Halloween spending to reach $9 Billion," National Retail Federation (website), September 20, 2018, https://nrf.com/media-center/press-releases/halloween-spending-reach-9-billion.

Fleeting lovebirds: Richard Johnson, "Mariah Carey quietly sold mega diamond ring from ex James Packer," Page Six, May 27, 2018, https://pagesix.com/2018/05/27/mariah-carey-quietly-sold-mega-diamond-ring-from-ex-james-packer/.

Acquisitive model, singer and performer Victoria Beckham: Mahalia Chang, "A look at all 14 of Victoria Beckham's insane engagement rings," Harper's Bazaar, October 31, 2017.

Liza Minnelli's fourth marriage to producer and gambling addict David Gest: Reuters Life!, "Liza Minnelli tops list of costly celeb weddings," *Reuters*, July 12, 2007, https://www .reuters.com/article/us-weddings/liza-minnelli-tops-list-of-costly-celeb-weddings -idUSN1235430320070712.

Vanisha Mittal, the daughter of Lakshmi Mittal: "Glimpsing a fairytale wedding," BBC *News*, June 22, 2004, http://news.bbc.co.uk/2/hi/south_asia/3830009.stm.

UNSHOPATHON

volatile actor Russell Crowe: Associated Press, "Russell Crowe's 'divorce' auction fetches millions for actor," CBC *News*, April 8, 2018, https://www.cbc.ca/news/entertainment/ russell-crowe-divorce-auction-1.4610370.

Music diva and overshopper Barbra Streisand: Alex Dobuzinskis, "Barbra Streisand auctions off objects for charity," *Reuters*, October 12, 2009, https://www.reuters .com/article/us-streisand/barbra-streisand-auctions-off-objects-for-charity -idUSTRE59B5KS20091012.

Elton John may be the king of the celebrity unshopathon: "Elton John talks about auctioning his personal collection," ABC *News*, August 8, 1988, https://abcnews.go .com/Entertainment/video/aug-1988-elton-john-talks-auctioning-personal-collection -52580042.
"Graham Kennedy's News Show," May 1988.
"Car auction 'thrills' Elton John," CNN, June 6, 2001, https://www.cnn.com/2001/ WORLD/europe/06/05/elton.auction.02/index.html.

John later launched an annual clothes sale: *Today*, April 10, 2006.

DESHOPATHON

deshopping phenomenon Marie Kondo: Jura Koncius, "The tidying tide: Marie Kondo effect hits sock drawers and consignment stores," *Washington Post*, January 11, 2019.

another Netflix show: Daniel D'Addario, "'Get Organized with The Home Edit' Makes Excess a Virtue: TV Review," *Variety*, August 31, 2020.

soul singer and writer Isaac Hayes: Ron Kisner, "The Money Problems of the Stars," *Ebony*, May 1977.

Big spender Sammy Davis Jr.: Terry Pristin, "Sammy for Sale: Entertainer Davis' Belongings to Be Sold at Auction," *Los Angeles Times*, September 18, 1991.
Gary Fishgall, *Gonna Do Great Things: The Life of Sammy Davis Jr.* (New York: Scribner, 2001), 378–81.

SHOPAGANDA

preposterous campaign stating that drinking McDonald's: McDonald's Canada, "Tiny bean, big impact: McDonald's Canada makes strong commitment to coffee sustainability with its McCafe brand," PR *Newswire*, July 3, 2019, https://www.newswire.ca/news-releases/tiny-bean-big-impact-mcdonald-s-canada-makes-strong-commitment-to-coffee-sustainability-with-its-mccafe-r-brand-805698011.html.

Donald Trump, who insisted his buildings were taller: Vivian Lee, "Donald Trump's Math Takes His Towers to Greater Heights," *New York Times*, November 1, 2016.

television star Ricardo Montalbán: Liberty Leather Goods, "Corinthian Leather – The Material with a Surprising Story," https://www.libertyleathergoods.com/corinthian-leather/.

Volkswagen's criminal scheme to sell "clean diesel": Brad Plumer, "Volkswagen's appalling clean diesel scandal, explained," *Vox*, September 23, 2015, https://www.vox.com/2015/9/21/9365667/volkswagen-clean-diesel-recall-passenger-cars.
"Volkswagen's 'clean diesel,'" *Truth in Advertising*, June 28, 2016, https://www.truthinadvertising.org/volkswagens-clean-diesel/.
Associated Press, "Volkswagen sued for false advertising over 'clean diesel' claims," CBC *News*, March 29, 2016, https://www.cbc.ca/news/business/volkswagen-lawsuit-ads-1.3510836.

Some shopaganda is dangerous to health: Stanford University, Research into the impact of Tobacco Advertising (website), https://tobacco.stanford.edu/.
"The Personal Reminiscences of Albert Lasker," interview by Dan Albertson and Allan Nevins, *American Heritage*, Volume 6, Issue 1 (1954).

OUTSHOP

hard-drinking womanizer Babe Ruth: Anthony Castrovince, "The 'Curse of the Bambino,' explained," MLB *News*, April 19, 2019, https://www.mlb.com/news/curse-of-the -bambino.

NFL *phenom Tom Brady:* ESPN Stats and Info, "Tom Brady falling to sixth round one of several forgettable draft moments," *ESPN*, April 16, 2020, https://www.espn.com/blog /new-england-patriots/post/_/id/4819844/tom-brady-falling-the-20th-round-one -of-several-forgettable-draft-moments.

"the prize" in a box of Cracker Jack: Randee Dawn, "Cracker Jack is replacing toy prizes inside with digital codes," *Today*, April 22, 2016, https://www.today.com/food/cracker -jack-replacing-toy-prizes-inside-digital-codes-t87811.

true story of Brian Molony: Gary Ross, *Stung: the Incredible Obsession of Brian Molony* (Toronto: Stoddart, 2011), 191.

BALKSHOP

Mean-spirited New York hotelier Leona Helmsley: Enid Nemy, "Leona Helmsley, Hotel Queen, Dies at 87," *New York Times*, August 20, 2007.
Howard Kurtz, "Leona Helmsley Found Guilty of Tax Evasion, Mail Fraud," *Washington Post*, August 31, 1989.
Leonard Buder, "Helmsley Jury Hears Closing Arguments," *New York Times*, August 24, 1989.
Howard Kurtz, "Take That, Leona! Trump Fires Missive at Hotel Rival Helmsley," *Washington Post*, April 20, 1989.

petulant landlord Donald Trump: Steve Reilly, "Hundreds allege Donald Trump doesn't pay his bills," USA *Today*, June 9, 2016.

author Juliet B. Schor: Juliet B. Schor, *The Overspent American: Why We Want What We Don't Need* (New York: HarperCollins, 1999), 29, 72.

teen idol David Cassidy: Christina Dugan Ramirez, "David Cassidy Denied Having Financial Issues 9 Months Before His Death," *People*, December 7, 2017.

singer and overshopper Willie Nelson: Kelly Phillips Erb, "Willie Nelson, Who Saved His Career And His House With The IRS Tapes, Turns 80," *Forbes*, April 29, 2013.

deadbeat dad Dennis Rodman: Sheila Marikar, "Dennis Rodman Is 'Broke,' Suffering from 'Drinking Problem,'" *ABC News*, March 27, 2012, https://abcnews. go.com/Entertainment/dennis-rodman-broke-suffering-drinking-problem/ story?id=16012846.

man-child Michael Jackson: Jeff Gottlieb, "Michael Jackson trial: Pop star was 'tapped out,' millions in debt," *Los Angeles Times*, August 12, 2013.

Jocelyn Wildenstein: George Rush, "Jocelyne's Revenge," *Vanity Fair*, March 8, 1998. Julia Marsh and Jennifer Gould, "'Catwoman' files for bankruptcy," *Page Six*, May 17, 2018, https://pagesix.com/2018/05/17/catwoman-files-for-bankruptcy/.

BLOTTOSHOP

Lululemon started serving draft: Abha Bhattarai, "Shopping under the influence," *Washington Post*, February 13, 2020.
Stephanie Clifford, "Online Merchants Home in on Imbibing Consumers," *New York Times*, December 27, 2011.

Belinda Carlisle admits: Ruth Huntman, "Belinda Carlisle: 'After three decades of cocaine use, I can't believe I'm not dead,'" *Guardian*, August 12, 2017.

Social media is alive with examples: Viktorija Gabulaitė, "90 Times People Shopped Online While Drunk and Regretted it Deeply," *BoredPanda*, https://www.boredpanda .com/funny-drunk-online-shopping-fails/.

CONTRASHOP

buying cheap counterfeit goods: "Fake goods, real dangers," U.S. Customs and Border Protection (website), October 4, 2019, https://www.cbp.gov/trade/ fakegoodsrealdangers.

for the purpose of increasing their status: Maria Eugenia Perez, Raquel Castano and Claudia Quintanilla, "Constructing identity through the consumption of counterfeit luxury goods," *Qualitative Market Research: An International Journal*, volume 13, Issue 3 (June 2010).

stuff such as elephant ivory: "Still poached for ivory," World Wildlife Fund (website), https://wwf.panda.org/knowledge_hub/endangered_species/elephants/african _elephants/afelephants_threats/.

Donald Trump once displayed a 'carved ivory frieze': Mark Singer, *Trump and Me* (New York: Tim Duggan Books, 2016), 80.
Mark Singer, "Trump Solo," *New Yorker*, May 19, 1997.

Jackie Siegel, co-builder: Jessica Pressler, "177 Minutes with Jackie Siegel," *New York*, April 26, 2013.

the helmeted hornbill: Rachel Bale, "Poached for Its Horn, This Rare Bird Struggles to Survive," *National Geographic*, September 2018.
"The Helmeted Hornbill crisis and BirdLife's conservation efforts," BirdLife International (website). (Article no longer available on website.)

Rhino horns are prized: "Rhino horn consumers, who are they?" summary by TRAFFIC of a study commissioned in 2013 under the WWF/TRAFFIC Illegal Wildlife Trade Campaign, https://www.traffic.org/site/assets/files/8094/rhino-horn-consumers-who-are-they. pdf.

The totoaba: Carlos Loret de Mola A., "Thanks to Mexico's inaction, a cartel is causing irreparable damage in the ocean," *Washington Post*, December 5, 2019.

populations of the vaquita marina porpoise: Christopher Joyce, "Chinese taste for Fish Bladder Threatens Rare Porpoise of Mexico," *All Things Considered*, NPR, February 9, 2016, https://www.npr.org/sections/goatsandsoda/2016/02/09/466185043/chinese -taste-for-fish-bladder-threatens-tiny-porpoise-in-mexico.

jewelry made from tiger teeth: Tiger facts, WWF (website), https://www.worldwildlife .org/species/tiger.

Even a simple cotton shirt can qualify as contrashopping: Tansy Hoskins, "Cotton production linked to images of the dried up Aral Sea basin," *Guardian*, October 1, 2014.

a 2017 paper by researchers: Wencke Gwozdz, Kristian Steensen Nielsen, Tina Müller, "An Environmental Perspective on Clothing Consumption: Consumer Segments and Their Behavioral Patterns," *Sustainability* (September 2017).

US *Congressman Duncan Hunter*: Jose A. Del Real, "Duncan Hunter Will Plead Guilty to Misuse of Campaign Funds," *New York Times*, December 2, 2019.
Hunter court documents: https://www.justice.gov/usao-sdca/press-release/file /1089516/download.

Trump . . . also qualified as a contrashopper: David Fahrenthold, "Trump agrees to shut down his charity amid allegations that he used it for personal and political benefit," *Washington Post*, December 18, 2018.
Trump court documents: https://ag.ny.gov/sites/default/files/court_stamped _petition.pdf.

High-living big spender L. Dennis Kozlowski: Andrew Ross Sorkin, "Tyco Details Lavish Lives of Executives," *New York Times*, September 18, 2002.
David A. Kaplan, "Tyco's 'Piggy,' Out of Prison and Living Small," *New York Times*, March 1, 2015.

Monumental swindler Bernard Madoff: Raquel Laneri, "Bernie Madoff's Shoe Fetish," *Forbes*, November 17, 2010.
Verena Dobnik, "Government sells spoils of Madoff's lavish life," *Associated Press*, November 13, 2010, http://www.nbcnews.com/id/40169595/ns/business-us_ business/t/government-sells-spoils-madoffs-lavish-life/#.Xp5DjZNKjOQ.

evangelical Christian Green family: Alan Feuer, "Hobby Lobby Agrees to Forfeit 5,500 Artifacts Smuggled Out of Iraq," *New York Times*, July 5, 2017.

Nicolas Cage outshopped fellow bone-collector Leonardo DiCaprio: Joseph Ax, "Actor Nicolas Cage returns stolen dinosaur skull he bought," *Reuters*, December 21, 2015, https://www.reuters.com/article/us-people-nicolascage-dinosaur -idUSKBN0U42MS20151222.

dubious political lobbyist and convicted felon Paul Manafort: Katelyn Polantz, "Manafort was only client to pay with international wire transfers, former clothing store manager says," *CNN*, August 21, 2018, https://www.cnn.com/politics/live-news/ manaforttrial/h_21f3d31af9300186337cac490e6329d7.

Rachel Weiner, Rosalind S. Helderman, Justin Jouvenal and Matt Zapotosky, "Paul Manafort trial Day 2: Witnesses describe extravagant clothing purchases, home remodels, lavish cars paid with wire transfers," *Washington Post*, August 1, 2018. Farnoush Amiri, "Paul Manafort's lavish suits and jackets are 'ludicrous' and 'excess,'" menswear experts say," NBC *News*, August 2, 2018, https://www.nbcnews.com/pop -culture/lifestyle/paul-manafort-s-lavish-suits-jackets-are-ludicrous-excess-menswear -n897121.

CONVERSHOPPING

convicted felon Conrad Black: Bryan Burrough, "The convictions of Conrad Black," *Vanity Fair*, October 2011.

MTV *Cribs*: Jessica M. Goldstein, "In 2000, 'Cribs' became a phenomenon. 20 years later, we're all living in an accidental reboot," *Washington Post*, July 24, 2020. Stephen LaConte, "'MTV Cribs' Was Pretty Much Fake, And Here Are the Receipts to Prove it," *BuzzFeed*, October 28, 2020.

David Geffen sparked outrage: Richard Luscombe, "Billionaire David Geffen criticized for tone-deaf self-isolation post," *Guardian*, March 28, 2020.

Elizabeth "Big girls need big diamonds" Taylor never hesitated: Mélanie Nauche, "The best of Elizabeth Taylor's jewelry," *Vogue*, March 23, 2020.

young people have embraced convershopping: Kit Yarrow and Jayne O'Donnell, *Gen BuY*, (Jossey-Bass, 2009), 48.

CYBERSHOP

Global internet sales are expected: "Retail e-commerce sales worldwide from 2014 to 2023," *Statista*, August 27, 2020, https://www.statista.com/statistics/379046/worldwide-retail-e-commerce-sales/.

And this was before Amazon declared: Brett Molina, "Wait, someone's hiring? Amazon, Walmart are among companies adding workers during coronavirus crisis," USA *Today*, March 20, 2020.

SHOPOSTLE

You may think of George Foreman: "Meet George," The Official Website of George Foreman, https://www.georgeforeman.com/pages/biography.

enthusiastic stuff-seller Ron Popeil: "About Ron Popeil," https://www.ronpopeil.com/.

comedian Vince Shlomi:
Ben Popken, "The 'ShamWow Guy' cleans up his act," NBC *News*, September 13, 2013, https://www.nbcnews.com/businessmain/shamwow-guy-cleans-his-act-8C11094914.

late loud-mouthed Billy Mays: Scott Mayerowitz, "The Seedy Underside of TV Pitchmen," ABC *News*, August 11, 2009, https://abcnews.go.com/Business/story?id=8306401.

culinary hero and kitchen wizard Jamie Oliver:
Potato Al Forno, by Jamie Oliver, YouTube, October 6, 2019, https://www.youtube.com/watch?v=mU2_CDcYwkI

what the highest bidder hired them to wear: Vanessa Friedman, "The Red Carpet Is Its Own Economy," *New York Times*, January 5, 2018.

Self-promoting clotheshorse Louise Linton: Maer Roshan, "Louise Linton, aka Mrs. Steven Mnuchin, Is Sorry," *Los Angeles Magazine*, June 13, 2019.
Chris Perez, "Mnuchin's wife unleashes Instagram fit after backlash," *New York Post*, August 22, 2017.

Kellyanne Conway famously raised the ire: Nolan D. McCaskill, Louis Nelson and Isaac Arnsdorf, "Kellyanne Conway under fire for promoting Ivanka's brand," *Politico*, February 9, 2017, https://www.politico.com/story/2017/02/kellyanne-conway-ivanka-nordstrom-234838.

loud-mouthed conspiracy theorist Alex Jones: Andrew Marantz, "Alex Jones's Bogus Coronavirus Cures," *New Yorker*, March 30, 2020.
Elizabeth Williamson and Emily Steel, "Conspiracy Theories Made Alex Jones Very Rich. They May Bring Him Down," *New York Times*, September 7, 2018.

Some ordinary shopostles: Ellie Flynn, "Multilevel marketing sells a dream. Don't buy it," *Globe and Mail*, August 30, 2019.

SHOPOCRACY

future crooked president Richard Nixon: Speech by Richard Nixon, September 13, 1960, https://www.presidency.ucsb.edu/documents/excerpts-from-remarks-vice-president -richard-nixon-lloyd-center-portland-or.

B-movie actor Ronald Reagan: Miller Center, "Reagan-Carter Oct. 28, 1980 Debate – 'Are You Better Off?'" YouTube video, https://www.youtube.com/watch?v=rU6PWT1rVUk.

president George W. Bush: CSPAN User, "October 12, 2001 | Clip of Presidential News Conference," CSPAN, https://www.c-span.org/video/?c4552776/user-clip-bush -shopping-quote.

Fashion icon Victoria Beckham once justified: This was widely reported at the time, attributed to the *Daily Star* newspaper.
"Posh spends up big in Milan," *West Australian*, January 10, 2010, https://thewest.com. au/news/world/posh-spends-up-big-in-milan-ng-ya-225234.

SHOPONOMICS

"After they leave my clutches": Betty Halbreich with Rebecca Paley, *I'll Drink to That: A Life in Style, with a Twist* (New York: Penguin, 2014), 138.

English economist Nicholas Barbon: Nicholas Barbon, *A Discourse of Trade* (The Lord Baltimore Press, 1690).

new perspective by Betty Halbreich: Betty Halbreich with Rebecca Paley, *I'll Drink to That: A Life in Style, with a Twist* (New York: Penguin, 2014), 138–39.

French economist Jean-Baptiste Say: *Traité d'economie politique* (1803).

Thorstein Veblen: *The Theory of the Leisure Class* (1899), Chapter 3.

Economic growth is a generally accepted imperative: Juliet B. Schor, *The Overspent American* (Harper Collins, 1999), 172.

"Abundance is the enemy of appreciation.": Elizabeth Dunn, *Happy Money* (Simon & Schuster, 2013), 34.

SHOPOMANIA

a certain item like toilet paper: Kyle Beachy, "'Rush on toilet paper' at local store causes fight; police called," *25 News Week.com*, March 21, 2020. (Article no longer available on website.)

Heather Navarro, "Deputies Actually Had to Respond to a Costco Over Coronavirus Buying," NBC *Los Angeles*, March 5, 2020, https://www.nbclosangeles.com/news/local/coronavirus-costco-chino-hills-deputies-panic/2323783/.

Antonia Noori Farzan, "'It's been nuts': Costco's sales spike amid coronavirus panic-buying of bottled water, hand sanitizer and toilet paper," *Washington Post*, March 6, 2020.

Ultimate Mega Balloon Drop: "Westfield Parramatta: Christmas shopping promotion ends in stampede – video," *Guardian*, December 26, 2019.

Organizers were clearly unaware of a similar incident: Associated Press, "10 injured in SoCal Black Friday mall stampede," November 25, 2006.

a Walmart employee was trampled to death: Kieran Crowely, "Worker killed in Walmart stampede," *New York Post*, November 28, 2008.

pepper-sprayed other shoppers at a Walmart in California: Hailey Branson-Potts, "Stores reach out to early birds," *Los Angeles Times*, November 25, 2011.

"customer-versus-customer shopping rage": "Wal-Mart pepper-spray attack caused 'total pandemonium,' says LAPD," *L.A. Now*, November 29, 2011, https://latimesblogs.latimes.com/lanow/2011/11/lapd-describes-choatic-dangerous-frenzy-at-wal-mart-black-friday-.html.

One explanation for the insanity: Emilie Le Beau Lucchesi, "What Turns Black Friday Shoppers Into Raging Hordes?" *New York Times*, November 21, 2017.

SHOPERATI

stand-up comic and social critic George Carlin: This is from a stand-up routine by Carlin in 1986 and is (still) really funny.

eccentric philosopher and brilliant economist Adam Smith: Adam Smith, *Of the Origin and Use of Money, An Inquiry into the Nature and Causes of the Wealth of Nations* (1776), chapter IV.

Leno has a collection of 180 cars: Paul Schrodt, "Jay Leno Is Worth $350 Million and Owns 181 Cars But Says He Still Lives Like Someone Who's on Their Last Dime," MSN, May 16, 2018. (Article no longer available on website.)

His fellow funny guy Jerry Seinfeld: Paul Henderson, "Jerry Seinfeld's Porsche collection is phenomenal," GQ, April 29, 2020.

In his book, Enough: John Naish, *Enough* (Hodder & Stoughton, 2009), 76.

Rolling Stones drummer Charlie Watts: James Raia, "Charlie Watts: A man and his cars and clothes but no driving," *Weekly Driver*, August 26, 2021, https://theweeklydriver .com/2021/08/charlie-watts-a-man-and-his-cars/.
Lisa Bowman, "Rolling Stones drummer Charlie Watts reveals the secret to his long marriage," NME, March 1, 2018.

Star Wars creator George Lucas: Patricia Leigh Brown, "Tour George Lucas's Office at Skywalker Ranch," *Architectural Digest*, October 7, 2016.
"Lucasfilm Research Library: Interview with Jo Donaldson, Manager, Lucasfilm Research Library & Robyn Stanley, Research Librarian," I Love Libraries (website), January 31, 2012, http://www.ilovelibraries.org/article/lucasfilm-research-library.

Priceline founder Jay Walker: Adrianne Jeffries, "Priceline's Litigious Founder Jay Walker: I Am Not a Troll," *Observer*, March 5, 2012.
The Walker Library of The History of Human Imagination (website), http://www .walkerdigital.com/the-walker-library_welcome.html.
Steven Levy, "Browse the Artifacts of Geek History in Jay Walker's Library," *Wired*, September 22, 2008.

idiosyncratic fashion pioneer Karl Lagerfeld: Laure Guilbault, "Karl Lagerfeld Delivers Master Class in Hyères," WWD, April 25, 2015.

famous nice guy Tom Hanks: Taffy Brodesser-Akner, "This Tom Hanks Story Will Help You Feel Less Bad," *New York Times*, November 13, 2019.

Southern gothic writer Cormac McCarthy: Sam Jones, "No typewriter for old men: Cormac McCarthy to part with beloved Olivetti," *Guardian*, December 1, 2009.

Thessaly La Force, "Great Writer, Great Machine," *New Yorker*, December 7, 2009.

Former rodeo champion Kiefer Sutherland: Chris Vinnicombe, "'Some people collect cars or art . . . for me, guitars are that': interview with Kiefer Sutherland," *Guitar.com*, May 27, 2019, https://guitar.com/features/interviews/some-people-collect-baseball -cards-some-people-collect-cars-or-art-for-me-guitars-are-that-kiefer-sutherland/.

Multi-instrument-playing peacenik and actor Richard Gere: "Richard Gere guitar auction fetches $936,438," BBC, October 13, 2011, https://www.bbc.com/news/entertainment -arts-15286982.

legendary rocker David Gilmour: Kory Grow, "David Gilmour's Guitars Sell for Millions at Charity Auction," *Rolling Stone*, June 20, 2019.

Basketball veteran Jarrett Jack once claimed: Carl Steward, "Sole Man: Warriors' Jarrett Jack owns 1,500 pairs of basketball shoes," *Mercury News*, December 3, 2012.

Roger Federer once owned more than 250 pairs: Elizabeth Gravier, "Roger Federer on his 250-plus sneaker collection: 'I think obsession can definitely lead to some good things,'" CNBC, November 26, 2019, https://www.cnbc.com/2019/11/26/roger-federer -on-being-obsessed.html.

The sneaker craze: Daisuke Wakabayashi, "The Fight for Sneakers," *New York Times*, October 15, 2021.

unlikely fashion icon Jonah Hill: "Jonah Hill And Sunny Suljic Go Sneaker Shopping With Complex," YouTube video, October 22, 2018, https://www.youtube.com/ watch?v=fLx7dq5cbg4.

Demi Moore's rumoured collection: Larry Hackett, "Domestic Drama," *People*, March 30, 1998. Lena Dunham, "Demi Moore Reveals All," *Harper's Bazaar*, September 12, 2019. *TV star Corbin Bernsen*: Heather John Fogarty, "Let It Snow," *Los Angeles Magazine*, December 24, 2013.

SHOPARRHEA

Reprehensible newspaper mogul William Randolph Hearst: W.A. Swanberg, *Citizen Hearst* (Charles Scribner's Sons, 1961), 465–68.

Lucy Magda, an extreme autoshopper: "Hidden riches amaze police: Clothes, gems cram house," *Hamilton Spectator*, April 26, 1997.

the car collection of Hassanal Bolkiah, the sultan of Brunei: Mark Seal, "The Prince Who Blew Through Billions," *Vanity Fair*, June 23, 2011.
Michael Sheehan, "The Sultan of Brunei's Rotting Supercar Collection," *Gizmodo*, March 15, 2011, https://www.gizmodo.com.au/2011/03/the-sultan-of-bruneis-rotting -supercar-collection/.
Thomas Fuller, "A Whopper of an Auction to Pay Off Prince's Creditors in Brunei," *International Herald Tribune*, August 8, 2001.
Associated Press, "Auction Nets $7.8 Million, Miffs Prince," *Los Angeles Times*, August 17, 2001.

shoparrhea also afflicted Roger Baillon: Benjamin Preston, "Trove of Valuable Antique Sports Cars Headed for Auction in France," *New York Times*, December 9, 2014.
Jay Ramey, "French Barn-Find Collection Brings $28.5 Million, Sets 10 Records," *Autoweek*, February 11, 2015, https://www.autoweek.com/car-life/events/a1863476/ french-barn-find-collection-brings-285-million-sets-10-records/.

the infamous brothers Collyer: "The Legendary Collyer Brothers Harlem NY 1881-1947," *Harlem World Magazine*, April 14, 2018, https://www.harlemworldmagazine.com /56456-2/.
"Strange Case of the Collyer Brothers," *Life*, April 7, 1947, 50.

SHOPITITIS

It describes Felice Campbell: "What Happened to the Mom Who Shopped Her Family Broke" *Oprah Winfrey Network*, October 3, 2015, https://www.youtube.com/ watch?v=3hbt_qOoO4E.

Erika Girardi, the free-spending star: Matthew Goldstein and Katherine Rosman, "The Real Trials of a 'Real Housewife,'" *New York Times*, October 9, 2021.

writer and former shopaholic Carla Sosenko: Carla Sosenko, "My Shopping Addiction Cost Me $98,000 in 6 Months," *Cosmopolitan*, July 26, 2018.

James Hammond: Lizzie Parry, "Male shopping addict, 19, jumped to his death from bridge after stealing thousands of pounds from his mother to pay for clothes and nights out," *Daily Mail*, March 28, 2014.

well-documented: Donald W. Black, "A review of compulsive buying disorder," *World Psychiatry*, February 6, 2007.

PROXYSHOPPER

Todd Klein, a New York decorator: Alex Kuczynski, "Lifestyles Of the Rich And Red-Faced," *New York Times*, September 22, 2002.

Los Angeles-based personal shopper Nicole Pollard: Julie Miller, "A Personal Shopper to the Rich, Famous and Royal Shares Tales of Holiday-Gifting Extravagance," *Vanity Fair*, December 21, 2016.

Adventure writer Brandon Presser: Brandon Presser, "Twelve Things I Never Knew About Clothes Until I Became a Personal Shopper for Barneys," *Bloomberg*, November 14, 2018, https://www.bloomberg.com/news/features/2018-11-14/secrets -of-a-barneys-personal-shopper-12-things-i-learned.

the renowned and beloved Betty Halbreich: Betty Halbreich with Rebecca Paley, *I'll Drink to That: A Life in Style, with a Twist* (New York: Penguin), 194.

". . . hundred-dollar Adele Simpson number . . .": Judith Thurman, "Ask Betty," *New Yorker*, November 12, 2012.

securing an old mattress: Juliet Eilperin, Josh Dawsey and Brady Dennis, "Scott Pruitt had aide do various personal tasks, including hunt for a used Trump hotel mattress," *Washington Post*, June 4, 2018.

SHOPACADEMY

Advertising is a $550-billion business: A. Guttmann, "Global advertising market – Statistics & Facts," *Statista*, November 12, 2019, https://www.statista.com/topics/990/global-advertising-market/.

diamond producer De Beers: J. Courtney Sullivan, "Why 'A Diamond is Forever' has lasted so long," *Washington Post*, February 7, 2014.
Uri Friedman, "How an Ad Campaign Invented the Diamond Engagement Ring," *Atlantic*, February 13, 2015.

"*converting tiny crystals of carbon into universally*": Edward Jay Epstein, "Have You Ever Tried to Sell a Diamond?" *Atlantic*, February 1982.

illusion they are a good way to preserve a fortune: Ira Weissman, "7 Reasons Why Diamonds Are a Waste of Your Money," *Huffpost*, January 23, 2014, https://www .huffpost.com/entry/7-reasons-why-you-shouldn_b_1720870.

vapid former tennis champion Andre Agassi: Andre Agassi, *Open, An Autobiography*, (Alfred A Knopf, 2009), 162.

author Rob Walker: Rob Walker, *Buying In: The Secret Dialogue Between What We Buy and Who We Are* (Random House, 2008), 78.

SHOPPING SHEEP

Hush Puppies: Malcolm Gladwell, *The Tipping Point*, (Little Brown & Company, 2000), 1–3.

"*I mean, once everybody gets on a trend*": Betty Halbreich with Rebecca Paley, *I'll Drink to That: A Life in Style, with a Twist* (New York: Penguin), 138–39.

"*Are we a nation of sheep?*": Véronique Hyland, "The Most Famous Personal Shopper in the World," The Cut, *New York*, September 4, 2014, https://www.thecut.com/2014/09/ most-famous-personal-shopper-in-the-world.html.

SHOPPING SHERPA

labelled her allegedly cheating husband: Stephen Brunt, "Tie Domi: The tough guy who wanted to be a player," *Globe and Mail*, September 30, 2006.

Engineers . . . have already invented a machine: Paul Sawers, "Gita is a $3,250 personal cargo robot that follows you around," *VentureBeat*, October 15, 2019, https:// venturebeat.com/2019/10/15/gita-is-a-3250-personal-cargo-robot-that-follows-you -around/.

AEROSHOP

"There's only one thing . . .": Tom Hanks: Viktor Navorski (Quotes section), IMDB (website), https://www.imdb.com/title/tt0362227/characters/nm0000158.

SHOP THERAPY

As Elton John says: Elizabeth Lambert, "Elton John's Houses in London and Nice," *Architectural Digest*, May 2000.

DESHOPPING CENTRE

When China decided in 2018: Philippa Duchastel de Montrouge, "Media Briefing: Canada's Plastic Waste Export Trends Following China's Import Ban," *Greenpeace Canada*, January 10, 2019, https://www.greenpeace.org/canada/en/qa/6971/media -briefing-canadas-plastic-waste-export-trends-following-chinas-import-ban/.
Saša Petricic, "China is no longer world's dumping ground, but cleaning up its own backyard is proving to be a challenge," *CBC News*, March 28, 2018, https://www.cbc.ca/ news/world/pollution-recycling-china-petricic-1.4593078.
Jan Dell, "157,000 Shipping Containers of U.S. Plastic Waste Exported to Countries with Poor Waste Management in 2018," *Plastic Pollution Coalition*, March 6, 2019, https://www.plasticpollutioncoalition.org/blog/2019/3/6/157000-shipping-containers -of-us-plastic-waste-exported-to-countries-with-poor-waste-management-in-2018.

Garbage exports to Africa: Hiroko Tabuchi, Michael Corkery and Carlos Mureithi, "Big Oil Is in Trouble. Its Plan: Flood Africa With Plastic," *New York Times*, August 30, 2020. Helena Varkkey, "By exporting trash, rich countries put their waste out of sight and out of mind," *CNN Opinion*, July 29, 2019, https://www.cnn.com/2019/07/29/opinions /by-exporting-trash-rich-countries-put-their-waste-out-of-sight-and-out-of-mind -varkkey/index.html.

garbage landslides: Stephanie Pappas, "Koshe Disaster: What Causes Garbage Landslides?" *Livescience*, March 17, 2017, https://www.livescience.com/58307-what -caused-ethiopia-garbage-landslide.html.

After that, it's clothing: "Fact and Figures about Materials, Waste and Recycling," US Environmental Protection Agency, 2017, https://www.epa.gov/facts-and-figures -about-materials-waste-and-recycling/textiles-material-specific-data.

Liam O'Connell, "U.S. apparel and footwear resale market - statistics & facts," *Statista*, August 13, 2019, https://www.statista.com/topics/5161/apparel-and-footwear-resale-in-the-us/#:~:text=A%202018%20survey%20found%20that,to%2011%20percent%20by%202027.

once is not enough to wear an outfit: "Seven celebrities who dare to rewear: recycling brings a touch of green on the red carpet," *South China Morning Post*, May 16, 2018. Lucy Siegle, "The Green Carpet Challenge: How it All Began," *Eco-Age*, January 17, 2020, https://eco-age.com/magazine/green-carpet-challenge-how-it-all-began/.

ECO-SHOPPING

Model-dating bachelor Leonardo DiCaprio: Robert Rapier, "Leonardo DiCaprio's Carbon Footprint Is Much Higher Than He Thinks," *Forbes*, March 1, 2016.

SHOP-O-EROTIC

In a study conducted in 2010: Francine Kopun, "Sex just as good as two-for-one deal: Study," *Toronto Star*, September 20, 2010.

George Harrison, "Shopping can be as stimulating as SEX for some people, according to a new study," *Sun*, September 28, 2017.

SHOPORNOGRAPHY

Sultry actor Lauren Bacall: KL Lum, JR Polansky, RK Jackler, and SA Glantz, "Signed, sealed and delivered: 'big tobacco' in Hollywood, 1927-1951," *Tobacco Control* 17, no. 5 (2008), 313–323.

Car manufacturers: Yeoman Lowbrow, "Sex Sells Auto Equipment In The 1970s And 1980s," *Flashbak*, August 27, 2014, https://flashbak.com/sex-sells-auto-equipment-in-the-1970s-and-1980s-19050/.

risky at best: Bridget Brennan, *Why She Buys* (Crown Business, 2009), 36.

Hardee's hamburgers: Charisse Jones and Zlati Meyer, "Sexy Burger Girls? No longer at Carl's Jr. and Hardee's," *USA Today*, March 29, 2017.

Kirthana Ramisetti, "Carl's Jr. CEO dishes on Kim Kardashian, Kate Upton's sexy burger ads," *New York Daily News*, May 30, 2015.

"Trump's Pick for Secretary of Labor: 'Ugly' Women Don't Sell Burgers," by Kristen Bellstrom, *Fortune*, December 9, 2016.

Vicky Valet, "Where Secretary of Labor Nominee Andy Puzder Stands on Employment and Jobs," *Forbes*, January 26, 2017.

neuromarketing study: Martin Lindstrom, *Buyology*, (Doubleday, 2008), 192–3.

SHOPITORIUM

the mall had become, as Gruen later sadly reflected: Malcolm Gladwell, "The Terrazzo Jungle," *New Yorker*, March 8, 2004.

Amy Crawford, "A Mid-Century Shopping Icon Makes Way for the Future," *Bloomberg CityLab*, December 22, 2017, https://www.bloomberg.com/news/articles/2017-12-22/what-will-become-of-victor-gruen-s-northland-center.

ANTI-SHOPPER

Plato was not likely the first: Plato, *The Republic*, Book II.

Lucius Annaeus Seneca . . . Epictetus: "The Highest Good: An Introduction To The 4 Stoic Virtues," *Daily Stoic*, https://dailystoic.com/4-stoic-virtues/.

"*. . . abundance of possesions . . .*": Luke 12:15

"*Jesus went into the temple of God*": Matthew 21:12–13

Italian philosopher Thomas Aquinas: Thomas Aquinas, *De Regno: On Kingship*, Chapter 3.

infamous anti-shopping or so-called sumptuary laws: Frank Trentmann, *The Empire of Things* (Penguin, 2016), 39.

Mao Zedong banned ownership of gold: "China's gold market: progress and prospects," World Gold Council (website), https://www.gold.org/sites/default/files/China%20gold%20market%20%20progress%20and%20prospects.pdf.

Adam Smith explained it: Adam Smith, *The Wealth of Nations*, Book II, Chapter III, 346.

PSEUDOSHOP

Some pseudoshoppers test-drive cars: "Test driving nice cars: a fun and free hobby,"
by Reddit user bogmire, https://www.reddit.com/r/ActLikeYouBelong/comments
/6d8gv7/test_driving_nice_cars_a_fun_and_free_hobby/.

SHOPAPALOOZA

Marty Brochstein, senior VP of industry relations and information: Dave McNary, "'Star
Wars' Movies Push Overall Licensed Merchandise Sales to $262 Billion," *Variety*,
May 22, 2017.

Today, the museum store: Karen Chernick, "Who Decides What You Buy in Museum
Gift Shops," *Artsy*, November 24, 2017, https://www.artsy.net/article/artsy-editorial
-decides-buy-museum-gift-shops.

SHOPTOMETRY

Paco Underhill: Paco Underhill, *Why We Buy* (Simon & Schuster, 1999), 31.

Laura Antonini: "Letter to Federal Trade Commission from #Represent," June 24, 2019,
https://www.representconsumers.org/wp-content/uploads/2019/06/2019.06.24-FTC
-Letter-Surveillance-Scores.pdf.
"Credit score 'on steroids': How your secret consumer score could be used against
you," *CBC Radio*, November 8, 2019, https://www.cbc.ca/radio/day6/saudi-aramco
-s-ipo-trump-nicknames-secret-consumer-scores-sesame-street-turns-50-ev-batteries
-and-more-1.5351327/credit-score-on-steroids-how-your-secret-consumer-score-could
-be-used-against-you-1.5351398.

SHOPOLOGY

to acquire and possess symbolic items: Kate Wong, "Cave That Houses Neanderthals
and Denisovans Challenges View of Cultural Evolution," *Scientific American*,
January 30, 2019.
Kate Wong, "World's Oldest Engraving Upends Theory of Homo sapiens Uniqueness,"
Scientific American, December 3, 2014, https://blogs.scientificamerican.com/
observations/world-s-oldest-engraving-upends-theory-of-homo-sapiens-uniqueness/.

". . . we make a parade of our riches . . .": Adam Smith, *The Theory of Moral Sentiments*, 44.

Douglas Coupland noted: Douglas Coupland, *Player One: What is to Become of Us: a novel in Five Hours* (House of Anansi Press, 2010), 231.

Libraries and industry journals are full: "The Market for Luxury goods: Income versus Culture," *European Journal of Marketing* 27, 1 (1993), 35–44.
"Luxury consumption factors," *Journal of Fashion Marketing and Management: An International Journal* 13, 2 (May 2009) 231–45.
Douglas B. Holt, "How Consumers Consume: A Typology of Consumer Practices," *Journal of Consumer Research* 22, 1 (June 1995, Oxford University Press), 1–16.
Liselot Hudders, "Why the devil wears Prada: Consumers' purchase motives for luxuries," *Journal of Brand Management* (2012).

The owner, Nile Niami: Nic Querolo and Olivia Rockeman, "This Could Be America's Most Expensive Home Ever—If It Can Find a Buyer," *Bloomberg*, January 29, 2020, https://www.bloomberg.com/news/articles/2020-01-29/this-could-be-america-s-most -expensive-home-ever-if-it-can-find-a-buyer.

Bloomberg News reported: James Tarmy, "Bored Rich People Shop Online For $500,000 Bracelets Amid Virus Outbreak," *Bloomberg*, April 23, 2020, https://www.bloomberg .com/news/articles/2020-04-22/bored-rich-people-are-buying-250-000-jewels-online.

". . . enormously powerful need for people to belong . . .": Kit Yarrow and Jayne O'Donnell, *Gen BuY*, (Jossey-Bass, 2009), 50.

what economist Harvey Leibenstein called: H. Leibenstein, "Bandwagon, Snob, and Veblen Effects in the Theory of Consumers' Demand," *Quarterly Journal of Economics* 64 (May 1950), 189.
Minas N. Kastanakis and George Balabanis, "Between the mass and the class: Antecedents of the "bandwagon" luxury consumption behavior," *Journal of Business Research* (October 24, 2011).
Yann Truong and Rod McColl, "Intrinsic motivations, self-esteem, and luxury goods consumption," *Journal of Retailing and Consumer Services* (September 9, 2011).
Bernard Dubois and Patrick Duquesne, "The Market for Luxury Goods: Income versus Culture," *European Journal of Marketing* 27, 1 (February 1, 1993).

Without such myths: Yuval Noah Harari, *Sapiens* (Harper, 2014), 131.

In his book Affluenza: Oliver James, *Affluenza* (Vermilion, 2007), 15.

Barbara Hutton . . . and her lifelong rival, Doris Duke: Stephanie Mansfield, "Inside the World's Richest Rivalry: Doris Duke and Barbara Hutton," *Town & Country*, April 26, 2017.
Women of Means: Fascinating Biographies of Royals, Heiresses, Eccentrics and Other Poor Little Rich Girls (Mango Publishing Group, 2019), 157.
Evalyn Walsh McLean with Boyden Sparkes, *Father Struck it Rich* (Little, Brown and Company, 1935), 308, Foreword.

"The lust for clothes": Betty Halbreich with Rebecca Paley, *I'll Drink to That: A Life in Style, with a Twist* (New York: Penguin), 194.

NECROSHOP

"King of Pop" peculiarity Michael Jackson: Ken Lee, "Michael Jackson Laid to Rest in a $35,000 Suit," *People*, November 10, 2009.

Jazz great and drug-abusing wife-beater Miles Davis: Greg Daugherty, "Nine Famous People and What They're Buried With," *Smithsonian*, October 29, 2014.

SHOPOCALYPSE

Amazon hired more than: Karen Weise, "Pushed by Pandemic, Amazon Goes on a Hiring Spree Without Equal," *New York Times*, November 27, 2020.

within months of the conflict's outbreak, Asma al-Assad: Robert Booth and Luke Harding, "Gilded lifestyle continued for Assad coterie as conflict raged in Syria," *Guardian*, March 14, 2012.

some anthropologists insist that shopping: Richard D. Horan, Erwin Bulte and Jason F. Shogren, "How trade saved humanity from biological exclusion: an economic theory of Neanderthal extinction," *Journal of Economic Behavior & Organization* 58, 1 (September 2005), 1–29.
Celeste Biever, "Free trade may have finished off the Neanderthals," *New Scientist*, April 1, 2005.
Yuval Noah Harari, *Sapiens* (Harper, 2014), 39–40.

SHOPTOPIA

reworn clothing sales: Lauren Thomas, "Resale market expected to be valued at $64 billion in 5 years, as used clothing takes over closets," CNBC, June 23, 2020, https://www.cnbc.com/2020/06/23/thredup-resale-market-expected-to-be-valued-at-64-billion-in-5-years.html.

Anna Wintour, the powerful editor: "Love your clothes and pass them on, says Vogue supremo Wintour," *Thomson Reuters*, CBC News, November 28, 2019, https://www.cbc.ca/news/entertainment/wintour-sustainable-fashion-1.5376506.

Activist actor Jane Fonda: Chelsey Sanchez, "Jane Fonda's Signature Red Coat Is the 'Last Piece of Clothing' She'll Ever Buy," *Harper's Bazaar*, November 8, 2019.

INDEX

diamonds, 186–88
DiCaprio, Leonardo, 79, 133, 208
Dickens, Charles, 96
Diderot Effect, 243
Dior, Christian, 242
Domi, Leanne and Tie, 192
downshop, 58–60
downtowns, 33–35, 216, 218–19
   See also shopification
Doyle, David, 63–64
Drake, 81–82
Dubai, 35, 193, 194–95
Duchovny, David, 151
Duesenberry, James, 50, 52
Duke, Doris, 240–41
Dunn, Elizabeth, 159
Duplantis, Jesse, 80
Dylan, Bob, 148

Eaton, Timothy, 49
Ebbers, Bernard, 87
Ecclestone, Tamara, 81
economy, 6, 7–8
eco-shopping, 208
El Chapo, 86–87
electronics, 11–12
Ellison, Larry, 53–54, 79, 88
Elrod, Suzanne, 24
endangered species, 127–29
English language, 6–7, 8
environment, 45, 129–31, 181,
   205–8, 251, 254–55, 256–57
Epictetus, 222
Epicureans, 242–43
Epstein, Jeffrey, 50, 70

Farrow, Mia, 183
fashion. *See* clothing; shopping
   sheep
Faye, Tammy, 80
Fayne, Maurice "Mo," 127
Federer, Roger, 164, 172
Feodorovna, Maria (empress), 99
Field, Marshall, 49
Firth, Livia, 206
fishing, 134
Flynn, Errol, 240

Fonda, Jane, 177, 254
Ford, Henry, 49
Ford, Rob, 13
Foreman, George, 145
Forster, E.M., 243
Fox, Louise, 101
Francis of Assisi, 222
Franco, Manuel, 82–83
Frank, Sidney, 43–44
Freeland, Chrystia, 69
Frick, Henry Clay, 49

Gable, Clark, 110, 244
gameshows, 138
garage sales, 18, 102, 107, 179
garbage, 45, 205–6, 257
Gates, Bill, 49
Geffen, David, 54, 77, 139
Gen BuY, 141, 237
Gere, Richard, 172
Gerety, Mary Frances, 187
Gest, David, 101
Getty, J. Paul, 25–26
Gibbons, Billy, 172
Gibson, Mel, 79
gifts, 95–101
Gilmour, David, 172
Girardi, Erika, 179
Giuliani, Rudy, 59, 184
Gladwell, Malcolm, 190–91
gold, 11, 17, 81, 83, 85, 86, 96, 99,
   130–31, 223, 245, 246
golf, 77, 88, 135
Great Depression, 248–49
Great Pyramid, 55
Green, Steve, 64
Gruen, Victor, 215, 216
Gucci, 40, 85, 156
guitars, 171–72, 173
Gupta, Sanjay, 74

haggling. *See* outshop
Halbreich, Betty, 75, 157, 183–84
Halloween, 99
Hammond, James, 180
Hanks, Tom, 164, 170–71, 198
happiness, 241–43

Harari, Yuval Noah, 239
hardware stores, 38
Harrod, Charles Henry, 49
Hayes, Isaac, 105
Hearst, William Randolph, 175
Helmsley, Leona, 119–20
Henry, O., 96
Hermès, 40, 81, 183, 198
HGTV, 110
Hill, Jonah, 173
Hillel the Elder, 243
Hilton, Paris, 20, 93, 140, 212
Hines, David T., 127
hoarders. *See* shoparrhea
hobbies, 134–36
Hobby Lobby, 132–33
The Home Edit (show), 104–5
Home Shopping Network,
   143–44
homes. *See* real estate
hospitals, 38
Houston, Whitney, 94
Hudson, Kate, 144
Hughes, Howard, 24–25
humans, ancient, 231–34, 239,
   245–47, 250
Hung, Stephen, 83–84
Hunter, Duncan and Margaret,
   131
Hupp, Millan, 184
Hush Puppies, 190–91
Hussein, Saddam and Uday, 86
Hutton, Barbara, 240–41

Ihlen, Marianne, 24
IKEA, 50, 213–14
India, 39, 155–56
Indus Valley, 193, 234
influencers, 138, 149, 165,
   190, 195
Inglehart, Ronald, 26
Inman, Walker II, 240
internet, 23, 123, 142, 144–45,
   149, 169, 229–30, 253
Iqaluit, 39
ivory, 127–28

shopocracy, 154–56, 249
shop-o-erotic, 120, 209–10
shopology, 227, 231–43
shopomania, 160–63
shopomatic, 89–91
shoponomics, 157–59
shopophobia, 28–29
shopopolis, 193–95
shopornography, 211–12
shoposphere, 125
shopostle, 143, 145–53, 188
shoppable
    defined, 37–40
    items, 37, 41–46
    regions, 38–41
    venues, 37–38
shopper, 22
    See also non-shopper;
        pseudoshop
shopping sheep, 190–91
shopping sherpa, 192
shopportunity, 203–4
shopreneur, 47
shoptometry, 228–30
shoptopia, 253–58
shopward, 196
Siegel, David and Jackie, 84–85,
    127–28
Simpson, O.J., 147
Simpson, Robert, 49
Singapore, 34–35
Smith, Adam, 166, 223–24, 236
snob effect, 237–38
Sosenko, Carla, 180
Spears, Britney, 147
Sphinx, 55
Stevens, Brooks, 67
storage. See predeshop
Streep, Meryl, 27, 183
Streisand, Barbra, 102
Stronach, Belinda, 192
Stronach, Frank, 56
supershop, 20, 71–72
Sutherland, Kiefer, 171–72

Taj Mahal, 246
Taylor, Elizabeth, 11, 141
teleshop, 142–43
Teplin, Joanna, 104–5
Terracotta Army, 246
Theron, Charlize, 147
Theroux, Justin, 81
Thoreau, Henry David, 222,
    243, 251
Timberlake, Justin, 173
Tirabassi, Sharon, 60
Tolstoy, Leo, 243
totoaba, 128–29
tourism, 40–41
toys, 2, 4–5, 65, 145, 162–63, 165,
    226, 227
trade, 193–94, 250
Travolta, John, 79
Trentmann, Frank, 223
Trump, Donald, 15, 20, 54–55, 56,
    108, 119, 127, 131, 132, 133,
    150, 155, 184, 213
Trump, Ivanka, 150
Tulip Mania, 64–65
Turner, Ted, 87
Tutankhamun, 246
typewriters, 170–71
Tyson, Mike, 81

ultrashop, 14, 20, 24, 39, 44, 54,
    57, 79–88, 105, 132, 139, 172,
    184, 192
    See also upshop
Underhill, Paco, 228–29
undershop, 76–78, 158, 183
unshop, 7, 8, 10–14, 16–17, 19, 44,
    52, 90, 126, 133, 155–56,
    169, 171, 177
    See also deshop; unshopathon
unshopathon, 102–3, 106
    See also deshopathon
upshop, 52–57, 158
    See also ultrashop
Urban, Keith, 226

vaccines, 42
Valentine's Day, 99
Vanderbilt family, 49, 241
Varna Necropolis, 245
Veblen, Thorstein, 52, 157–58
Venice, 30, 194, 199–200
vodka, 43–44, 148, 150
Volkswagen, 108–9
von Hahn, Karen, 239

Wahlberg, Mark, 212
Walker, Jay, 169
Walker, Rob, 189
Walmart, 40, 49–50, 131, 141, 144,
    161, 219, 230
Walton, Sam, 49–50
Wanamaker, John, 49
Wang Sicong, 82
war, 249
Warhol, Andy, 43, 173
watches, 11, 13–14, 59, 68–69, 82,
    85, 126, 132, 164, 167, 170,
    183, 232, 244
water, bottled, 44–46
Watts, Charlie, 167
Wayne, John, 79
weddings, 100–101, 102, 106, 162,
    186–87, 207
West, Kanye, 16, 99, 173
Wexner, Leslie, 50
Wildenstein, Jocelyn and Alec,
    121–22
Winfrey, Oprah, 179–80
Wintour, Anna, 206, 253–54
Witherspoon, Reese, 104–5, 144
Woodhead, Lindy, 96
Woodward, Joanne, 13–14
Woolworth, Frank, 49, 215

yachts, 24, 53–55, 59, 79, 86, 132,
    139, 176, 208
    See also boats
Yarrow, Kit, 141, 237

Appendix Bibliography

Biographies Cited or Consulted

Barr, Nancy Verde. *Backstage With Julia: My Years with Julia Child*. Hoboken, NJ: John Wiley, 2007.

Bourne, Peter G. *Jimmy Carter*. New York: Scribner, 1997.

Bradford, Sarah. *The Reluctant King: The Life & Reign of George VI, 1895-1952*. New York: St. Martin's Press, 1989.

Buckley, David. *Elton: The Biography*. Chicago: Chicago Review Press, 2007.

Burnett, Carol. *One More Time*. New York: Random House, 1986.

Buss, Dale. *Family Man: The Biography of Dr. James Dobson*. Wheaton, IL: Tyndale House, 2005.

Byrne, Paula. *The Real Jane Austen: A Life in Small Things*. New York: Harper Collins, 2013.

Carpenter, Humphrey. *J. R. R. Tolkien: a biography*. Boston: Houghton Mifflin, 1977.

Carwardine, Richard. *Lincoln: A Life of Purpose and Power*. New York: Knopf, 2006.

Clinton, Bill. *My Life*. New York: Knopf, 2004.

Clinton, Hilary Rodham. *Living History*. New York: Scribner, 2004.

Cohen, Morton N. *Lewis Carroll: A Biography*. New York: Knopf, 1995.

Cousteau, Jean-Michel. *My Father, the Captain: My Life With Jacques Cousteau*. Washington, D. C.: National Geographic Society, 2010.

Dembling, Sophia and Lisa Gutierrez. *The Making of Dr. Phil: The Straight-Talking True Story of Everyone's Favorite Therapist*. Hoboken, NJ: John Wiley and Sons, 2004.

Dougan, Andy. *Robin Williams*. New York: Thunder's Mouth Press, 1998.

Ellmann, Richard. *Oscar Wilde*. New York: Random House, 1984.

Emery, Noemie. *Washington: A Biography*. New York: Putnam, 1976.

Falkner, David. *Great Time Coming: The Life of Jackie Robinson from Baseball to Birmingham.* New York: Simon & Schuster, 1995.

Ferrer, Sean Hepburn. *Audrey Hepburn, an Elegant Spirit*. New York: Atria Books, 2003.

Frank, Jeffrey. *Ike and Dick: Portrait of a Strange Political Marriage*. New York: Simon and Schuster, 2013.

Fultz, Jay. *In Search of Donna Reed*. Iowa City, IA: University of Iowa Press, 1998.

Garrow, David J. *Bearing the Cross: Martin Luther King, Jr., and the Southern Christian Leadership Conference*. New York: William Morrow, 1986.

Gerth, Jeff and Don Van Natta Jr. *Her Way: The Hopes and Ambitions of Hillary Rodham Clinton*. New York: Little, Brown, 2007.

Gleick, James. *Isaac Newton*. New York: Pantheon, 2003.

Gray, Charlotte. *Reluctant Genius: Alexander Graham Bell and the Passion for Invention*. New York: Arcade, 2006.

Gunn, Tim. *Gunn's Golden Rules: Life's Little Lessons for Making It Work*. New York: Gallery Books, 2010.

Hawking, Jane. *Travelling to Infinity: My Life with Stephen*. Richmond, Surrey, UK: Alma Books, 2000.

Hemingway, Ernest. *A Moveable Feast*. New York: Charles Scribner and Sons, 1964.

Hendrickson, Paul. *Hemingway's Boat: Everything He Loved in Life, and Lost: 1934-1961*. New York: Alfred Knopf, 2011.

Hill, Pamela Smith. *Laura Ingalls Wilder: A Writer's Life*. Pierre, SD: South Dakota State Historical Society Press, 2007.

Hillman, William. *Harry S. Truman In His Own Words*. New York: Bonanza Books, 1984.

Huxley, Elspeth. *Florence Nightingale*. New York: Putnam, 1975.

Isaacson, Walter. *Einstein: His Life and Universe*. New York: Simon and Schuster, 2007.

Israel, Paul. *Edison: A Life of Invention*. New York: John Wiley & Sons, 1998.

Kalush, William and Larry Sloman. *The Secret Life of Houdini: The Making of America's First Superhero*. New York: Atria Books, 2006.

Kessler, Ronald. *Laura Bush: An Intimate Portrait of the First Lady*. New York: Doubleday, 2006.

King, Larry. *My Remarkable Journey*. New York: Weinstein Books, 2009.

King, Stephen. *On Writing: A Memoir of the Craft*. New York: Pocket Books, 2001.

Kremer, Gary R. *George Washington Carver: In His Own Words*. Columbia, MO: University of Missouri Press, 1987.

Lelyveld, Joseph. *Great Soul: Mahatma Gandhi and His Struggle With India*. New York: Knopf, 2011.

Levinson, Peter J. *Puttin' on the Ritz: Fred Astaire and the Fine Art of Panache*. New York: St. Martin's Press, 2009.

Lewis, C. S. *Surprised by Joy: The Shape of My Early Life*. New York: Harcourt Brace Jovanovich, 1963.

Lofton, Kathryn. *Oprah: The Gospel of an Icon*. Berkeley: University of California Press, 2011.

Ma, Marina and John A. Rallo. *My Son Yo-Yo*. New York: Chinese University Press, 1996.

Madonna, "Truth or Dare," *Harper's Bazaar*, November 2013, 254.

Maraniss, David. Clemente: *The Passion and Grace of Baseball's Last Hero*. New York: Simon & Schuster, 2006.

Metaxas, Eric. *Bonhoeffer: Pastor, Martyr, Prophet, Spy*. Nashville: Thomas Nelson, 2010.

Migel, Parmenia. *Titania: the Biography of Isak Dinesen*. New York: Random House, 1967.

Miles, Barry. *Paul McCartney: Many Years From Now*. New York: Henry Holt, 1997.

Miller, Nathan. *Theodore Roosevelt: A Life*. New York: William Morrow, 1992.

Milne, Christopher. *The Enchanted Places*. London: Bello, 1974.

Montefiore, Simon Sebag. *Young Stalin*. New York: Vintage, 2008.

Montville, Leigh. *At the Altar of Speed: The Fast Life and Tragic Death of Dale Earnhard*t. New York: Doubleday, 2001.

Morton, Andrew. *Madonna*. New York: St. Martin's Press, 2001.

Orwell, George. *Homage to Catalonia*. New York: HBJ, 1952.

Oz, Mehmet. *Healing from the Heart*. New York: Dutton, 1998.

Pausch, Randy and Jeffrey Zaslow. *The Last Lecture*. New York: Hyperion, 2008.

Philbin, Regis. *How I Got This Way*. New York: Harper Collins, 2011.

Pryor, Elizabeth Brown. *Clara Barton: Professional Angel*. Philadelphia: University of Pennsylvania Press, 1987.

Roe, Sue. *Private Lives of the Impressionists*. New York: Harper, 2006.

Shlaes, Amity. *Coolidge*. New York: Harper Collins, 2013.

Smith, Sally Bedell. *Diana In Search of Herself*. New York: Random House, 1999.

Smith, Sally Bedell. *Elizabeth the Queen: The Life of a Modern Monarch*. New York: Random House, 2012.

Smith, Sally Bedell. *Grace and Power: The Private World of the Kennedy White House*. New York: Random House, 2004.

Smith, Sean. *J. K. Rowling: A Biography*. London: Michael O'Mara Books, 1999.

Spada, James. *Julia: Her Life*. New York: St. Martin's Press, 2004.

Spink, Kathryn. *The Miracle of Love: Mother Teresa of Calcutta, Her Missionaries of Charity, and Her Co-Workers*. San Francisco: Harper and Row, 1981.

Starkey, David. *Elizabeth: The Struggle for the Throne*. New York: Harper Collins, 2001.

Thomas, Donald. *Robert Browning: A Life Within Life*. New York: Viking Press, 1983.

Thompson, Clive. "The BitTorrent Effect," *Wired*, January 2005.

Tomalin, Claire. *Charles Dickens: A Life*. New York: Penguin Press, 2011.

Wapshott, Nicholas. *Reagan and Thatcher: A Political Marriage*. New York: Sentinel, 2007.

Welch, Jack with John A. Byrne. *Jack: Straight from the Gut*. New York: Warner Business Books, 2001.

Wilder, Laura Ingalls. *A Little House Traveler: Writings from Laura Ingalls Wilder's Journeys Across America*. New York: HarperCollins, 2006.

Wozniak, Steve with Gina Smith. *iWoz: Computer Geek to Cult Icon*. New York: Norton, 2006.

General Research Works, Cited in the Text

Berns, Gregory S., Bell E., Capra, C. M., Prietula, MJ, Moore, S, Anderson, B., Ginges, J., Atran, S. "The Price of Your Soul: Neural Evidence for the Non-utilitarian Representation of Sacred Values." *Philosophical Transactions of the Royal Society* B, 5 March 2012, vol. 367, no. 1589, 754-762.

Blair, James, Derek Mitchel and Katrina Blair. *The Psychopath: Emotion and the Brain*. Malden, MA: Blackwell Publishing, 2005.

Blumstein, D. T., Daniel, J. C., Griffin, A. S. and Evans, C. S. "Insular Tammar Wallabies (Macropus eugenii) Respond to Visual but not Acoustic Cues From Predators." *Behavioral Ecology* (2000) 11 (5): 528-535.

Coss, R. G. "Effects of relaxed natural selection on the evolution of behavior." In S. A. Foster and J. A. Endler (Eds.), *Geographic variation in behavior: Perspectives on evolutionary mechanisms*. New York: Oxford University Press, 1999.

Cruz, A., Prather, J. W., Wiley, J. W., and Weaver, P. F. "Egg Rejection Behavior in a Population Exposed to Parasitism: Village Weavers on Hispaniola." *Behavioral Ecology* (2008) 19 (2): 398-403.

Deloache, J. S. and Lobue, V. "The Narrow Fellow in the Grass: Human Infants Associate Snakes and Fear." *Developmental Science*, 2009 Jan; 12 (1): 201-7.

Fisher, Helen. *Why Him? Why Her?* New York: Henry Holt, 2009.

Foster, Susan Adlai, and Engler, John A. *Geographic Variation in Behavior: Perspectives on Evolutionary Mechanisms*. New York: Oxford University Press, 1999.

Gazzaniga, Michael S. *Who's In Charge? Free Will and the Science of the Brain*. New York: HarperCollins, 2011.

Gray, Jeffrey. Consciousness: *Creeping up on the Hard Problem*. New York: Oxford University Press, 2004.

Grigsby, Jim and David Stevens. *Neurodynamics of Personality*. NY: Guilford Press, 2000.

Gottman, John Mordechai. *What Predicts Divorce? The Relationship Between Marital Processes and Marital Outcomes*. Hillsdale, NJ: Lawrence Erlbaum, 1994.

Hunnius, Sabine, Tessa C. J. de Wit, Sven Vrins and Claes von Hofsten. "Facing threat: Infants' and adults' visual scanning of faces with neutral, happy, sad, angry, and fearful emotional expressions." *Cognition & Emotion*, 2011, 25:2, 193-205.

Kemp, Anthony E. *The Musical Temperament: Psychology and Personality of Musicians*. New York: Oxford University Press, 1996.

Leppänen, Jukka M., Moulson, Margaret C., Vogel-Farley, Vanessa K., and Nelson, Charles A. "An ERP Study of Emotional Face Processing in the Adult and Infant Brain," *Child Development*, 2007 ; 78(1): 232–245.

Libet, Benjamin. "Unconscious Cerebral Initiative and the Role of Conscious Will in Voluntary Action," *Behavioral and Brain Sciences*. 1985:8, 529-526.

Marler, Peter and Miwako Tamura. "Culturally Transmitted Patterns of Vocal Behavior in Sparrows." *Science*, New Series, Vol. 146, No. 3650. (Dec. 11, 1964), pp. 1483-1486.

Massey, Brent. *Where In The World Do I Belong?* (Jetlag Press, 2006).

Murray, Gregg R. and J. David Schmitz. "Caveman Politics: Evolutionary Leadership Preferences and Physical Stature." *Social Science Quarterly* 2011, 92:5, 1215-1235.

Myers, Isabel Briggs, McCaulley, Mary H., Quenk, Naomi L., and Hammer, Allen L. *MBTI® Manual, A Guide to the Development and Use of the Myers-Briggs Type Indicator*, 3rd edition. Mountain View, CA: CPP, 2003.

National Institute of Mental Health website:

"Statistics." http://www.nimh.nih.gov/health/statistics/index.shtml

Öhman, Arne. "Of Snakes and Faces: An Evolutionary Perspective on the Psychology of Fear." *Scandinavian Journal of Psychology*. December 2009. Vol 50, issue 6, pp 543-552.

Peltola, Mikko J., Leppänen, Jukka M., Mäki, Silja, Hietanen, Jari K. "Emergence of Enhanced Attention to Fearful Faces Between 5 and 7 Months of Age." *Scandinavian Journal of Psychology* (2009) 4,134–142.

Peltola, Mikko J., Leppänen, Jukka M., Vogel-Farley, Vanessa K., Hietanen, Jari K. and Nelson, Charles A. "Fearful Faces But Not Fearful Eyes Alone Delay Attention Disengagement in 7-Month-Old Infants." *Emotion*. 2009 August ; 9(4): 560–565.

Rakison, David H. "Does Women's Greater Fear of Snakes and Spiders Originate in Infancy?" *Evolution of Human Behavior* 2009 November 12; 30 (6): 439-444.

Ripple, William J. and Beschta, Robert L. "Trophic Cascades in Yellowstone: The first 15 years after wolf re-introduction," *Biological Conservation*, 145 (2012): 1, 205-213.

Skarda, Christine A. and Walter J. Freeman. "How Brains Make Chaos in Order to Make Sense of the World," *Behavioral and Brain Sciences* (1987) 10, 161-195.

Strathearn, Lane, Fonagy, Peter, Amico, Janet, and Montague, P. Read. "Adult Attachment Predicts Maternal Brain and Oxytocin Response to Infant Cues," *Neuropsychopharmacology*. 2009 December, 34(13): 2655–2666.

Strathearn, Lane, Jian Li, Fonagy, Peter, and Montague, P. Read. "What's In a Smile? Maternal Brain Responses to Infant Facial Cues." *Pediatrics* 2008; 122, 40-51.

Steele, Howard, Steele, Miriam and Croft, Carla. "Early Attachment Predicts Emotional Recognition at 6 and 11 Years Old." *Attachment & Human Development*, Vol. 10, No. 4, December 2008, 379-393.

Wiseman, Rosalind. *Queen Bees and Wannabes: Helping Your Daughter Survive Cliques, Gossip, Boyfriends and the New Realities of Girl World.* New York: Three Rivers Press, 2009.

Literary Quotation Sources

Adams, Douglas. *The Hitchhiker's Guide to the Galaxy.* London: Pan Books, 1979.

Austen, Jane. *Pride and Prejudice.* London: 1813.

Austen, Jane. *Persuasion.* London: 1818.

Austen, Jane. *Sense and Sensibility.* London: 1811.

Berendt, John. *Midnight in the Garden of Good and Evil.* New York: Random House, 1994.

Burnett, Frances Hodgson. *A Little Princess.* New York: Scribner's, 1905.

Crichton, Michael. *Jurassic Park.* New York: Knopf, 1990.

Descartes, Rene. *Discourse on Method.* Paris: 1637.

Dickens, Charles. *A Tale of Two Cities.* London: 1859.

Didion, Joan. *The Year of Magical Thinking.* New York: Knopf, 2005.

Dillard, Annie. *An American Childhood.* New York: Harper and Row, 1987.

Dinesen, Isak. *Out of Africa.* London: Putnam, 1937.

Doyle, Arthur Conan. *A Study in Scarlet.* London: 1887.

Eliot, George. *Daniel Deronda.* London: 1872.

Eliot, George. *Middlemarch.* London: 1872.

Franklin, Benjamin. *Autobiography.* New York: Modern Library, 1942.

Hemingway, Ernest. *The Sun Also Rises.* New York: Scribner's, 1926.

Jacq, Christian. *The Wisdom of Ptah-Hotep.* London: Constable & Robinson, 2004.

Jung, Carl. *The Archetypes and the Collective Unconscious.* Princeton: Princeton University Press, 1969

Jung, Carl. *Psychological Types.* Princeton: Princeton University Press, 1971.

King, Martin Luther, Jr. "Letter from Birmingham Jail," *The Christian Century* (June 12, 1963).

Lennon, John. "Imagine," *Imagine* album. Capitol Records: 1971.

Lewis, C. S. *The Magician's Nephew*. London: Bodley Head, 1955.

Montgomery, Lucy Maud. *Anne of Green Gables*. Boston: 1908.

Orwell, George. *The Road to Wigan Pier*. London: Victor Gollancz, 1937.

Orwell, George. "Shooting an Elephant," *A Collection of Essays*. San Diego: HBJ, 1981.

Proust, Marcel. *In a Budding Grove*. Translated by Scott Moncrieff. London: 1924.

Proust, Marcel. *The Way by Swann's*. Translated by Lydia Davis. New York: Penguin, 2002.

Scott, Walter. *Rob Roy*. London, 1817.

Shakespeare, William. *Hamlet*.

Smith, Alexander McCall. *The No. 1 Ladies' Detective Agency*. New York: Anchor Books, 1998.

Solzhenitsyn, Aleksandr. Thomas P. Whitney, trans. *The Gulag Archipelago*. New York: Harper & Row, 1974.

Twain, Mark. *Life on the Mississippi*. Boston, 1883.

Ward, Candace, ed. *Great Short Stories by American Women*. New York: Dover, 1996.

Washington, Booker T. *Up From Slavery*. *The Christian Century*, 1901.

Welty, Eudora. *The Optimist's Daughter*. New York: Random House, 1972.

INDEX

124-31; imbalance in, 240-1; as King, 177-8; literary examples of, 128-31; as movie director, 143-6; in negative environment, 154-6; in politics, 127-8; as Prime Minister, 172-3; as script writer, 147; sense of safety in, 125, 152-3, 156

Introverted Sensing: defined, 106-13; as evolutionary advantage, 135; frequency of, 109; imbalance in, 240; as King, 171-2, 177; literary examples of, 110-3; as movie director, 140-3; in negative environment, 154-6; as Prime Minister, 173-4; as script writer, 149-51; sense of safety in, 107, 109, 136, 152-3, 156; in team with Extroverted Sensing, 135-6

Introverted Thinking: in conscience, 86-90; defined, 63-8; imbalance in, 238-9; in Japanese culture, 94; as King, 175-6 ; literary examples of, 67-8; as Prime Minister, 172-4; sense of safety in, 63

Intuition (N): abbreviation for, 115-6, 169; in academic work, 138-9; and change, 137-8; characteristics of, 115-8, 137; defined, 22, 25, 133; as hunch, 116-7; in marriage, 298-305; as minority, 134, 136; in temperament, 263

inventor, 120, 221, 224-5

ISFJ: dominance, 286; imbalance, 240; profile,193-5; related opposite, 315

ISFP: dominance, 286; imbalance, 239; profile, 205-7; related opposite, 315

ISTJ: dominance, 283-4; imbalance, 240; profile, 187-9; related opposite, 316

ISTP: dominance, 284; imbalance, 238; profile, 199-201; related opposite, 316

It's a Wonderful Life, 190

James, Bill, 57
Jane Eyre, 219
Japan, 94-5
John, Elton, 206
journalist: in documentaries, 147; ESTP, 197; INFJ, 218; Introverted Intuition in, 126, 128, 155; Orwell as, 131

Judging: balance of Thinking and Feeling, 81; defined, 21; imbalance, 238-9; in marriage, 292-8; as part of MB letter code, 179

Jung, Carl: life and works, 17-20, 178; rules of, 27-8, 81, 161-2, 164, 167; terms as used by, 24-7, 45, 237

Jurassic Park, 266

Kangaroo Island, 36
Keirsey, David, 262-3

Kekulé, August, 117, 127
Kerr, Deborah, 141-2
King, Larry, 204
King, Martin Luther Jr., 131, 214, 268
King, Stephen, 231
King's Speech, The, 200
Koch, Robert, 18

Lang, Fritz, 143
"Last Lecture," 221
lawyer: in case study, 248; ENTJ, 208; ESTJ, 186; Extroverted Thinking, 57-8, 177; INFJ, 218; INTJ, 212; Introverted Intuition, 186; ISTJ, 187; NT temperament, 266

leadership, 271, 273, 279
"Letter from Birmingham Jail," 131
Lennon, John, 131, 219, 315
Lewis, C. S., 123, 231
Lewis, Michael, 57
libido, 25
Life on the Mississippi, 103
lifetime tasks, 255, 295
Little Princess, A, 112
Lincoln, Abraham, 209-10
Lister, Joseph, 18
Long Good-bye, The, 145

Ma, Yo-Yo, 215
Madonna, 198
Magician's Nephew, The, 123
Maltese Falcon, The, 144
Mandela, Nelson, 217-8
Marler, Peter, 33-4
marriage: archetype of husband and wife, 106, 141-3; Bubble dominance and, 276; challenges of, 291-2; checkerboard model of, 306-9, 316-7; conscience in, 292-4; and divorce, 91-2; Extroverted Intuition personality types in, 223, 225, 228, 231; Extroverted Sensing personality types in, 198, 201, 204, 209; family control of, 134; feudal model of, 309-11, 315-6; gender roles in, 305-6; Introverted Intuition personality types in, 209, 213, 216; Introverted Sensing personality types in, 187, 189, 192, 195; Judging functions in, 85, 294-8; Perceiving functions in, 156, 298-305; related opposites in, 314-7

Maslow, Abraham, 268
mathematics: dominant Intuition, 139; ENTP, 220; Extroverted Intuition, 119; Extroverted Thinking, 56; Florence Nightingale's

innovation in, 175; INTP, 224; Introverted Thinking, 64, 66, 175

Matrix, The, 148, 150

"Maxims II," 113

McCain, John, 315

McCartney, Paul, 221-2, 315, 317

McCartney, Linda, 315

McGraw, Dr. Phil, 197-8

Mean Girls, 185

mechanic, 199-200, 284, 316

Memento, 150

Meno, 47

memory: in animals, 34, 37; in babies, 43; in Extroverted Sensing, 101; in INFP personality, 231; in Introverted Sensing, 108, 110-1; in rabbit experiment, 7-8; in unconscious mind, 4, 6

Merchant of Venice, The, 62

Milne, A. A., 231

Middlemarch, 68, 74, 79, 111-2, 231

Midnight in the Garden of Good and Evil, 103

mind: attractors and repellers in, 10; connection with body, 215; conscious and unconscious, 3-4, 116-8; defined, 5-6; dominance in, 272, 286-7; extroverted and introverted, 49-52; Freud's model of, 18-19; functions of the (mental functions), 24-5, 27-8, 51-2, 134, 162, 179; 'I don't know' state of, 7; Intuition dominant in, 136-8; Jung's model of, 20, 21-6; King and Prime Minister of the, 171, 174; as living system, 8; mobile as model of, 162-6; need for balance in, 150-1, 237, 243; organization of, 161-2, 166; perceiving the world, 99-100; rules balancing functions of, 27-8; seen from outside, 170

model: advantages of dynamic, 11, 13-5; of behavior, 111-3; of conscience in churches, 93-4; Freud's, 18; Jung's, 20; purpose of, 29-30; of related opposites, 314-7; working, 161 (*see also* checkerboard model, feudal model, *and* role model)

Moneyball (film), 57, 201

Moneyball: The Art of Winning an Unfair Game, 57

morality: in churches, 93-4; under stress, 153-6; in Thinking, 64-5, 88

Mother Teresa, 194, 195

Mr. Smith Goes to Washington, 140-1

musician: in case study, 250-3; ENFJ, 215-6; ENTJ, 209; INFJ, 219; INFP, 316; Introverted Intuition, 126; ISFP, 206; NF temperament, 268; songwriting team, 315

Myers, Isabel, 25, 178-9, 262

Myers-Briggs personality framework, 11, 27, 178-9

Myers-Briggs Type Indicator (MBTI), 20, 178, 262

Myers-Briggs Type Indicator Manual, 82, 183, 278

N (*see* Intuition)

Narcissistic Personality Disorder, 256-7

National Institute of Mental Health, 257

Nazi Party, 154, 218

Negotiation, *see* NF temperament

Nepal, 94-5

neural network: in childhood, 236; in Extroverted Sensing, 100-1; in Intuition, 116, 137; organization of, 9-10; unpatterned activity of, 6-7

neuroscience: definition of mind, 5; definition of unconscious thought, 4, 116; experiments, 4, 41; hormones and, 262; mental functions and, 21; and sacred values, 50; and Sensing, 100

neurology: early developments in, 18; Freud trained in, 17; testing in, 254

"A New England Nun," 110

Newton, Isaac, 224

NF temperament: description, 267-8; in marriage, 301

Nightingale, Florence, 211-2

Nixon, Richard, 212

No. 1 Ladies' Detective Agency, The, 74-5, 191

normal personality, 13, 254-5

NT temperament: description, 266-7; in marriage, 301

nurse: in case study, 246; ESFJ: 190; ESFP, 282; ISFJ: 193; Soul Dominance, 286; Thinking and Feeling tasks, 83

Obsessive-Compulsive Disorder (OCD), 240

Ono, Yoko, 315

optimism: in Extroversion, 24, 51, 134-5, 139; in Feeling, 70-1; in role, 107; in Intuition 118-9, 147-50, 157; in Thinking, 59-62, 90; in Sensing, 102-3, 135-6, 147

Orwell, George, 104, 130-1, 218

Out of Africa, 62-3

Oz, Dr. Mehmet, 215

paranoia, 256

Paranoid Personality Disorder, 256

parent: Bubble Dominant, 284-5; in checkerboard model, 307; difference in N and S, 303-4; ESFJ, 192; ESFP, 204; ESTP, 197; in feudal model, 310; influence of in conscience, 92;

INFP, 231; INTJ, 213; INTP, 225; ISFJ, 195; ISFP, 207; ISTJ, 189; ISTP, 201; patterns and habits of, 90-1; and temperament, 269-70

Pasteur, Louis, 18

Pausch, Randy, 221

peer pressure, 71-2, 78

Perceiving: as camera lens, 139-51; in culture wars, 320; defined, 21, 133; imbalance, 239-40; in marriage, 298-305; part of conscience, 151-58; part of MB letter code, 179

personality: abnormal, 253-7; assessing, 269-70, 288-9; balance in, 50, 81, 85, 140, 142, 150, 236; case studies of, 243-53; chart of, 263, 278, 294, 314; in children, 30, 92, 234-5; competition in, 55, 58, 66, 83; conscience in, 90, 97, 157; defined, 3, 5, 8, 10; disorders of, 255-7; and dominance, 271-4, 288; dominant function in, 58, 82, 134, 136-7, 162; environmental factors shaping, 30, 134; extroverted, 171; factors in considering marriage, 292; Feeling in, 69-79, 89; five trait theory of, 19; flexibility of, 29, 304; gender similarity in, 59, 305; genetic basis of, 19; influence of introversion on, 52; Intuition in, 115-31, 149; Jung's mental functions of, 20-8; rules for balance of, 27-8, 161-2; imbalanced, 158, 237-43; N and S, 136-7, 298-305; names for types of, 178-80; normal, 254-5, 320-1; as living system, 11-14, 27, 233; profiles, *see individual entries by type name*; related opposite pairs of, 314-17; Sensing in, 99-113, 147, 157; stress effect on, 30, 234-6; and temperament, 262-3; Thinking in, 55-68; worldview created by, 140-3, 153-4

pessimism: in infant mind, 43; in Judging, 64, 67; in movies, 144, 145, 150; in Perceiving, 102, 109, 127, 136, 147, 149

Philbin, Regis, 191

Plato, 47

Please Understand Me: Four Temperament Types, 262

police: archetypal ideas of, 48; Extroverted Sensing, 102, 234; in Film Noir, 144-5; ISTJ, 187

political attitudes, 95-6, 127

Postman Always Rings Twice, The, 144

pragmatism: about truth, 71, 74-5; in conscience, 85-90; defined, 24; in Extroverted functions, 51-2, 63, 157; in Feeling, 69-70, 74; in frontal lobe activity, 50; in relationships, 85; in Sensing, 101-2, 136; in Thinking, 56, 58, 60

prejudice, 128

President: archetypal image, 107; ENFP, 227; ESTJ,

185-6; ESTP, 197; height of candidates, 46; Horizon Dominance, 287; ISTJ, 188-9; wife of, 195

Pride and Prejudice, 67, 79, 231

Proust, Marcel, 110,

Psychological Types, 17, 20, 24-6, 162, 178, 237

psychopathy, 87, 256, 257

"Queen Bee," 185-9, 191-2

Queen Bees and Wannabes, 185-6

rabbit experiment, 7-8

Rational, *see* NT temperament

realism, 145, 147, 316

Reed, Donna, 190

related opposites, 314-7

repeller, 9-10, 235

Road to Wigan Pier, The, 104-5

Rob Roy, 68

Roberts, Julia, 228

Robinson, Jackie, 196-7

Rogers, Carl, 268

role model, 197, 235, 244, 279, 280

role-playing games, 108-9

Room Dominance: defined, 275-6, 281-3; in marriage, 306-9, 312-3

Roosevelt, Theodore, 197

routine, 120

Rowling, J. K., 231

rules: Feeling attitude toward, 77, 89, 94, 174; Introverted Sensing respect for, 185-6; in math, 59; moral rules, 48-9, 51; of order, 58; pragmatism about, 90, 102, 198-9, 201, 203, 227, 231; in proverbs, 65-7; in science fiction, 150-1; temperament and, 264-9; Thinking respect for, 64-6, 88, 93, 95, 153, 158, 174, 191, 219

Russell, Cameron, 57

Russia, 155-6

Ryan, Nolan, 200

sacred values, 50, 76, 108

safety, *see* template: of danger and safety

salesmen, 101, 197, 204, 226

Samuel (Biblical prophet), 46

science fiction, 121, 123, 138, 148

scientific method, 126

scientist: ESFP, 203; INTJ, 211, 316; Introverted Intuition, 126; Thinking and Feeling, 83

Scott, Walter, 68

Search of Time Past, In, 110

self-organizing, *see* system, self-organizing

Sense and Sensibility, 67, 74

Sensing (S): defined, 22, 100, 133; frequency of Extroverted or Introverted, 134; in marriage, 298-305; in work, 135-6

Shakespeare, 62, 128, 143

SJ temperament, 264-5

Skarda, Christine, 7-8

Smith, Alexander McCall, 74

snakes, fear of, 37-9

social justice, 127, 131

society: archetypes in, 152; and conscience, 94-5; as negative influence, 153-6

Socrates, 47

Solzhenitsyn, Aleksandr, 130

Soul Dominance: defined, 276-7, 283-8; in marriage, 309-12, 313

Soviet Union, *see* Russia

SP temperament, 265-6

space opera, 150

sparrow, white-crowned, 33-4

spiders, fear of, 37-9

Star Wars, 150

Stewart, Jimmy, 140

Study in Scarlet, A, 61-2, 129

stories: and ENFPs, 228; folk, 48-9, 65; idealism in, 65, 79; and INFPs, 230; Intuition in, 118, 126, 138

Sun Also Rises, The, 105-6

superstition, 116, 128, 198, 201

Swann's Way, 110-1

system: ants' communication, 32; conscience as, 82, 89, 91, 97; defined, 8; dynamic, 28; hormonal, 41, 305; graph as, 126; Intuition, 115, 130; Jungian/Myers-Briggs, 20, 23-5, 178-80; living, 8-14, 27-9, 81, 161, 233; warning, 50, 77, 156; temperament, 262-3, 269; Thinking, 55; Feeling, 59, 73, 77; for managing relationships, 78; self-organizing, 5, 7-8, 81, 86-7, 115, 161; societal, 155, 184, 218, 269

syzygy, 46

Tale of Two Cities, A, 80

Tamura, Miwako, 33-4

teacher: archetypal role, 48, 107; case study, 244-5, 251-2; ENFJ, 214-5; ENFP, 226; ESFJ, 190, 316; ESFP, 204; INFJ, 317; ISFJ, 193-4; ISTJ, 187, 316; Room Dominance, 279, 281-3; SJ temperament, 264; Thinking and Feeling, 83

temperament: defined, 262; interaction among

groups, 269-70 (*see also* NF, NT, SJ and SP as individual entries)

template: in communication, 34-5; of danger and safety, 40, 42-4, 48, 151-2, 156, 235; for learning, 33, 44; for "mother," 41-2, 45; for moral ideas, 48-9, 88; of predators, 35-7

teenage years, 84, 158

temporo-parietal junction, 50, 76

terrorism, 156

Thatcher, Margaret, 210

Thinker: using Feeling, 85; at work, 82-3

Thinking (T): in conscience, 88; defined, 22, 55; as dominant function, 82-5; and emotion, 85; in marriage, 85, 294-8; variations, 234

Tolkien, J. R. R., 230-1

trophic cascade, 12, 312

Truman, Harry S, 188

Twain, Mark, 103

unconscious mind: defined, 4; in Intuition, 117, 125

Up From Slavery, 122

variation in personality, 233-4

visualization, 271-2

wallabies, tammar, 36-7

warm conscience: in American culture, 95; chart, 294; defined, 88-9; effect in parenting, 90; in relationships, 91, 157

Washington, Booker T., 122

Washington, George, 185

weaver birds, African, 39-40

Welch, Jack, 208

Welty, Eudora, 75

Wilde, Oscar, 227

Wilder, Billy, 143-4

Wiley, James, 39

Williams, Robin, 227

Winfrey, Oprah, 215

Wisdom of Ptah-Hotep, The, 67

Wiseman, Rosalind, 185-6

wolves, 12

work: academic, 138-9; dominance and, 279, 283-5; dominant function in, 82-3; in psychopathy, 257; roles and appearance, 107; Sensing in, 135-6

worldview: challenged by totalitarian society, 153-6; as conscience, 151-2; of Extroverted Sensing, 146-7; of Introverted Intuition, 143-6; of Introverted Sensing, 108-9, 113, 140-3; in personality, 21

CPSIA information can be obtained at www.ICGtesting.com
Printed in the USA
BVOW09s0300160416

444309BV00001B/1/P